THE WAKE UP CALL

The Wake Up Call

—◦◦◦—

BETH FITZGERALD

Dedication

Dedication is derived from the Latin word dedicare: the giving of oneself to some purpose. Writing a book requires a great deal of dedication and it is certainly more than anyone could possibly anticipate at the onset. For an author to purposefully dedicate herself entirely to a book it often requires that other people in her life must either pick up the slack or go without which was definitely the case in my home.

As a sign of my sincerest gratitude, I dedicate this book to my incredible husband Doug and my four fabulous children Devon, Liam, Katie, and Clare—all of whom sacrificed a great deal for this book to be written.

And to you, the reader, how could I not dedicate this book to you? I wrote this book *for* you. There is not one page in this book that did not have your best interest at heart. So thank you from the bottom of my heart for the inspiration you gave me all along the way to deliver to you my very best work!

With Gratitude

I am incredibly grateful to my family, Doug, Devon, Liam, Katie, and Clare, without whom this book would never have been completed. They remained silent when multiple copies of the rough draft were spewed across the kitchen table for long periods of time forcing us to eat dinner huddled in the corner at the other end. They took matters into their own hands when I proclaimed "Dinner is fend for yourself" yet again. They supported and encouraged me when things got over-whelming and disheartening. When you read the cover of this book it will always state the author is Beth Fitzgerald, but don't be fooled. It would never have come to fruition without the love and support of my family and friends.

I am grateful to my four editors and friends: Jen Madej, Bonnie Hurley, Susan Niedt, and Mary Ellen Pina. All four of these brilliant women did incredible editing on my behalf. Jen unfortunately received the roughest of rough drafts—she was a trooper and I am so grateful she still calls me "friend!" She and I will forever refer to the rough draft of the book as *the white brick*. Bonnie, Susan, and Mary Ellen edited over 400 pages of text as well. I can't imagine the amount of time they put into this effort. I learned so much from each of them. Absolutely noth-ing got past Bonnie. She caught every mistake and she made my writing better. Susan also made my writing better and she taught me that no one "should" be forced to do anything.

I am so grateful to Jen Madej and Amy Fitzgerald for putting this compilation of inspirational writings in order! For me, that task seemed

Herculean, but for these two women, it was like riding a bike. When they were done I felt as though the weight of the world had been lifted. "Forever grateful" doesn't even come close.

I am also grateful to Terry Lynch, Kerri Croland, and Maureen Westerman who never stopped encouraging and supporting me throughout this journey.

I would also like to thank Tim Pitts and Mark Green. Both of these men, published authors in their own right, readily provided every resource they had, took every one of my phone calls, and answered every question. These men gave me the guidance I desperately needed about an industry that was completely foreign to me. With their help I was able to take the next step.

Preface

It was rather ironic how this book came to fruition. I was in the midst of finishing up writing *another* book when my daughter, Devon arrived home from college. We were enjoying each other's company over lunch at our kitchen table when it happened. I started to tell her how happy I was about almost finishing the rough draft of my very first book when she lowered the boom. "Honestly Mom, I think a better book would be if you compiled all your daily motivational posts that you have already written into one book that would essentially *coach* someone for a full year!" As I looked across the table at her I thought, "She might be right. I have almost five years of daily posts that are already written. This will be easy, just compile the best 365 posts. It's as if the book has already written itself. This is a brilliant idea!"

Me thinking "the book has already written itself" was wrong. Her idea though was, in fact, brilliant; my first book should be (and is) a compilation of my daily posts. What was entirely wrong was my miscalculation of the time it would take to not only find the best 365 posts over a 5-year period, but also compile them as well as edit each one so it read as if it were written for a book and not a daily blog. What I did not know when I sat at my kitchen table with Devon was that it would take the better part of 2 more years until all that work was completed. So back to my original thought: "This will be easy"—I would like to retract that statement if I may.

I understand now why authors refer to their books as *a labor of love* and *my baby*. Writing a book is an intense process that becomes incredibly time consuming, but in a very fulfilling way. I am the mother of four children and all of them, I am sure, would attest to the two-year time period while I wrote this book when they were convinced they had a *fifth sibling.* They might even argue that she was my *favorite* given how much time I spent with her. Fortunately, she never cried nor needed a diaper change—just time with mom. But just like being a parent, there is no greater satisfaction than when your work is done.

My intention for writing this book—In addition to Devon's encouragement, the driving force behind this book was the burning question I had which was, "What would happen if a person truly followed and acted upon the coaching advice in this book for one full year?" The writing of my daily post was definitely grounded in inspiration and motivation, but it arrived each day as either an email or a random post on someone's Facebook feed. How would things change if each person had, at their fingertips, 365 motivational ideas to choose from and be inspired by daily? Converting this daily virtual encouragement into a tangible guidebook and resource would have the potential to change the trajectory of someone's life. I knew then I needed to create this book.

Why this book is important—I believe it is incredibly important for everyone to live into their own truth—their blueprint of why they are here. But it is certainly not possible for everyone to hire a coach and definitely not a coach that shows up every day. This book provides each one of us an opportunity to challenge our comfort zone daily, forcing us to think outside the box. It firmly puts us in a position for growth that wouldn't otherwise be there.

This book does have one limitation that working with a coach does not have and that is that there is no accountability—the book acts as coach but I can't be there to make sure the reader acts. Although, creating a book club would be a brilliant way around this limitation. Just a thought!

About the Author

Beth Fitzgerald is a certified life coach, certified John Maxwell Coach, Master EFT Practitioner, Positive EFT Practitioner, international speaker, and trainer. She brings years of experience from her time working on Wall Street at a small boutique hedge fund, then at Prudential Financial in the Portfolio Management Department, and finally in The World Trade Center where she managed the internal sales force for Oppenheimer Management. In addition to her corporate experience she has twenty plus years as the mother of four. She has been coaching clients and writing her blog for over six years now. She has worked with every client from recovering drug addicts to Wall Street executives and she has identified one common thread amongst us all— although we all want to be happy and successful, we first need to be loved and accepted. This book was written with that in mind.

How to Use This Book

Although this book was designed as a full year of daily inspirations, beginning on January 1st, there is no particular order in which it absolutely needs to be read and/or applied. Insert yourself into the text when the timing is right for you; there is no right or wrong spot. There are a few times when the topic is relevant to a particular time of year or holiday, but otherwise the entire book is date-neutral.

Even though there is no particular order in which this book needs to be read, there is a key to its success. The key to successfully reading this book and reaping the benefits is going to be ACTION. Reading the book and not following through on the action steps is best summed up in a quote I love by Mary Morrissey: "Inspiration without action is merely entertainment." Having said that, this book, due to its nature of providing a daily dose of motivation, can quickly become overwhelming for some.

This book was never written with the intent to overwhelm but it is completely understandable how it could happen. This book has a tremendous amount of content and not all may be applicable to each reader. Some readers may act on every daily post, while others may only focus on one or two posts that resonate with them each month. There is no right or wrong answer, but it is important to be honest with yourself and to go at the pace that feels right for you.

As you follow along with this book for the next year, you will be asked to spend about 5 minutes per day journaling. Please don't ignore those five minutes; spend the time journaling about what you just read. Five minutes seems like nothing, but it will surely add up if you are doing it for a full year. It totals 1,825 minutes or slightly over 30 hours! Imagine what we could accomplish if we were given 30 hours. If you would like to take this book to the next level, get a partner to follow along with or create a book club with many readers. The more you discuss the ideas within the text the more opportunity you will have to grow!

THE WAKE UP CALL

The Reference Point

—∞—

Do you have the right mindset to take on this year's New Year's Resolution? Have you, like me, made the same New Year's Resolution year after year? Why has success eluded us? Why are we trying to overcome this resolution yet again?

I cannot speak for you, but I do not want to repeat a resolution ever again. "Resolute" means determined, strong-willed, and uncompromising, but I have shown in years past that I can be anything but. This year will be different because in years past I have started strong, then somewhere along the way, I didn't think I had the willpower to carry on. I was wrong.

Let's take a moment and ask ourselves, "When in life was I determined? Strong-willed? Uncompromising? Tenacious?" When we can put our finger on those times in our life (and there were those times), we will know from the deepest part of our soul that we can do this thing!

Every time it gets tough or we fall off the wagon, we need to visualize that time in our life when we were seriously and extraordinarily unshakable! We have a reference point. We have shown how strong we truly are and we need to tap into that past strength. Repeat after me, "This is the **last** year that I repeat a resolution! Never again! This year, I will prevail."

———

ACTION STEP: Find your reference point. When were you determined, strong-willed, uncompromising, and tenacious? Spend a few minutes journaling about that time. Write down how you felt, looked, acted, your posture, your breathing, your voice—close your eyes and visualize that exact state of being.

A Year from Now

—∞—

Where do you want to be in your life a year from now? If you have not stopped to think about this, I invite you to take five minutes in some quiet place to mull over what you would like to happen over the next year.

Once we know where we want to be a year from now, we can ask an even better question: "What skills do I need to get there that I do not currently have in my arsenal?" This answer gives us the weapon we need to slay this dragon. It will be an uphill battle if we are not prepared. We need to arm ourselves with the most powerful weapon possible, our mind. We can take a class or read a book, but we must invest in ourselves.

Let us all agree there is at least one thing we need to learn in order to get us to where we want to be at the start of next year. We will need to write it down, commit to it, and learn it. It will be time well spent. We cannot get there without it. It's time to get this thing done. Let's go!

———

ACTION STEP: Spend the next few minutes journaling about where you want to be one year from today. This is more than a want, it is a declaration that you **will** make this happen. A deadline can come in very handy here. Pick a deadline to sign up for a class or finish a book.

Happy New Year!!

—⚬—

"New Year is not about changing the dates but direction; it's not about changing the calendar but commitment; it's not about changing the actions but attitude." —UNKNOWN

May each and every day of this new year be filled with happiness that comes from within.

———

ACTION STEP: Today begin reflecting and journaling on each of the three parts of the quote above; what does each section mean to you, and how can you make this new year different from last year or any other year.

New Year is not about changing the dates but direction:

It's not about changing the calendar but commitment:

It's not about changing the actions but attitude:

Happiness Quotient

—◊◊◊—

Have you ever paused to consider the greeting, "Happy New Year"? As this year begins, I am reading some amazing research from Harvard Medical School on happiness. I love research and statistics and this particular publication has astounded me.

Believe it or not, our happiness (in part), is inherited. 50% of our happiness is genetic! 10% is circumstantial (job, home, spouse, etc.), which leaves 40% completely under our control. Obviously, these percentages fluctuate given each person's individual life experiences. What will you choose to do with your 40%? How can you maximize your 40%? Don't dismiss this research because it has been proven that happier people live longer by almost 10 years.

The research also shows that money and material things are not the way to happiness. Although there are many ways of achieving happiness, here are a few: lower our daily stress, exercise and eat healthy, be more flexible and resilient, maintain a positive outlook, and find a meaningful way to give back to society. As broad as these may seem, really take a moment to examine this powerful list of five. These are five really important ways to drive our happiness quotient up. Remember, we can just as easily describe it as our 40% of unhappiness. We are behind the wheel on this one, let's be sure we know in which direction we are driving.

———

ACTION STEP: Pick one thing that has made you unhappy recently. Spend a few minutes journaling on all the ways you could look at this differently. Steer your thoughts in the direction of happiness. This is a strategy you might want to continue using throughout the year until it becomes rote.

The Best of Intentions

—m—

Have you ever set an intention? Intention setting is an extremely powerful tool and, once you get the hang of it, you will want to set intentions daily. Intention is a higher-consciousness thought and it allows us to use the mind for a higher purpose.

By setting an intention, we are planting a seed. It is the seed form of that which we wish to create. The intention is focused on how we wish to be; it is not goal-setting.

For example, I could start the day by saying, "My intention is that I remain positive and upbeat regardless of what crosses my path today." Essentially, I just told my mind, my subconscious, and the universe how my day is going to proceed. I don't need to do another thing. I released that intention into the world and I simply let my intention manifest itself.

It sounds so simple! Let us take a look at the same day without intention. I will drift through the day on autopilot, like I have every other day. When a confrontational or unpleasant event arises, I will likely allow it to upset me. I did not plant the seed of positivity in my higher consciousness.

Intention is an energetically powerful tool. If we choose to set an intention daily, we will give our life direction. Otherwise, we are choosing to allow our life to run on autopilot. Here are some great intentions:

Today, my intention is:

I will be kind to everyone around me, including myself.
I will be focused and driven.

I will be happy.
I will be calm and peaceful all day long.

These are just a few intentions to trigger some thoughts within yourself. Give it a try. This idea of intention setting will not only affect you but those around you. It could not be simpler! Simple is good.

———

ACTION STEP: What is your intention for today? Will you add *Intention Setting* to your daily routine?

Capture One's Imagination

—ᗰ—

The hardest part of my job is getting people to act. You know the adage, "You can lead a horse to water, but you can't make him drink." This is too often true.

In my Strategies for Success class, we cover imagination. At first glance, you may believe you do not use your imagination very much anymore. Perhaps you believe you stopped imagining when you left elementary school. I thought that was true for me, too, when I first read the chapter on imagination in Napoleon Hill's *Think and Grow Rich,* but I was wrong.

Each of us has a fabulous imagination. Not only is it active but it is creating unbelievable thoughts. Unfortunately, our imagination is too often used to imagine the worst. Our imagination creates all the scenarios under which we will fail, lose money, stumble and fall. It creates worry, fear and anxiety. Rarely do we allow our imagination to transport us to the land of success and happiness.

What if we allowed our imagination to go to those incredible places of achievement, success and prosperity? What would happen then? Maybe we would take that first step, that one step we have not taken because of every pessimistic scenario we imagined. We need to cultivate our imagination to head in the direction we want to go!!

———

ACTION STEP: Use the words *achievement, success* and *prosperity* to flip the switch on your imagination. Write down all the things that come to mind when you read those words. Which word spoke to you? Which word will compel you to move forward?

The Root of the Problem

—m—

Let us agree, we all have problems. There is no one out there who can boast a "problem free" life, or at least no one whom I have met. Aren't we all striving for serenity? I do have moments of it, but it continues to be fleeting. I have started to notice a pattern with problems, not only my own, but those of my clients as well.

The revelation is that no one is ever upset about what they think they are upset about. Whether this is you, your spouse, your child, or your boss, try to dig deeper to find the true source of the emotion. When we find the root, then we can begin to address the problem. Uncovering this truth has changed everything for me.

Once we agree with the following premise, "You are never upset for the reason you think you are upset," then we can start to unearth the real reason. When we start to reflect, the underlying reason will jump out at us. Most people will take the problem at face value. Now, when we ask the question, "Why am I really upset?" we can get to the root of our unhappy emotion. All the answers rest here, not where the problem originated. And when we get here we can address the real problem and we will usually approach it with more compassion than would have otherwise been the case.

I will add, if you have teenagers, "What are you really upset about?" is the question we could all benefit from asking them.

———

ACTION STEP: Journal for a few minutes about one of your problems with the premise, *you are never upset for the reason you think you are upset.* Start by answering the question, "Why am I upset?" I like to answer that same question five times, digging deeper each time. Here is an extra bonus, the emotion anger is rarely ever anger, it is almost always fear. So if you find yourself angry, what is it that you are fearing?

Are You Managing or Are You Leading?

—m—

Everyone is in a leadership role, even if you have chosen to live the life of a hermit or a recluse because, even then, you would be leading yourself. The questions is, "Are you choosing to lead or are you choosing to manage?"

Managing is making sure a company runs smoothly, so essentially we are an administrator. Underlying the definition of management is the word, "maintain." Leading a company is quite different and it is more dynamic. Leading implies movement and change in a positive direction.

Today I am asking all of us if we are leading or managing? Are we affecting change in our home or our workplace? Here is a powerful question we can ask ourselves: "Who can I help grow and develop and how?" Leadership requires intention and vision. Management requires task completion. Are you a manager or are you a leader?

———

ACTION STEP: Today, as you journal, focus only on the word leadership. Spend 5 minutes writing about who you lead at work and at home. After each name, ask yourself, 'How can I help this person develop and grow?'

My Social Media Rant

I am not sure where you stand on the effects of social media, but I blame this prolific electronic communication for a lot! I definitely commiserate with my husband and friends on the downside of this medium, with full knowledge and appreciation of its upside.

Yesterday, in the middle of my disparaging remarks about social media, I gave pause. I realized I had personified it. I made it the evil doer, but that is not true. Social media is a tool like any other tool. Take a hammer, for instance. Properly used, it is a fabulous tool, but if it is misused, someone can easily get hurt. It is all based on the user.

We can say social media wastes valuable time, makes people feel badly about themselves, diminishes face-to-face conversations, etc., but one thing is also true; social media is all within our control.

Our electronic devices, with their immediate access to almost anything, are supposed to be just like a hammer, a tool at our disposal. But when social media grabs our attention, when it makes us feel inadequate, when it diminishes our self-worth, when it consumes us and causes us to fret, it is no longer working for us. Like most things in life, we are in control, if we choose to be. "Off" is always an option.

ACTION STEP: Does social media play a role in your life that could easily be turned off? Are you using this tool to enhance your life or has it become a hindrance? Journal for a few minutes about the role these tools play in your life. Think about what you might gain by turning it off occasionally like more time, peace of mind, or maybe even self-satisfaction.

The Bar

Have you ever heard the expression, "Raise the bar"? I'm sure you have. It comes from the high jump in track and field. The bar is raised after each jumper completes a jump; thereby making each jump more challenging.

I have been known to use a variation of this expression with my children. I borrowed this idea from a book I read. I used it again as my son left Sunday morning for a week in Arizona with his lacrosse team. My parting words were, "Do not forget, our bar is higher." He has heard this before. He knows what I mean. I do not care what everyone else is doing; I expect more from him. At his age (18 at the time), it is more about his behavior, but I instantly thought about how it applies to my life, too.

We can raise the bar on anything. It is our choice. By raising the bar, we separate ourselves from the crowd. Wherever the masses are, we need to aim higher. We are not shooting for mediocrity. Excellence is our target. What would change if we picked one thing each week we committed to raising the bar on? As we all head into this week, "Do not forget, our bar is higher." Choose excellence.

ACTION STEP: Where do you need to raise the bar? Home? Work? Be specific. Spend a few minutes writing about where and how you will raise the bar.

Smooth Sailing

—m—

Assume, for a second, you are sailing a boat. You are the captain and the only person on the boat. Returning to land is not an option; you must sail. You have everything you will need and the boat is amazing. Where will you sail? What will be your strategy? Will you chart a course or just drift in the ocean?

Essentially, that is what we have been given with our life. We have been provided with a fully stocked boat that is incredible, yet the course, the strategy, and the direction are all up to us, the captain. We can choose to simply drift in our boat, that is our prerogative. We will still lead a good life. Or we can choose to chart a course, maximizing what we want to see and do on this blessed journey. We can stay in one port or circumnavigate the globe! We are the captain, and the only one on the boat. The journey is entirely up to us.

Most of us drift because we never take the time to plot the course. We do not have to plot the whole trip around the globe today, but can we all agree to charting our course to the next port? We can all do that, right, one port? Sailing will be a lot more fun (and rewarding) than drifting, I can promise you that!

———

ACTION STEP: Spend a few minutes charting your course to the next port. What is the next port for you in your life? Do not get overwhelmed, you are simply plotting the course to a port not so far away. Breathe. Dream a little. This is supposed to be fun. The journey is going to be spectacular.

The Tribe

I had the pleasure of attending a private bible study last night. If you are about to tune-out because bible study is not your thing or you are not Christian, stay with me for a little bit longer. I walked away from this night lighter, happier, and more hopeful and I want to share with you why.

These women have been getting together for years. They drank and ate. They talked and listened. They became vulnerable. They laughed . . . a lot! They were compassionate and authentic because it was safe. Nothing was off limits here. It was beautiful to witness. In the self-help space, this is called a tribe.

We all need a tribe. All of humanity seeks a sense of belonging. We all want to be accepted and loved for exactly who we are, with all our imperfections. This night filled my tank and I am not even in their tribe! It reminded me to reconnect with my tribe. Why am I not getting together with them more often? Why am I letting "busy" get in the way?

Men and women alike, we all need our tribe. Reconnecting with our tribe and making it a priority has so many fabulous health benefits: happiness, joy, laughter, camaraderie, a sense of belonging, and love. Call your tribe. Make a plan. I am definitely calling mine.

ACTION STEP: Spend a few minutes journaling about who is part of your tribe and how can you get together with them more often?

Burn the Boats!

—⚭—

A long while ago, a great warrior faced a situation which made it necessary for him to make a decision which insured his success on the battlefield. He was about to send his armies against a powerful foe, whose men outnumbered his own. He loaded his soldiers into boats, sailed to the enemy's country, unloaded soldiers and equipment, then gave the order to burn the ships that had carried them.

Addressing his men before the first battle, he said, "You see the boats going up in smoke. That means that we cannot leave these shores alive unless we win! We now have no choice—we win, or we perish!

(An excerpt from *Think and Grow Rich* by Napoleon Hill).

How do *you* retreat from battle? For me, it is the "fat pants." You know the ones I am talking about, the ones that always fit, no matter what. It is the pair I keep handy, just in case. They are at least a size larger than I am now and certainly a size larger than I want to be. If I am really going to commit to the win, I have to burn the boats!

I used an example most of us could relate to, but replace my word *pants* with your retreat. I have to get rid of the *pants* or I will always have an out. It will be really difficult to let them go, but it is time. When we get rid of the *pants,* we can proclaim, "I can and I will win!" If we keep the *pants,* we are saying, "But maybe I won't be successful." **Burn the boats!**

————

ACTION STEP: Before you look at personal retreat tactics, you must first know what you want. Maybe you want weight loss too, or perhaps it is something more work related like talking to your boss about compensation or a promotion. Once you determine what you want, then you can focus on how your retreat prevents you from achieving it. Spend 5 minutes writing about ways to burn the boats! It is likely this is not the first time you have used this retreat.

Martin Luther King, Jr.

—ɯ—

I hope this Monday has you off from work, celebrating Martin Luther King Jr. Day. I stand in awe of this man and what he accomplished in his prematurely short life. I cannot hear his famous, "I Have A Dream" speech without crying. I love so many of his quotes, but if I had to choose just one as my favorite, I believe it would be: "Darkness can't drive out darkness, only light can do that; hate can't drive out hate, only love can do that."

As I try to do with every holiday, I try to remember what I am supposed to be celebrating. It is not just another day off. We observe this day because an extraordinarily passionate man wanted to end racism using non-violent civil disobedience. He fought for what he believed. He made a stand.

We cannot be silent about what matters. What matters to you? Who are you advocating for? Thinking of MLK today reminded me of who I advocate for and that I had dropped the ball. I let my "full plate" be my excuse. Whoever you advocate for, thank you for making a stand! What would the world look like if we all took one giant MLK step?

———

ACTION STEP: Spend a few minutes answering the following prompts:

What matters to you? Is it climate change, endangered species, or inner-city youth? Write down who or what matters to you.

How can you be better about giving of your time, talent, and treasure to what matters most to you?

How Are You?

—ɷ—

I was in New York City having dinner with a friend. Neither of us even came close to finishing our individual gourmet pizzas so we asked for them "to go". My friend gave his pizza to me because he was about to enter into the high holy day of Yom Kippur and he would begin his fast thereafter.

I took the pizzas with me in a brown shopping bag and headed down into the train station. As soon as I entered the building, I could sense someone close by. As I looked over my shoulder, I saw a young man who appeared to me to be homeless. I could feel myself tense up instantly. He said, "How are you?" in a very kind voice. I perfunctorily responded, "I'm well, how are you?" His response floored me. "I can tell you but you don't really care about the answer." Wow! As I went to respond, the truth of his words stung. Not just coming from him, but from anyone. I said, "No, I do care," but he called me on it again and said, "Um, maybe, but I don't think so."

At this point we reached the area where we were going to part ways. I said, "Have a great night!" and he responded in kind. As I turned away, I felt the weight of the pizzas dangling from the shopping bag in my right hand. I quickly looked back to my new friend and yelled, "Hey!" He turned and I jogged over to him, wanting to protect his dignity, I whispered. "Are you hungry?" He quickly nodded yes. I handed him the bag of pizzas and he was profusely grateful. We laughed a little bit and we wished each other well again. As I walked away, he yelled, "And I love your hair!" I don't know where that thought came from, but he made me laugh out loud.

I am so glad I chose to face my fear when he first spoke to me. He taught me a valuable lesson about asking, "How are you?" Am I really asking because I care or are my words mechanical and uninterested? I will carry him in my heart for a long time.

––––––––

ACTION STEP: Spend 5 minutes journaling about how this story applies to you. Maybe it is about the greeting, "How are you?" or the homeless, or maybe it is about something else altogether. You decide, but tune in to what spoke to you. This exercise is about awareness.

How Does Your Garden Grow?

—◊—

You may think it is winter, but it is not. It is spring. If you are in an area where snow is currently blanketing your yard, you may be seriously questioning my declaration.

January is when we start the year by setting new goals. So January is our spring as we set out to plant the seeds for the new year. If we do not plant any seeds now, there will be nothing to harvest later.

> "You're frustrated because you keep waiting for the blooming of flowers of which you have yet to sow the seeds."
>
> —STEVE MARABOLI

If you have not planted anything yet, now is the time to do so. It is certainly not too late. We reap what we sow. We must intentionally plant our garden now so we can harvest our dreams in the future. Just as a seed produces a plant, so do our actions produce results. Gardens do not grow by wishing them so. It is spring. What are you going to plant?

———

ACTION STEP: Today, you are the gardener. Journal for a few minutes about what you would like to plant so that later this year you will be able to reap a bountiful harvest. We reap what we sow. Sow away!

I Don't Eat Cake

In our attempt to achieve any goal, it will require us to change our ways. We will need to break old habits and develop new ones, both of which are difficult. Willpower alone will not do the trick, but willpower connected to a strategy is highly effective.

Here is a particularly useful strategy that was recently discovered by researchers at Boston College and the University of Houston. They found word choice to have a profound psychological effect. The phrases, "I can't" versus "I don't" seemingly have a subtle difference but can have very powerful effects on our thoughts, feelings, and behavior.

We would tend to say, "I can't have cake, I'm on a diet," but if we change that statement to, "I don't eat cake," we are far more likely to be successful. "I don't" is experienced as a choice, so it feels empowering. It is an affirmation of our determination and willpower. "I can't" is not a choice—it is a self-imposed restriction. So thinking "I can't" undermines our sense of power.

In the study, 8 out of 10 women using the "I don't" strategy were successful in achieving their goal, versus 1 out of 10 in the "I can't" group.

Here is an extra bonus: when talking about the gym or exercise, choose "I get to" versus "I have to". "I get to" changes our perspective on exercise.

ACTION STEP: Where do you need to implement this "I don't" strategy? Spend 5 minutes journaling on where you are currently using "I can't" when "I don't" might be a better choice.

The Greatest Generation

—◦◦◦—

Recently, I attended my Aunt Joan's 85th surprise birthday party. She comes from a very small family; it was only her and my father, who has already passed. This beautifully intimate luncheon was attended by all of her children and grandchildren, my siblings, and me.

We all sat around my aunt and had the privilege of listening to her tell stories of the past which I had never heard. She told of my dad meeting General MacArthur as he arrived via ship in New Guinea and how the General pulled rank on my father, making him unload his furniture before he unloaded the food that was on the ship for the men. This contentious meeting began my father's lifelong hatred of the General.

She also told a story of my dad creating a code on the face of his letters to his mom during the war so she could decipher where he was actually stationed, which was classified information. I sat next to my aunt, riveted to her every word about all of this rich history I was learning for the first time.

On our way home, Doug said to me, "Our parents lives were so much more interesting than ours will ever be." His words struck a chord with me. The Greatest Generation is sitting on a treasure trove of amazing stories that will remain there unless we ask them to share it with us.

I am headed on a trip with my mother-in-law soon and I cannot wait to ask her so many questions I have about her childhood. Is there a treasure trove in your life waiting to be unearthed? It will not be there forever. It is precious and rich and only requires that we ask, "Please, tell me about your childhood."

———

ACTION STEP: Who will you call and make a date with to hear all the stories of the past?

The Top 4%

—〰—

Over the weekend, I had the honor of attending our dear friend's Eagle Scout Celebration. If you have never been to one, all I can say is, "Wow! I want to be a Boy Scout now!"

Eagle Scout is the highest achievement attainable in the Boy Scouting program. The designation "Eagle Scout" was founded over 100 years ago. Only 4% of Boy Scouts have earned this rank. The requirements necessary to achieve this rank take years to fulfill. To do so speaks volumes about the character of the individual Scout. These young men are remarkable.

Why do only 4% achieve this rank? Some of the reasons are: fear, time required, lack of confidence, lack of drive, lack of persistence, etc. All of these "excuses" that the 96% use are really just roadblocks in their minds!

You and I might not be Boy Scouts, but we can certainly take a page from their handbook. I want to be in that 4%, what about you? The top 4% are always remarkable, exceptional, and uncommon. I want that. Thank you Andrew, my favorite Eagle Scout, for inspiring me to reach for that top 4%.

————

ACTION STEP: Where in your life would you like to achieve "Eagle Scout" status? Is it your marriage or at work? Where do you want to be "remarkable, exceptional, and uncommon"? Spend the next few minutes journaling about how you can get yourself into that top 4%.

Flex Your Muscles

—ɯ—

Willpower. What is willpower? Is it a virtue that you are born with? Do some people have more of it than others? Can we increase it?

There are two things we need to know about willpower. First, everyone has it, some more than others. Willpower is like a muscle though, it will increase in direct proportion to how much we use it. The second thing we need to know is willpower comes in limited supply throughout the day. It is at its peak first thing in the morning and will continue to wane all day long, which is good to know if we plan our daily exercise for after work.

How can we increase our willpower:

1. Get enough sleep
2. Eat a healthy breakfast
3. Exercise
4. Meditate
5. Find Inspiration (scientifically proven to boost motivation)

Knowing motivation will continue to decline all day long, it is important to make sure we front load our day. Try to avoid things at the end of the day that will be very hard to resist. If we cannot avoid it, then we will need to find inspiration to empower us.

———

ACTION STEP: Spend 5 minutes writing about willpower. How and when is willpower failing you? Now that you know more about willpower, can you manipulate it to your advantage?

You Can Heal Your Life

—⚉—

Eastern medicine has long held the belief that the physical manifestation of an illness always has an emotional root. In simpler terms, our own thought patterns (unresolved psychological/emotional issues) affect the health of our body. Each emotional thought pattern is really an underlying cause of a physical illness. If we can identify and address the cause, we are far more likely to be able to rid the body of the ailment.

My "bible" on this subject is *You Can Heal Your Life* by Louise Hay. In her best-selling book, originally printed in 1984, she lays out each ailment, a probable emotional cause, and a new thought pattern. Let me be brutally clear, if you are sick you should seek medical attention. This book is not in lieu of seeing your doctor, it is in addition to seeing your doctor. Adding this book to any treatment plan is a way for you to heal your body with your mind and to heal your mind with your body.

Let me share an example from Louise Hay's book:

PROBLEM: Lower back pain

PROBABLE EMOTIONAL CAUSE: Financial woes and concerns

NEW THOUGHT PATTERN: I trust the process of life. All I need is taken care of. I am safe.

If any of this resonates with you, consider adding the affirmations Ms. Hay's book offers to help change your thought pattern. I know this may be a completely foreign concept. My goal is to expose you to another way of looking at the process that is not so mainstream. I have used her book, without fail, for years now. This book has always been spot-on with every one of my physical ailments and those of others.

———

ACTION STEP: I am strongly encouraging you to get this book. In the meantime, Google some of your ailments, along with Louise Hay, and see what surfaces. I will give you one warning; you must be clear on the ailment. A friend had a tumor in her neck; I researched neck when I should have researched tumor.

I'll Show You

—✺—

Tom Brady is amazing. At the time of this writing he has taken the New England Patriots to the Super Bowl nine times. Of the nine appearances, the Patriots won six and lost three. He is arguably one of the greatest quarterbacks of all times, and let the record show, I am a Philadelphia Eagles fan.

Here is what you need to know about Tom Brady, regardless of whether or not you are a football fan: in the 2000 draft, Tom Brady was not chosen until the 6th round. To put that into perspective; 198 players were chosen before him. There are only 256 players chosen in total, so only 57 players came after him. 80% of the draft was complete when New England took Brady.

What does Brady's story mean to you and me? It doesn't matter where we start, what matters is how we finish. Our past does not define us, unless we let it. Being chosen so late in the draft gave Brady a chip on his shoulder, an "I'll show you" attitude that we all could use to our benefit.

Is there a place in your life where you have accepted your *draft number* as your lot in life? Brady absolutely did not accept that and neither should we! Today, join me in saying, "I'll show you!" about something in our life we wholeheartedly are unwilling to accept, and now let's go change it!! It is one powerful thought away.

———

ACTION STEP: Before you can say, "I'll show you," you need to pinpoint exactly what the *late draft pick* was in your life. Was it your education or job choice? Spend a few minutes journaling about where you think you and Tom Brady have had similar journeys and what you could do about it now.

Jar of Success

—⚭—

I was reviewing last year's goals yesterday to assess how successful I had been in achieving each of them. I realized quickly, while reviewing my Health and Wellness Goals, some goals are not quantifiable if I do not keep a record. My memory does not qualify as a reputable source of valid information, but that was all I had to use. I declared, "I definitely did a better job working out last year than the previous year." That statement is true but it did not shed a whole lot of light on the level of my success.

Had I kept a solid record of the number of times I had gone to the gym, I would have then been able to truly feel successful and proud. Documenting gives us a sense of accomplishment, but it does not have to be very official, it can be fun. I read about a woman who put a marble in a jar for every workout and, as the jar overflowed, so did her pride. There was another woman who put a dollar in a jar for every workout, and would withdraw her coffers every few months to treat herself to something special.

If we are not keeping track of all our hard work, we are missing a very valuable motivational tool. If neither of these ideas excite you, go to Pinterest and start browsing there, but keep track of your progress in some way. January is almost over, can we imagine how full our jar would be right now?

P.S. After I wrote this, I started putting a dollar in a jar after every workout. For a while things were looking great, until one day the jar was no longer looking full. I realized my children were *borrowing* from it so they could buy snacks at lunch. You might want to hide your jar!

———

ACTION STEP: Today, spend your 5 minutes journaling about ways you could document your successes. If you decide on a money jar, I highly recommend hiding it!

Hooah!

—◁∭▷—

I am an enormous fan of the book *Think and Grow Rich* by Napoleon Hill. I teach a class on this book, and my favorite chapter is entitled "Persistence." This chapter changed my life. Persistence is the difference between success and failure. People give up far too quickly on goals and dreams that are achievable if only they would apply a bit more determination and persistence. Do you know that only 2 out of 100 people will continue after a second failure? Two percent will have the persistence to carry on. I always want to be that 2% and I hope that you do too.

Persistence is a habit. It is a mental decision we can make to persevere, regardless of how bumpy the road gets along the way. The Navy Seals are a great example of this. Two-hundred men go into training and only 20 graduate. All two-hundred are qualified to succeed but the goal of the training is to find the sailors who will not quit. Those with enough mental toughness to get through the seemingly impossible.

Naval instructors make it extremely hard to do what they ask, and they also make it easy to quit. At the main office sits a bell. If the pain and misery and coldness and fatigue become too much, all they need to do is ring the bell and they are done, permanently. No questions asked. Nobody gets upset. No judgments. The bell gets shined every day, every Seal touches it every day, and every day there are more helmets lined up of those that have rung the bell—reminding the others of those who have quit.

The Seals are not looking for the best athlete, they are testing their resolve. They want to see how deep their desire goes. They need to know that when they serve they will not quit, they will never ring the bell. On this journey called life, remember this, you may stumble and you may fall. That is when you need to get up and move forward, but DO NOT ring the bell! Hooah!

———————

ACTION STEP: Today you get to journal as if you are a Navy Seal. Think of something in your life you really want. It may be a difficult road, but it is achievable. Spend a few minutes writing about how you will use the mindset of the Navy Seal, as well as the information you just received on persistence, to accomplish this desired goal. DO NOT ring the bell.

TGIF or Is It TGIT

—m—

Which is the best day of the week? Automatically, almost everyone would likely say Friday, but it depends on what we mean by "the best" day. If we are looking for "happy," then Friday is our day. But, if we are looking for inspiration, then Tuesday is a much better choice. Tuesday is the king of inspiration, and not just by a little bit. A recent study found that inspiration is 79% more likely to occur on a Tuesday than on a Friday.

So, for now, go with happy if you are picking the best day of the week. Enjoy all of the weekends that are surrounded by freedom and autonomy, but if you are working on anything that will need inspiration and you are not feeling it, fear not, Tuesday is right around the corner!

———

ACTION STEP: Today, regardless of the day of the week, is a day off. Simply enjoy it knowing that Tuesdays **and** Fridays are awesome days!

The Leash

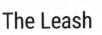

As I was walking the dog last week, I was intrigued by her leash. Of course, part of me loved that she could not run away or get into the street, but there was another part of me that felt apologetic for her tight restrictions.

I watched her try to wander off and explore but the leash did not offer her that luxury. She pushed the limits of her leash for a while, but then a sad thing happened, she stopped challenging the leash. She accepted her restrictions. She toed the line and remained safe for the rest of our walk. I cried, not for the dog, but at the thought of the "leash" I had put on my children and the "leash" that had been put on me at a young age.

The leash has a big price tag. If we are always on a leash, how do we learn to take risks? What are we missing just beyond the length of our rope? The leash can be subtle. Sometimes we forget that it is even there, but it most certainly is there, holding us back. Do you have a leash on yourself, your children, or your employees? It is within our control to let both others and ourselves off the leash, or at least lengthen the rope.

Success does not simply occur; it must be actively pursued by taking risks. Dreams are not achieved by those on a leash. I doubt anyone ever achieved greatness by playing it safe. So take some risks. Failure is definitely a possibility, but so is success. Let's agree to get rid of the leash!

ACTION STEP: Today, spend a few minutes thinking about the leash that is on you. It is keeping you "safe," it does not allow risk-taking, and it is holding you back. When you are done, consider journaling for another few minutes on the leash you may possibly be putting on your family or employees.

One Word

—ɷ—

As you begin this new year in earnest today, I want to share one word with you that I had previously shared with each of my individual clients. The word is *invincible*. Webster's Dictionary defines invincible as incapable of being conquered, overcome, or subdued.

I share this word today because many of us, although determined to succeed, have in the back of our mind a nagging fear that maybe we will fail with our resolutions, goals, and objectives. I wanted to offer a new thought to battle that nagging fear. What if we are *invincible*? What if we are truly incapable of being conquered? Both failing and invincible are just a thought away and I want all of us to engage in the more empowering thought.

This new year will not fly by without its fair share of challenges. When these challenges come, and I mean *when* not if, because they are coming, we all need to have a powerful line of defense. It is important to know you are *invincible*. How do we become invincible? Simply by choosing to be so. Today, please join me in choosing to be invincible!

———

ACTION STEP: What would this new year look like if, every day, you said to yourself, "As I begin this day toward my resolutions, goals, and objectives, I must remember I AM INVINCIBLE"? Spend a few minutes journaling about those three words.

Stronger Still

—〰—

The New Year has arrived! It is the dawn of a new day for all of us. Shedding last year has made us lighter, good or bad. It is gone, finished, behind us. Well, not so fast. Unless we really came to terms with what we left behind, we may find it has followed us into this new year and it is most unwelcomed.

Here is a simple exercise that will rid us of any residual from last year that we do not want latching onto us like a barnacle at the bottom of a boat.

STEP 1: Write down any large negative experience from last year. If there are more than one, write them all down.

STEP 2: Below each experience, write all the strengths that served you well during these times, as well as any lessons you may have learned, no matter how hard they were to learn.

STEP 3: Read through this paper one last time so you recognize how much stronger you have become after having had such an experience. Now, destroy the paper in a fireplace (disposing of it in the trash is not enough).

Have you ever thought or said, "You don't understand what I am going through." Pay attention to the word choice. "Going through" means you will come out on the other side, presumably stronger than before. Perhaps you already did come "through," and if so, accept all your new strengths as gifts.

———

ACTION STEP: It is a brand new year which is liberating. Choose today to release yourself of anything from last year that will weigh you down and limit your freedom to move forward.

"Begin with the End in Mind."

STEPHEN COVEY

—⁂—

Forrest Gump takes it one step further by adding, "If you do not know where you are going, then you probably will not end up there." Today we are focusing on how stress is impacting our health. One really great way to not only reduce stress but also to become massively productive, is to begin with the end in mind. What do I mean by that?

First, for anything we want to accomplish, it is critical that we pick a *by then* date and this date cannot be changed. Once the date is set, we can work within that window of time to accomplish the task. This is an extremely effective tool. *By then* changes everything.

Second, it is imperative that we plan our day, every day, and work from the plan. Once we have written down what needs to get accomplished, we are less likely to get distracted or pulled off course.

For me, planning my day makes me massively productive. I find there is nothing more satisfying than checking things off my list. Planning also makes me efficient, and when I end the day accomplished, focused, and efficient, I am invariably less stressed.

———

ACTION STEP: Do you plan your day? This is a *must*! If you do not have a planner, please purchase one. It should be big enough to jot down not only your commitments but also your daily tasks or priorities. I use Franklin Planner, but there are so many to choose from. Give yourself a *by then* **date** to order your new planner—it should be no more than a week out.

Come Monday

—ɯ—

Research shows that more heart attacks occur on Monday morning than on any other day of the week. Furthermore, they occur between 5am and 10am. According to researchers, an outpouring of stress hormones, such as cortisol and adrenaline, occurs within working people on Mondays. The data led researchers to conclude that Monday is the most stressful day of the week when it comes to risk factors for a heart attack.

So, how is that motivational? Well, knowledge is power and stress is real. Regardless of whether or not we like our job, Monday is stressful, so we need to address this stress. What steps are you taking to reduce your stress as you head into Monday? My guess is none. If you are like most people, you already start checking emails before your feet hit the floor in the morning. Are you frantically trying to get work done before you even get to the office? Is your mindset, "Work, work, work"?

Here are some Monday morning stress-reducing tips:

1. Do not leave it for Monday. On Sunday night, make a plan for the week.
2. Listen to a 10-minute guided meditation before getting out of bed. (This is a very powerful de-stressor).
3. Make a playlist of songs that have a happy memory for you and listen to them either in the car or on the train on your way to work.
4. Exercise (doctor approved, of course)! Go outside and get some fresh air, if that is an option.
5. Deep breathing exercises are helpful as we so rarely breathe deeply.

———

ACTION STEPS: Go back to the stress reducing tips and circle the three you are most likely going to do! I believe tip #2 and #5 are the most powerful.

Success Tip

—⚭—

Here is a tip that will increase your success, whether it be at home or at work. Every day, write down the most important thing you can do today and then get it done.

This is not a to-do list. "Pick up dry cleaning" is not the target. It might be, "Get into work earlier so I can get some critical work-related reading done before the day begins" or stay late if you are not a morning person. Or it might be, "Be aware of how much I am yelling at the kids and target more household peace daily."

I do not know what your most important items are, but I do know if we do not put them down on paper and tackle them every day as a **priority**, rarely, if ever, will they get done. Write down three things a day, but start with one, one really great thing you want done in your life. Make it important. What will take you to the next level professionally or personally? These are done-in-a-day tasks. You can do this!!

———

ACTION STEP: From now on, write down in this book, the most important task (or more) that will raise you up as an individual. Create an acronym for this if you would like, or simply use My Top 3. This one tip has made me significantly more productive. It is my override button for procrastination.

An Overnight Success

—⚊—

"Opportunity is missed by most people because it is dressed
in overalls and looks like work."   —THOMAS EDISON

Brilliant!! At first glance it appears as though Edison was alluding to laziness being the cause of missed opportunity. But I do not think he was saying that at all.

Many people will say how lucky successful people are because they invented something or were in the right place at the right time, but rarely is that true. That is usually not the whole story, and it certainly was not the whole story for Thomas Edison. All of these accomplished people rolled up their sleeves and worked tirelessly, sometimes for years, to become an "overnight" success.

You might think you want to be an overnight success, but there is nothing like the satisfaction that accompanies hard work. Opportunity is sitting at our doorstep right now! We need to put on our overalls and get to work. It will not be easy, but I promise it will be worth it. Actually, the journey may be as much fun as the success. Edison would agree, I'm sure.

———

ACTION STEP: Revisit, in your mind, the times you remember hard work, mental or physical, that paid off. Spend 5 minutes journaling about that memory, and specifically remember how you felt.

Get Smart

—))(—

"Education is the most powerful weapon which you can use
to change the world." —NELSON MANDELA

Even at a very early age, my children started to educate me. I loved when they brought home facts from school that I did not know. Am I smarter than a 5th grader? LOL, maybe not.

One night, I was talking with my son, Liam, who was a senior in high school at the time. Liam was taking a marine science class that really captured his attention. He started telling me about orcas and how Sea World, and others like them, have outright abused these beautiful animals. He said, "You should really watch the documentary *Blackfish*." So I did.

Wow! It was a powerful movie and, as a result, I don't foresee me ever visiting Sea World. Having this particular conversation with Liam and then watching the movie reminded me that there is no excuse not to be educated. Powerful information is sitting at our fingertips. Maybe you do not care about orcas but you care about the rainforest. Take a pass on Grey's Anatomy once a month and watch a documentary. What do you want to learn about? Fracking? The Meat Industry? Cartels? Global Warming? There is a documentary about almost anything. If we all watched one documentary a month, imagine how informed we would be after just one year? Nelson Mandela was spot-on: "Education is the most powerful weapon which you can use to change the world." But only if we use it.

ACTION STEP: No journaling today! I want you to watch a documentary. It sounds simple but wait until you see how many documentaries are available to watch. The good news is documentaries are generally shorter than movies. Make some popcorn, kick back and enjoy!

It's About Time!

—⟋⟍—

Do you find yourself repeatedly saying, "I just need more time!"

Here are five ways to capture more time:

1. Get organized.
2. Plan your day in advance.
3. Eliminate interruptions.
4. Turn off the internet (1–10 hours is wasted each day).
5. Stop multi-tasking. Multi-tasking will drain your mental energy by 40%. Complete the task at hand, then move on.

I always need more time and this five-step approach has made an enormous difference in my productivity. I am certain this strategy will help you as well.

———

ACTION STEP: Look at the list of five items above and circle the one that could be the most helpful in capturing more time for you. Now, take 5 minutes to journal about this idea and how you can best implement it in your life.

The Lost Art of the Handwritten Note

Gratitude is an emotion expressing appreciation for what one has rather than what one wants. Gratitude is getting a great deal of press nowadays. Studies show that we can increase our well-being and happiness by deliberately cultivating gratitude. Gratefulness—and especially expression of it to others—is proven to be associated with increased energy, optimism, and empathy.

We talk about gratitude and we say we are grateful, but it is not the same as expressing it to others. Recently, I wrote a thank you note to my husband and I clandestinely placed it in his car at night so he would find it on his way to work in the morning. I thanked him for everything for which I was feeling grateful. I thanked him for all he provides for our family, for his long daily commute, for his intense loyalty, etc. Writing that letter brought me so much joy to definitively express how much I appreciate Doug and all he does for our family.

I know you are grateful for many people and things in your life. If you have a free moment, write someone a thank you note expressing your gratitude. Writing it down allows you time to genuinely incorporate all of your thoughts and feelings. Maybe it is not a spouse, but someone else. Let them know. You will both receive the powerful effects of gratitude.

ACTION STEP: Spend a few minutes today writing a thank you note to someone close to you. Those closest are rarely the ones we send a genuine and heartfelt handwritten note. They deserve it.

A Really Big Question

—∿—

Each day I post on Facebook. Very often, if not daily, I hear from someone who says, "I loved your post! I feel like you wrote it just for me. I needed to hear that today." Although compliments like that are wonderful to hear, it still does not answer a big question I have lingering in my mind.

Many of the things I write about, I think you already know on some level. Maybe not the way I posture them, but your gut was already telling you what I just affirmed in writing. So the big question I have is this: "Why don't more people act?" The information is "speaking to you," yet there is a big disconnect between hearing the words and actually taking the next step forward. Why?

I think about this all the time. What is holding us back? Is it fear? Is it procrastination? Is it the packed schedule? We need to figure out why we are not taking the next step. Sometimes in life we have to dig deep, muster up our bravery, and just do it. Not doing it certainly has not helped, so let's try doing it instead and see what happens. But please do not say, "What if . . ." The pessimistic scenarios we create in our heads are most often not even remotely plausible. We need to act. Let's go!

ACTION STEP: You have read this book for over a month now. Are you one of those people who love the advice but do not act? If that question spoke to you, then journal for 5 minutes about why you do not act. Make sure you journal not only about the problem of moving forward but also journal on the solution.

My Biggest Obstacle

—✺—

"Get out of your own way. Seriously. Move."
—AUTHOR UNKNOWN

More often than not, with myself as well as with my clients, I find the biggest obstacle standing in the way of **my** success and attaining what **I** want is **me**. I want the roadblock to be an outside source; I want to blame something or someone else, but truthfully it boils down to me getting in my own way.

Maybe it is anxiety, doubt, or a lack of confidence. Maybe it is my ego or my critical inner voice that stands between me and what I want. Unfortunately, what I do to avoid acknowledging that it is really me getting in my own way is I pass the blame onto someone or something else. I have blamed previous failures on everything from PowerPoint to Oprah!

If I really want to be truthful, Oprah didn't do anything wrong. She's lovely. It's me. I got in my own way. And, the quicker I acknowledge my own hindrance, the quicker I can get moving again.

Does this ever happen to you? Ask yourself now, "Is it possible that I am the one standing in my own way?" If the answer is "Yes," the best part is you are easier to move than anyone else! So seriously, move!

———

ACTION STEP: Today, journal for a few minutes on how you are in your own way. Now that you know that, how will you get out of the way?

Oranges to Avocados

—∿—

Do you ever find yourself comparing yourself to others? With social media, it is almost impossible not to compare. I have found, when I compare myself to others, I invariably make myself miserable. The self-talk that ensues is cruel and merciless. Heading down that rabbit hole rarely pays off.

Here is the truth about comparisons, you will never win. Never. The second truth about a comparison is that any comparison will be unfair. Our gifts, talents, successes, contributions and value are entirely unique to us and our purpose in this world. They can never be properly compared to anyone else. It is like saying the orange is more visually beautiful than the avocado. The only fair comparison is comparing the us of today to the us of yesterday.

We have been given a unique set of gifts. These gifts have been given to us so we will use them to the best of our ability. This world needs us to tap into those gifts immediately and start sharing them. So we must stop looking left and right and wishing we were someone else. Look inside, grab your God-given gifts and start sharing them with the world. We are unique for a reason. Our comparisons are wasting precious time and energy as well as making us very unhappy. Be grateful for, not jealous of, everyone's unique giftedness.

Post Script: I will share a quote from my friend Kim who is perhaps the happiest person I know. She said, "I find it most helpful to continuously be grateful for what I have, not focus on what I don't have, and not compare my life with others."

ACTION STEP: Today, spend 5 minutes focusing on what you do have. Reread the last paragraph. What are your gifts? The world needs those gifts.

Kindness Begets Kindness.

———ᴡ———

No truer words have ever been said, but I will be the first to admit, it is easier said than done. As you look at the quote, you might be thinking, "Beth, what is your problem? Just be kind and kindness will come back to you." I agree, except, that is only the case if you are starting from a level playing field.

When "kindness begets kindness" really comes into play is when there is anything but kindness happening. I would love to say this only happens at the local coffee shop or the parking lot of the mall at Christmas time, but very often it is happening in my own home.

Yup, I went there. The inside of my house is not always an episode from Leave it to Beaver. So the challenge is, how can we remain kind when we really want to defend our position, make our point, and most of all, be right?

Well, like most things in life, we have a choice. I know it is difficult, but we have a choice to remain calm and offer kindness or jump into the disagreement and fight fire with fire. Rarely does that end well. I certainly know that first hand. It tends to makes more fire.

The resolution lies with the person who chooses the higher ground, the person who can control his or her emotions and the person who leads with kindness. It is a miraculous neutralizing agent. Fire does not know what to do with kindness. So, if you have your own battles at home like I do, would you like to join me on a *kindness crusade*? We can rally together. The kids won't know what hit them. I am sure we will get a few comments thrown back at us like, "You're acting weird." It will be our little secret.

———

ACTION STEP: Today we simply have marching orders: Do NOT engage in the fight. Kindness only. Extinguish all fires now.

Spontaneity

—⟫⟫—

Infuse your life with happiness! Do not wait for it to happen. Make it happen.

Interesting fact: Spontaneity has a direct correlation to happiness. There is something about the flow of spontaneity that breeds happiness. We live in such a planned society, rarely do we allow for spontaneity. We say, "No," even before we have mentally processed the spontaneous thought. We have become so conditioned to following a plan that we feel uncomfortable in the absence of one.

We have made planning a habit, therefore it falls within our comfort zone. Spontaneity lives a vivacious life just outside our comfort zone, waiting for us to open the door and jump in. Happiness and fun are so conveniently and fortuitously located that all we have to do is open the door. Say, "Yes," to a spontaneous idea and experience the resulting joy, happiness, and fun.

A word of warning for my ardent planners out there (me included): you cannot plan a spontaneous idea. I know you were planning the entire time you were reading this post. It does not work that way. Synonyms of spontaneous are unplanned, instinctive, impromptu, ad-lib, without premeditation, and extemporaneous. I hope these words help. They certainly helped me.

———

ACTION STEP: When were you last spontaneous? Is there a recent memory or is it in the distant past? Spend 5 minutes journaling about the word *spontaneous* and how it has or will fit into your life. Here is one way to be spontaneous with only a little premeditation: pick a time that works for you to be spontaneous. When that time arrives, go do something completely free-spirited and perhaps out of character.

Where Is the Richest Place on Earth?

—✺—

I am certain you have heard this question before. Is it the diamond mines of South Africa? The gold mines in the U.S? Or the oil fields of the Middle East?

> "The graveyard is the richest place on earth, because it is here that you will find all the hopes and dreams that were never fulfilled, the books that were never written, the songs that were never sung, the inventions that were never shared, the cures that were never discovered, all because someone was too afraid to take that first step, keep with the problem, or determined to carry out their dream." —LES BROWN

What do you have burning inside of you? What dream have you talked yourself out of? I know it is in you, we all have something inside of us that we need to breathe life into. How much longer are we going to suppress this dream? All we need to do is take the first step. Promise yourself today that you will take the first step. Do not take *it* with you to the graveyard. What good would that do?

———

ACTION STEP: What is *your* dream? Write it down here. Why are you not moving forward with your dream? Spend 5 minutes writing about it. Be honest with yourself, are you the one standing in the way of your own dream? Can you commit to one action step to move toward the realization of your dream? Take just one baby step forward.

It Was Nothing

—⚇—

"No worries," "It was nothing," and "Don't mention it" are phrases I often responded with when I was being thanked by someone for lending a helping hand. Little did I know what an enormous mistake I was making.

When I dismissed someone's appreciation with a quick "it was nothing," I did not *receive* the "thank you" that was genuine and heartfelt and directed toward me; but, more importantly, I missed the opportunity to tell my friend how much it meant to me to be able to help.

Going forward, I will be using a few new phrases, phrases that authentically represent how I felt about helping, and they will sound more like this . . .

"It was my complete pleasure," "I am so glad you asked me to help," or "The pleasure was all mine."

ACTION STEP: If you are not already using them, consider using these responses next time you do someone a favor. These words are much better at completing the give and receive equation.

The World Is Flat

—ᵐ—

I spoke at Prudential recently and one of the topics I discussed was *Beliefs*. Beliefs drive everything. Our beliefs determine our potential; they drive our actions and, therefore, our results. But here is the catch about beliefs: they are not necessarily true or factual and, therefore, are very often limiting and misleading.

For example, many years ago everyone believed the world was flat. You and I believed there was a Santa Claus (I still kind of believe that one!) So what if a lot of our beliefs are just like these two? What if our beliefs are holding us back and limiting us and they are not even true?

I graduated from Rutgers University. If I had graduated from Harvard, would I have a different belief in myself? You betcha. We all create a self-image of "Who I am" based on our beliefs. Most of these beliefs were formed from past experiences, successes and failures, and many came from our early childhood.

What if I told you the limiting belief you currently have of yourself is as true as "the world is flat" and Santa Claus exists? We can really challenge ourselves by asking pointed questions like, "What if my belief about me is wrong?" and "What if my belief of who I am is not even close to what I am truly capable of?" When you get the true answers to these questions, then we can make things happen!

———

ACTION STEP: What limiting beliefs are you living under? What do you say internally about yourself and your potential that is unkind, limiting, and/or self-deprecating? Here are a few doozies I have said to myself:

I do not have enough time.

I am too old.

It is too late to change.

I have too many responsibilities.

Journal for a few minutes today on any of the above limiting beliefs (which are not true, by the way), or any other limiting beliefs you can think of. The goal of this exercise is to write about all the ways this limiting belief is not true.

Life Can Be Tough

—∽—

Have you noticed that life is tough sometimes? OK, maybe it is tough more than just sometimes. Life can be downright cruel. But here is what I have noticed with myself and my clients and maybe this will resonate with you as well: often, I find that after taking the blow in life, people suffer in that dark place for a long time. My job, as a coach, is to get them back to where they were and then on to an even better place, but I always wonder where they would be if they were not seeking some kind of assistance.

If you are in that space now, please do not feel the need to go it alone. Our culture has this "I can't show any sign of weakness" mentality that, quite frankly, is ridiculous because the strong person is the one who takes the risk to ask a friend for some support during a rough patch. Two heads are always better than one. Always!

If it is not you going through a rough patch, maybe it is a friend. Our lives are so busy, we rarely stop to think. What would happen today if we all reached out to one person? Do you know someone who is grieving? Is there someone who is struggling with their children or their spouse? Do you know anyone who has a health issue (mental or physical)? Do you know anyone out of work? Who could use a phone call?

I know at least one person in each of these categories so I am guessing you do, too. Diana Ross' song says "Reach out and touch somebody's hand, make this world a better place, if you can." That's great advice. We need to actively connect more often so we can give and receive support. Let's go make it happen.

———

ACTION STEP: Pick one person in your life right now who could use a phone call. Write their name here. Commit to making that phone call today. It is as simple as, "I was thinking about you today. How are you?"

Happy Valentine's Day

I am going to take a very nontraditional approach to Valentine's Day this year. First, I have never been a fan of Valentine's Day as a complete marketing ploy nor am I a fan of the price-gouging that goes along with it. Second, it's not celebrated by everyone which makes me uncomfortable. And third, for those who do celebrate, it can very quickly (on social media) become a "keeping up with the Joneses" kind of day—and I REALLY HATE THAT!

So today, I am going to have a very private Valentine's Day. I am going to reach out to those that I love and take a moment to tell them so—thoughtfully, privately, and without contributing to Hallmark, Godiva, or the local floral shop.

Love is an incredibly powerful emotion and it can be shared in many more ways than just romantic love. Actively spreading love changes everyone psychologically and physically; it also creates a sense of safety, increases positivity, and reduces fear.

ACTION STEPS: Today, take a moment and spread the love!

Solitude

—⚉—

With Valentine's Day barely behind us, I may be jumping the gun by talking about solitude. In today's fast-paced world, we rarely take time to be alone. Even when we are alone, we are not alone. We are constantly checking emails, Facebook, texts, Snapchat, Twitter, etc. We check these things even when we know we just finished checking and there was nothing new.

Genuine solitude has tremendous benefits and I am not even going to dwell on the increase in creativity, the decrease in depression, the boost in self-esteem, and the improvement in memory and concentration. I am encouraging each of us to spend time alone so we will finally slow down (stop, really) and allow ourselves to just be. Recharge our battery. Reboot and declutter our mind. It is important to give ourselves time to reflect, take stock, and think deeply. Find our voice again. Reflect on the course of our life. We cannot keep going at this pace.

Even on the best road trip, stopping for fuel, nourishment, and rest is essential. Life is the ultimate road trip. We must make sure we stop along the way. Running out of gas, as well as being hungry and tired makes the journey arduous and the traveler miserable. The choice is ours.

———

ACTION STEP: Today, spend a few minutes planning your getaway. Choose a date. Put it on your calendar. Do not relinquish this date for any reason. Where will you go? Maybe it is a day trip to the beach or a library. Or maybe you can really get away and spend an overnight somewhere. Regardless, it is time to recharge the battery.

Compassion Is a Sign of Strength

—⚡—

The other night, my son played in the semifinal round of a local ice hockey tournament for his high school. It was an intense game that remained within a goal or two until the very end. My son's team won. It was a tough loss for the opposing team as the win was within their reach the whole time.

As the young men came off the ice, they walked up a ramp to the locker room. As all the fans watched, I saw a young man all clad in the opponent's regalia, high-fiving his friends and supporting them after their painful loss. Two of the seniors on the team stopped and hugged this young man. One of the seniors said, "Bud, you have no idea how much it means to me that you were here for this game. Thanks so much."

I could not help but ask myself, "Who is this kid?" After such a loss, how could these teenagers show so much composure to stop and thank one fan? Finally, it was my turn to go up the ramp. I looked over to see who this diehard fan was, and then it all made sense. He was a young man with Down syndrome, standing on the bench intensely searching for more of his team. It was clear he felt compelled to support each and every one of them.

I instantly got choked up. These two senior hockey players amazed me. At such a young age, they get it. They recognized something bigger than themselves. Hockey doesn't matter and neither does winning, but love, compassion, and kindness, now that is how we change the world.

As I watched these three young men share a moment, energetically, it changed the room. Love changes things. There was no better end to

Valentine's Day than being witness to this beautiful moment. Do you want to change the world? Go spread some love!

––––––––

ACTION STEP: Lessons from two seventeen-year-old boys is not an everyday occurrence. Journal today for a few minutes on what you learned from these two young men and how you can spread the love.

Hitting the Brakes

—∞—

Do you know why roller coasters do not have individual brakes for each rider?

Because they know we would apply them! Almost immediately actually. We know in advance the ride is going to be scary. We are somewhat comfortable with our decision to take the ride because we boarded the roller coaster of our own free will. Yet, if they gave us the ability to brake, many of us absolutely would.

Have you ever seen anyone exit a roller coaster after the ride? They are usually smiling and laughing with a look of exhilaration. The journey was scary but fun. They were forced to go through the scary parts with no brakes.

Life is so similar to a roller coaster, but unfortunately, we have a brake. Some of us never take our foot off the brake. Some of us stop and start repeatedly and, as a result, we aren't getting very far. Is your foot on the brake? You cannot move forward if it is and you certainly won't have any fun. Imagine what would change if you took your foot off the brake! Wow!

———

ACTION STEP: Spend your time today answering a few questions:

Is my foot on the brake?

How is my foot on the brake?

What would happen if I took my foot off the brake?

What Are Your *Top 3*?

—⚉—

What are your top three attributes? What do you excel at doing? Have you ever given those questions any serious thought? Take the time to put the answer into writing so you can definitively capture the essence of your giftedness. Most of us will never take the time, but if we do, it will be a ten minute exercise we will not regret taking the time to complete. We need to tell our children to do it as well.

It is only after we really nail down what it is we excel at that we can ask the next obvious question, which most people will not ask themselves; "Am I using all of my top qualities and attributes?" Not using our giftedness is like trying to fly a 747 with one engine. The plane will still fly but it will only fly at its peak when all four engines are functioning at full capacity. Would a pilot ever shut down the other three engines and just make due with one? No. The thought is ridiculous for both the pilot as well as for us.

If you are a natural born leader and you are not leading people, you have shut down an engine. If you have amazing organizational skills and they are not being utilized, you have shut down an engine. No one shuts down an engine on purpose; it usually happens involuntarily, over time. But it will remain shut down until we intentionally coax it back to life. If we want to fire on all cylinders, we need to be using all of our top qualities and giftedness. Let us make sure everyone around us is firing on all cylinders as well; we want everyone operating at full capacity, not just us.

———

ACTION STEP: List your top 3 attributes.
1.
2.
3.

Answer this question, "What am I truly gifted at?"
Am I using all of my gifts?

We Are All Capable of More

—⚋—

"If you treat an individual as he is, he will remain as he is.
But if you treat him as if he were what he ought to be and
could be, he will become what he ought and could be."
—JOHANN WOLFGANG VON GOETHE

If you are a parent, a coach, a teacher, a manager, or you lead people in any way, this quote is for you! In that capacity, think of your children or your staff and know they have not even scratched the surface of their potential. Even if we know what they are capable of, can we challenge them for more? We are all 100% capable of much more than we think we are.

Can the student raise their grade from an 80 to an 84? Yes. Can the athlete produce one more goal a game? Yes. Can the employee up their performance? Yes. What is holding them back? Is it because we have not asked them to be or do more? Is it because they are simply meeting the expectation? Is it because their current results are good enough? Or, is it because no one told them, "I see a lot more in you than you see in yourself. I know you can deliver more than you are currently delivering and I need you to challenge yourself to get there. It is in you. You may not see it, but I do. We need to set the bar higher for you; you are capable of far more than this."

There is no excuse for not living up to our potential. Sometimes, we need a parent, teacher, coach, or boss to see it in us first. That person can set the expectation of our greatness.

Oh, and by the way, to all of the parents, coaches, teachers, and bosses, there is more in you as well. Set the bar higher. You have so much more potential! Challenge yourself.

ACTION STEP: Pick one area in your life that you know you are not operating at 100% and journal about how you can increase your performance just one percent. Raise the bar just one notch.

Roadblocks

—◆—

Have you ever felt like you hit a roadblock in your life?

Do you know that statistically 98% of the population will quit after 1–2 unsuccessful attempts at doing something? We can all relate to quitting after things appear to not be going as planned. We couch it by saying, "Well, I guess it wasn't meant to be," or "Clearly this is a sign," or maybe even "I tried, but it didn't work out."

A roadblock is not a stopping point, metaphorically or literally. If we arrived at a roadblock in real life, we would not abandon the car and walk away. We would take the detour or choose a different route. A roadblock is an opportunity disguised as misfortune. We *will* hit roadblocks in our lives and when we do, we should be grateful and inspired.

Grateful and inspired? Yes, we were saved from going down the wrong road possibly for a long time, and ultimately having to turn around anyway. A roadblock is a blessing but only if we stop and ask ourselves a few really good questions. What is this roadblock trying to tell us? Do we need to make a minor adjustment or a major one? Pause and be grateful for the roadblock and take the time to absorb the *why*.

When we find ourselves at a roadblock, we must not quit. We need to be the 2% who will forge ahead anyway. And, most importantly, when faced with a roadblock, do not think with your mind, because the mind isn't always truthful; stop and listen to your heart and your gut. That is where the truth lies. Be the 2%.

———

ACTION STEP: What roadblock are you currently experiencing? Spend 5 minutes journaling about this roadblock and all the various routes you could take. What is this roadblock trying to tell you? Make sure you answer that question. Even a bad crop has some good fruit. Harvest the good.

No News Is Good News

—∞—

If you begin each day watching the news on the television, you might want to reconsider that decision.

Only reconsider if you want to begin each day happier and with less worry, as watching the news has been scientifically proven to have an adverse effect on our mood as well as heightening our tendency to worry about our own specific problems.

Many years ago, newscasters delivered an impartial news, but this is not the case today. The news, even the weather report, is sensationalized to some degree. Today newscasters emotionalize their news and do so by emphasizing any potential negative outcome, regardless of how minute the probability is of that outcome. In addition, we now have twenty-four hour news coverage and many of these stations are battling against entertainment programs for their viewership.

So why am I telling you this? You don't have to stop watching the news outright if you're enjoying it, but you should be aware of the scientifically proven psychological effects of watching the news on a regular basis. Knowledge is power.

Negatively interlaced news broadcasts are likely to make us sadder and more anxious. In addition, they are also likely to intensify our own personal worries and anxieties. None of us want to be sad, anxious, or worry more!

One option is to read the news. The written form of news eliminates the emotion. If you watch the news on television, then consider reducing the amount you watch, and do not leave the news channel on all day.

Trust me when I tell you, if something big happens, you will know about it!

————

ACTION STEPS: If you typically start your day watching the news, for the next week, change your routine. After a week, check in with yourself and see if you are feeling less anxious and perhaps happier.

Goals

—꿈—

Goal setting is a way for us to reach for what we want. If it is simple, it is not a goal, it is a task. Goal setting is for the big things. The ultimate reason for setting goals is to encourage us to become the person it takes to achieve these bold, audacious goals.

Every person is filled with untapped talent and potential. The ultimate goal in life is to accomplish all that we can with all that we have been given. If you do not have any goals written down, why not? Can you think of just one goal you would like to accomplish this year? Now, imagine one year from today with that goal accomplished! How does it feel? It will not happen by itself, we need to make a plan, but it can be done.

Get serious about writing just one goal. It's all about commitment. We must commit and we must act. Let's do this thing!

———

ACTION STEP: Spend 5 minutes thinking about one goal you would love to accomplish. Put that one goal in writing here. Give it a deadline. Do not get scared because you gave it a deadline. Now plan one action step. We got this!

Food for Thought

—✹—

Lessons on the importance of and the need for gratitude sometimes have a way of sneaking up from behind and walloping me over the head. Somehow, they never arrive in a straightforward fashion.

Yesterday, while meeting with a friend, I was made aware of someone who had really fallen on hard times. So hard, that she had not eaten in a few days and needed to visit a food pantry. This woman does not fit into the box of food pantry recipients, she is not homeless or lacking education. In fact, she is likely more educated than both you and me put together.

This is not something I thought I was going to share with you, but this situation really unraveled me and I now know that it is more common than I had previously thought. If you are like me, when I am asked to donate to the food pantry I do so, but rarely do I think to do so on a regular basis. If you are so inclined, fill a bag with some really good stuff (not the nearly-expired stuff) and drop it off at the food pantry near you. I'm sure it will be well-received.

———

ACTION STEP: Consider calling your local food pantry today to see if they are accepting food donations. Make a plan to complete this worthy task. If you're like me, *later* almost always means never.

One Traffic Light

—✻—

Yesterday, I travelled to Trenton, New Jersey for a meeting. Part of my journey was through the heart of the city. As I sat at a stoplight, I watched seven teenage boys who had clearly just left school, walk down this less-than-inviting street; I could not help but think of my own kids who are essentially the same age.

It was as if the time at this traffic light stood still and only the boys kept moving. My motherly instinct immediately ignited and I was concerned for their safety. I would never let my children walk down this street. Then I thought about the path of these boys future in comparison to that of my own children and how different it likely was going to be.

I felt like this traffic light was intentionally forcing me to stop and reflect. So many emotions bubbled over while I unwillingly sat there: compassion, sadness, gratitude, hope, and fear, just to name a few. This may be the only world these teenagers know, but I know there is another world in which my kids live.

Finally, the traffic light let me go, maybe she knew I had completely received the message she had held me in place for. I believe she wanted me to remember to always be grateful for all of my blessings that I over-look daily. I am grateful for that reminder. I also believe she wanted me to remember to help those who daily walk down a less fortunate street than I do. One traffic light. One transformational traffic light. I am grateful she made me stop.

———

ACTION STEP: Today is a free day. Journal about whatever came to mind as you read my story. What message did you receive?

Peace of Mind

—⚮—

Do you meditate? The most common response I hear when I ask that question is, "I don't have the time to meditate. Plus, I think it is weird." But what if I told you that you are already meditating every day? By definition, to meditate is to think deeply or carefully about something.

We are meditating when our mind slips into worry about finances. We are meditating when we beat ourselves up mentally over our weight gain. And we are certainly meditating when we perseverate on our life, our job, and our future. It is not healthy meditation but, do not be fooled, it is meditation nonetheless.

I tell all my clients, "You don't *not* have time to meditate." I use an app for guided meditation. I usually wake up sometime after five a.m. and meditate for about fifteen minutes, preparing my mind for the day. That fifteen minutes gives me such peace. If this kind of productive and healthy meditation is not for you, then at least be aware of the self-deprecating, destructive meditation that is currently going on in your head and proactively engage in shutting it down.

Meditation is a wonderful gift you give your mind. It can be so powerfully restorative and rejuvenating that once you experience its benefits, you will happily make the time to do it every day. It will prove to be the best way to start the day or to recharge your batteries during the day.

———

ACTION STEP: Today, download one free meditation app and do it for ten minutes. The apps I use are *Relax and Rest* or *Calm*. The best time to meditate is early in the morning. Remember, sleeping is not meditating; meditation is quieting the active mind. To see the most powerful image of a brain scan before and after ten minutes of meditation, go to www.mdmindfulness.com.

Sweet Serendipity

—⚬—

A few years ago our eldest daughter, Devon, was in her senior year of high school, buried in homework and trying to finish her college applications. Doug and I agreed we had to find a way to spend more time with her. We discovered Devon loved a new Thursday night television show, *Scandal,* and we decided it would be fun to watch the show with her.

We had no idea what was about to come from that single decision. We reconnected with Devon, sitting down each Thursday night to watch the show and speculate on what would happen every week. Devon has now graduated from college and *Scandal* is off the air, but it remains an incredibly fond memory for us—thank you Kerry Washington for bringing us all together! Doug and I have maintained this Thursday night ritual, now watching *This Is Us.* It has morphed into a much-coveted date night. I have looked forward to Thursday night for six full years now, first to spend time with Devon and now to spend time with Doug.

I never planned to create a date night with Doug (or Devon), but that is what transpired. I wish I could say I was wise enough to know how important a date night is to a marriage (as well as a stressed-out teenager), but it was serendipitous. Every Thursday night I can count on a few things: a good glass of wine, an hour of *This Is Us,* and a date with my husband! I love Thursdays! Here's to date night!

———

ACTION STEP: Spend 5 minutes today journaling on who could benefit from a date with you! Is it your child, your spouse, or someone else? After you have answered who, answer where and when. Our date night very often takes place in our family room. Sometimes, when the kids come into the family room on Thursday night, I jokingly say, "Are you coming on our date with us?"

Put Your Thinking Cap On

—◊◊—

Fat Tuesday!

For all those non-Christians, this is the day some Christians engage in excessive eating and drinking before the fasting of Lent begins the following day. The history behind the Lenten fast is quite interesting.

In ancient times, it was only practiced by those adults who were in the process of becoming Christian. Under the threat of Roman persecution, becoming a Christian was serious business, so their process of preparation was intense. Their final period of "purification and enlightenment" was the forty days before their baptism at Easter. Eventually, the rest of the Church began to observe the season of Lent in solidarity with these newest Christians.

These observances, which have been in existence since the earliest of times, have been a way for the faithful to turn away from whatever has distracted or derailed them. It has been a way of positively turning one's life back toward God. I suspect every faith has some form of Lent, like the Jewish atonement, Yom Kippur.

Regardless of your faith, it is always important to stop and reflect. Are you on track? Is derailment a possibility, a probability, or a reality? Are you distracted or focused? Are you living the life you dreamed of living or are you just going through life on autopilot? There is a lot to be gleaned from time spent on introspection, soul-searching, and reflection. Don't be afraid to take an honest look at your life, the answers you receive will be worth it.

"Never be afraid to sit awhile and think."

—LORRAINE HANSBERRY

———————

ACTION STEP: Spend 5 minutes today thinking about any of the questions I postulated in the paragraph above. Set a timer on your phone so you don't stop before 5 minutes have expired. Stay focused. When the 5 minutes are up, it may be helpful and telling for you to write down your answers.

The Fun Committee

—⁓—

We added another dog to the house in September. Doug and I were not on board at first, but now we cannot imagine life without both Sophie and Ella. So here is the deal with Ella . . . she is all about the fun. As soon as we walk into the house, she literally scans the immediate area to see what she can grab and brings it to us as if to say, "Wanna play?" We get shoes, laundry, socks, umbrellas, anything so that we know she is ready to play.

Sometimes we play and other times we say, "I have to make dinner," or "I have to study," or "Not now." Hmm. I understand all of those things are important, but Ella reminds me constantly that I do not play enough. Richard Branson has a great quote, and I am paraphrasing, that fun is not a reward, it is a responsibility. Well, Amen to that!

How can we take Ella's advice and add *fun* and *playful* to our day? If you are at work, create a Fun Committee or at least invite everyone out for happy hour after work every once in a while. If you are at home, can you surprise the family with something fun? We are way too serious, almost incurably so. Ella is right; we should all have the mindset of, "Let's play!" It is contagious!

———

ACTION STEP: There are two action steps today.
1. Think of something fun for work or home.
2. Implement the fun!

Pick Your Top 3

—∞—

What are the top three things you need to get done today? Did you write them down? When I say top three, I hope "picking up the dry cleaning" is not one of them. By top three, I mean the three things that will really propel you along in your career or help you attain a big goal or dream.

We get caught up in busy stuff like emails and texting. This era is so fixated on being busy we not only allow the frenzy but pride ourselves on it. We boast about our ability to multitask (which is inefficient, by the way). But most importantly, everyone has access to us 24-7 and although we are supposed to be our own gatekeeper, most of us are not doing such a great job. We allow everything in, which is at our own expense.

So today, as keeper of the gate, lock the door. Decide what really needs to get done. Pick three really important things that, if they get done, will advance you in some way and then go do them! This is a habit we should all be doing every day. The **top three** every day. Once the three are written down, nothing supersedes them. Do not be distracted by what is quick or easy; stay focused on these three things. Unfortunately, the digital age has trained us to focus in short spurts (Snapchat, Twitter, texts). We need to retrain our mind to remain focused and most importantly, limit who and what has access to us and when. All of this technology was created for **our** convenience, not for that of someone else. Choose wisely. Guard your gate.

———

ACTION STEP: Write down your top three "Get 'Er Done" ideas that will propel you forward. And then immediately get started! Remember this is an everyday list.

   1.

   2.

   3.

The Highlight Reel

—⁓—

I had a revelation recently. I was working with my teenage son in preparation for a big lacrosse tournament. I decided part of his *mental prep* should be to watch his highlight reel. His highlight reel is approximately four minutes of him excelling at the sport of lacrosse. He does everything correct, he wins every face-off, and scores on every shot he takes! Pretty sweet, huh? There are no errors and no missed shots; there is nothing but perfection.

After about three nights of watching this with him I thought, "Wow, I wish I was watching my highlight reel every night!" Instead, I have a habit of playing my blooper reel. I replay (and regret) the words I should or should not have said, the phone call I did not make, or the cake I should not have eaten.

Not anymore! I am done with the blooper reel. I now know the impact of a highlight reel, even when it was not my own, and it is very powerful. I may not have physical footage of my days, but I certainly can remember those things I did exceedingly well. I may not always have four minutes of reel, but I will always have some highlights I can play back for myself before I go to sleep at night. I am going to feed my subconscious the highlight reel from now on. The blooper reel will be left on the cutting room floor.

———

ACTION STEP: Keep a journal by your bed. Every night jot down the wins for the day. If you do not have a bedside journal, then go through the various wins in your head. There should be no better way to prepare yourself for a good night's sleep than by reviewing your highlights!

A Lost Art

—m—

Ash Wednesday is a Christian holiday observed by fasting. I know I should never talk about religion, politics, or money but please indulge me for a moment.

Ash Wednesday is the beginning of the observance of Lent which will last until Easter Sunday. During these 40 days (it is 46 really but it excludes Sundays), Christians are supposed to engage in penance, reflection, and fasting. As I reflected on these three components this morning, I said to myself, "It is unfortunate that I essentially only do this once a year. This would be a great practice (even if just for a day), if I did it once a month". Reflection alone is a lost art.

Regardless of your faith, these are three really great practices to consider at any time of the year. It is always a good practice to take some time to acknowledge what we have done wrong, reflect on what we could do to make this world a better place, and indulge a little less. We live in a very busy world. Stopping to reflect might be just the thing this bustling world needs. Just thinking of it brings me peace.

———

ACTION STEP: Today is an action day. Decide how you will engage in all three of these actions. Will you do it just for today or maybe more often?

PENANCE:

REFLECTION:

FASTING: (Please do not take this literally. Perhaps you refrain from eating desserts for the day, or maybe you spend a day being vegetarian, or you could even eliminate processed snacks from your diet)

"I Am Still Learning."

MICHAELANGELO

—⚊—

Inspiring words spoken by Michelangelo at 87 years old.

Now he was a man after my own heart. Regardless of how old we are, I believe, we need to keep learning and growing. But in today's world, it is difficult to find the time. So if there is no extra time, how do we add learning and growing to an already full docket?

Here are three ways to add time to our day for growth. First, we can make our car a mobile classroom. We can listen to podcasts while driving. We spend a lot of time in the car, we might as well make good use of it. I now look forward to all the time I spend in the car. Currently, my mobile classroom is being taught by Jim Rohn.

The second way is to watch an informational video like a TED talk while doing some mindless activity, like making dinner or folding clothes. I certainly feel twice as productive when performing these mundane acts if I am also learning something new.

The third way is to download a book to your phone. When I go for a walk to get some exercise, I always grab my headphones and listen to a book on tape.

We have to find the time to continue to educate ourselves. Our formal education usually ends when we are in our mid-twenties. We cannot let that be the end of our learning.

———

ACTION STEP: What will you do to begin learning and growing? Will you make your car a mobile classroom? Will you download an audible book? Today, journal about who you might like to teach you and what you might like to learn. Then make it happen.

Make Some Memories

—⚉—

In our very busy lives, we forget to breathe. I can only speak for myself, but most often I put my family and work first (which is solid prioritizing) but when it comes to friends, they tend to fall a distant third. One of my goals for this year was to be a better friend, which also linked up well with the theme of, "Say 'yes' to everything."

In an effort to spend more time with my friends, I invited a bunch of them up to Vermont for a short getaway. A few of them were able to make it, but in the days leading up to our departure, everything started to unravel. My puppy had major surgery and needed constant care and my son lost the only set of keys to the car we were taking (just to name a few of the obstacles). I was ready to cancel numerous times but I kept hearing my daughter Katie's voice, "Just go Mom! You never go away with your girlfriends!" Those words kept gnawing at me. What message was I sending to my kids?

I made it to Vermont! More things went wrong, but I am so glad I listened to Katie. My friends and I laughed for the whole five hour ride up; then we sat in front of the fireplace with cheese and crackers from Cumberland Farms, because it was the only place open when we arrived, cue more laughter. We shared a great bottle of wine and caught up with each other. Two more friends arrived the next day. We skied a little, but mostly we made memories.

Friends are really important. Being away from our families is really important too. It may be challenging, but they will survive (might even thrive) in our absence. You might be wondering, "How's the puppy?" She came to Vermont with us. If there's a will, there's a way. Call your friends. Plan a getaway. Dinner and the movies does not cut it. It is the overnight part that changes everything. Go make some memories.

———

ACTION STEP: Please call your friends and make a plan to go away. Away can even be at someone's home. The sleepover is the best part, allowing everyone to completely relax.

Carpe Diem

———

I believe there are risks associated with living a *safe life;* the safe life may actually be riskier than taking risks. Do you remember the expression *better safe than sorry?* Is it really? Because by doing so, we likely remain stagnant. So today I am asking you to take a risk.

When you read, "take a risk", did you know exactly what risk you should be taking? If you did not know the exact risk, perhaps you knew the exact area of your life in which you need to take a risk. Has this potential risk-taking idea festered in you for a while? Today is the day! Carpe Diem, my friend!

How many times have you gone to the end of the proverbial diving board, only to turn around and climb back down? Not today—today, we jump! Pick the risk that has been eating away at you for a while now and do it. Make the phone call, send the email, start to write that book you have always talked about, or walk into that office. The fear you have of taking this risk is far greater than the risk itself.

I cannot promise you that your risk will pay off, but I can promise you this: you will get a feeling of exhilaration and euphoria after the risk has been taken. I liken it to a runner's high. Not all of my risks have paid off, but every risk I have taken has expanded my comfort zone and grown me as a human being. I want that for you as well! Carpe Diem!

———

ACTION STEP: Seize the day! Journal for 5 minutes on this idea. It does not need to be anything huge, just something you have been afraid of doing like making a phone call, sending an email, or talking to your boss. Remember, the fear is almost always greater than the risk!

"No" Is a Complete Sentence

—◇—

Saying yes is easy, it is no that is difficult.

Here is a quick tip. Saying yes is easy (at first) because we are often trying to be the people pleaser. We feel a compulsion to meet everyone else's needs before our own. The result of our yes will likely be at our own expense because it will increase our stress. We need to ask ourselves this question first, "Do I actually have excess time to spend on this activity?" If the answer is no, then our answer should be no.

Saying no is all about our time management habits and how exposed we are to attacks on our schedule. We can create appropriate boundaries which will protect our time. Saying no, leads to the prioritizing of our most important activities. No is hard to say at first, but what we are verbalizing is, "I have priorities too, and they must come before anything else I choose to do."

Saying no will quiet the people pleaser within. "No" is a powerful word and the sooner we learn how to use it effectively and without regret, the sooner we will be in control of our own time. Some will argue, "But it is beyond my control." This is an excuse and it is rarely, if ever, true. Today, we must begin to say no to some things. We need to grab the wheel.

———

ACTION STEP: Spend a few minutes thinking about something you have recently said, yes to that really needed to be a no. Become aware of the many things you have a knee-jerk impulse to say yes to. Awareness is the first step. Next time, you can say no.

*If no is too difficult at first, try "Let me get back to you," or "Let me check." They are great place holders until you can teach yourself to say no.

Dig Yourself Out of a Hole

—⚏—

All of us are in some form of a hole. Some holes are deeper than others, some people have been in their hole longer, but we all have a hole. Our hole is our story. Today I want all of us to *stop digging*.

There is a beautiful quote I live my life by which was shared with me years ago by my friend, Terry, "Life is happening for you not to you." No matter what is happening in my life, I repeat this quote to myself. If everything is happening for me, then everything, good or bad, is in some way a gift. Sometimes it is difficult to see the gift, but if we look deeply enough, it is there.

Yesterday would have been my mom's 88th birthday. My mom had dementia. Watching her decline was perhaps the most difficult thing I have ever had to witness. My mom's dementia taught me how to be intensely present and to love unconditionally, and it taught me how to give from the deepest place in my soul. She may not have known what I was doing for her, but I knew. It was the very least I could do for my incredible mom. I ultimately saw her dementia as a gift. Of course I would have preferred no dementia, but the dementia gave me the gift of profoundly and unconditionally loving her.

So today, stop digging. You know your story and it is not an easy one. None of our stories are easy, but life is happening for us. Find the gift. Look for the silver lining. When we stop digging and focus on the gift, we may find the hole just got a little bit smaller and not so deep. A hole or a gift? We get to choose.

———

ACTION STEP: What hole are you in? Please journal for 5 minutes about the quote, "Life is happening *for* you not *to* you," and how you can apply it to the current hole you are in. Find the gift; it's there, I promise. And keep this quote handy, it will remain very useful while you are here on this earth.

Eye on the Prize

—◆—

There is nothing like a good paradox to make us think. For example, we place little value on the things we get for free and we value those for which we pay money. But the reverse is also true. Everything that is really priceless to us has been given to us for free.

We value the nice car, the jewelry, and the bank account but truly they can be replaced. We take for granted our minds, our bodies, our ambitions, our dreams, our intelligence, and even our family. These are treasured possessions, they are irreplaceable and they are free.

Have you taken any of your free gifts for granted? Look over the list. It has been scientifically proven by major universities that we only use a very small percentage of the operating capacity of our minds. What about dreams and ambitions? Are we moving forward in these categories? How about the body? I know personally I am not treating mine like the priceless and irreplaceable gift it is. So I suppose the question is: "Are we treating our car better than we are treating ourselves"? Hmm. If you are looking for a focal point, this may be it!

———

ACTION STEP: Spend 5 minutes or more thinking about the paradox. We place little value on the things we get for free and we value that which we pay money for. Have you taken any of your free gifts for granted? This is worth a few minutes of your time.

Poisonous Pals

—⟋⟋⟍—

Recent research conducted by TODAY.com and SELF magazine suggests that 84% of women have at least one toxic friend. The study further identified the top five venomous "friends" as: the narcissist, the chronic downer, the critic, the underminer, and the flake. Ironically, nobody in the study admitted to being a bad friend themselves. Do you have one of these "friends" in your life? Statistically, it is highly likely that we all have one of these *poisonous pals.*

Perhaps even more surprising, 83% of women admitted to staying in a friendship with a 'frenemy,' simply because it felt too difficult to end the friendship. They did not want to come off as "not nice."

Women are dealt a daily dose of stress from finances, work, family, and health. Friends are supposed to be a source of strength, support and positive emotional well-being. If a friendship adds stress and anxiety to our life, it is a warning that a change is necessary. Toxic friends negatively impact our health. We need to take measures to protect ourselves against these lethal ladies (or men). If we cannot eliminate them from our life completely, then we must make sure we exponentially reduce our exposure to them.

To get complete clarity, ask yourself, "How would I advise my child, spouse, or friend, if they shared the details with me of their toxic friend?" Then follow your own advice.

————

ACTION STEP: List at least one "friend" whom you would consider toxic. Jot down some notes about this person and how they are negatively impacting you. Ask yourself some powerful questions like:

1. Do I see clearly now how they are negatively impacting me?
2. Why do I keep this person in my life?
3. Is there a way to reduce my exposure to him/her?

Heart and Soul

—〰—

I was asked a question recently that sounded something like this, "How do I handle the struggle of being satisfied with what I have versus wanting more?"

I have two answers for this question. If our desire to have more comes from a place of jealousy and keeping up with the Jones', then we need to focus on gratitude. Jealousy is one of the ugliest of human emotions.

If, on the other hand, our desire to have more comes from someplace other than jealousy, we need to stand up and take notice. It means our soul is screaming to be heard! Well, the soul actually whispers, so I guess it is me who is screaming.

I firmly believe we have been put on this earth for a reason. It is our job to discover our giftedness. The feeling of *desiring more* is the universe's gentle way of creating unrest deep inside us so we will actually begin our search in earnest.

If you have ever been in any of my classes, you know I will tell you that I care deeply about you finding your giftedness. Do you know why I care so much? Because your giftedness is not for you, but for you to share with all of us. The world needs your giftedness!

———

ACTION STEP: Today, spend 5 minutes journaling on the questions, "Do I desire to have more? And is my soul speaking to me?"

A Warm Welcome

—∞—

I was truly excited to attend our dear friend, Sara's bat mitzvah. I arrived at the ceremony with my daughter and a few of her friends. They instantly abandoned me and found their home with all of Sara's 7th grade class, which was what I had expected. As I sat down, a nearby woman caught my eye and said, "You're alone? Come sit with me. My name is Donna."

Donna proceeded to guide me along this three-hour journey which was almost entirely in Hebrew. She changed my experience completely because she reached out with a warm hand of welcome. She taught me about the Torah and the Ark, the Jewish mourning period, and many other incredibly interesting traditions and facts. In addition to Donna's unexpected welcome, I was also greeted by the Rabbi as he followed the Torah around the synagogue. He looked me straight in the eye, shook my hand, and said, "I hope she (Donna) is taking good care of you?" To which I replied, "She is taking *great* care of me!"

I had no expectation of receiving all this kindness. I expected to sit alone and be witness to Sara's bat mitzvah. Instead, Donna and the Rabbi made certain I was welcomed and enveloped in the entire ceremony. My experience would have been completely different without them.

Who are we repeatedly walking past that needs to be welcomed? Is it the new hire at your job? Is it someone at your church or synagogue or school? We see the new person or the visitor, but how many times do we engage, really engage? Donna did not hesitate. I often do. I hope I will never forget the lesson she taught me recently. Feeling welcomed is a really wonderful feeling and it is never too late to welcome someone.

————

ACTION STEP: Who can you welcome? Don't hesitate; channel Donna and make them feel truly welcomed. Donna taught me a wonderful lesson, and I hope she taught you one too.

Lessons from a 16-Year-Old

—⚉—

Sometimes we all need a reminder of what is truly important in life. I know I do. And I always find it refreshing when the reminder comes from a sixteen-year-old. The reminder I need, as I re-engage with this crazy world each morning, is that what everyone wants more than anything else is to be loved and accepted.

It sounds so simple, right? We should all be able to do that, right? Well, when I ask myself, "Could I do better? Could I be more loving and accepting?" The answer is always, "Yes." So, back to the astute teenager. My daughter entered her high school the other day to unexpectedly discover 3000 post-it notes throughout the school, on every locker, in the bathrooms, in the halls, etc. Each note was a note of inspiration and love. One read simply, "You're beautiful." Another declared, "The world is better with you in it."

This sage young lady and her friend spent countless hours writing these notes and then more hours strategically placing them about the school, simply to make everyone happy! She is extraordinary and I believe we all would benefit from taking a page from her playbook.

Ok, so her idea was not original. It has been done before, but who cares? She took matters into her own hands and made about 1500 students and teachers happy! Her actions remind us all that loving and accepting others is just one post-it away. ONE post-it! She has inspired me. I know I can do better. I *will* do better. She, for sure, changed someone's life that day. Incredible. Sixteen years old. Wow!

P.S. My favorite post-it was, "Be the Fruit Loop in a bowl of Cheerios!"

———

ACTION STEP: How can you expand your *love and acceptance* band beyond where it extends to now? I keep post-its in my handbag now and very often write an encouraging note and leave it surreptitiously in public places. Journal ways in which you can extend love and acceptance.

Listen Up!

—⟋⟍—

Do you want to be more charismatic? The Greek word charisma means "divine favor" or "gift from God." Charisma is always a mix of presence, warmth, and power. There are some people who are naturally charismatic but, if you, like me, are not one of them, it can be learned.

> "True charisma is basically when you disappear and allow something loving to come through you for the other person." —MARTHA BECK

Here is a quick life hack to increase charisma. If you have a cocktail party or family function you will be attending soon, try arriving with one goal: "All I am going to do is ask questions." If you are asked a question, be polite and answer, but be brief. When you ask your questions, just listen to the answers. Studies show, really good listeners are perceived as very charismatic.

I tried this at a family function this past weekend. It is important to note, I am a Chatty Cathy. When I focused on asking questions and intentionally listening for the answer. It changed everything for me. I was laser-focused on what the other person was saying, not thinking about what I was going to say next. Give it a whirl. It was truly amazing.

ACTION STEP: Is there an event looming on your calendar during which you could be intentional about listening to others? It could be a night out with a friend, a work event, or a family holiday. Commit to practicing the lost art of listening. Remind yourself daily to be a better listener.

Targeting Our Thoughts

—⬯—

Great thoughts have the potential to bring about great things. The best thoughts to have are those that create a philosophy on life that allows us to make the best decisions and take the best action. It is possible that our current "philosophy" plays a far bigger role in messing up our life than the actual challenges we are experiencing. What do I mean by that?

Ask yourself, "What is the greatest thought I could have about my life today?" Really think about the answer to that question, then repeat it tomorrow and then the next day. You will develop a transformative habit that can result in a change in the course of your life.

Here is a philosophy: I am just scratching the surface of my potential. I have so much more potential than I can even comprehend. When I believe in myself and my abilities, the world is my oyster. I really do believe in me.

———

ACTION STEP: Spend a few minutes creating a positive and well thought out answer to the question, "What is the greatest thought I could have about my life today?" What would happen if you replayed that thought all day?

Best Advice

—〰—

One of the best pieces of advice I have ever heard was from the author and motivational speaker, Jim Rohn. To almost any problem presented to him, he responded with this one simple retort, "Sounds like a personal problem to me."

Jim Rohn is the godfather of personal development. What he knew, when he said those seven simple words was, "You cannot change the circumstances, the seasons, or the winds, but you can change yourself." Most people will blame external reasons for what is going wrong in their life well before they will look inside themselves. The answer is *always* inward because it is the only thing we have complete domain over.

Work is not going well? Sounds like a personal problem to me. The test was not even on what we studied in class? Sounds like a personal problem to me. Struggling with a relationship? Sounds like a personal problem to me. Adopting this seven-word sentence, for ourselves or those who come to us with their problems, is masterful. For both ourselves and others, when we change our perspective toward the problem, that is when we can actually take strides toward fixing the problem. Choosing to be the victim relinquishes all our power. When we make it a personal problem, we chose to own it and, in doing so, we put all the power back in our own hands. It is always our choice. Choose to own it.

———

ACTION STEP: How can you adopt Jim Rohn's advice? Spend a few minutes today journaling on his seven-word statement, "Sounds like a personal problem to me." His premise is that we may have an ownership problem.

A Good Night Sleep

—⚎—

A hear everyone talking about lack of sleep like it is a badge of honor or a secret society, but I just do not get the attraction. We have enough stress in our lives, so lack of sleep is not a badge I am looking to acquire.

Although it may seem impressive to tell others we only get five hours of sleep a night, but it is not impressing anything inside our body. Lack of sleep takes a toll on our body regardless of what our colleagues think. What exactly does happen to the body when it is repeatedly abused with lack of sleep?

- more susceptible to colds and the flu
- increased risk for heart disease
- increased risk of diabetes
- altered brain function and mental health
- increased risk for obesity

If we maintain a punishing schedule that limits our nightly sleep, we should consider making some adjustments. Our health and our productivity will be the beneficiaries of our commitment to a good night sleep.

———

ACTION STEP: Be honest, how many hours of sleep a night do you average? If it is less than six, you need to make an adjustment in your life. The research shows adults actually need 7–9 hours of sleep a night.

Are You All-In?

—∽—

What does an old-time baptism and your goal have in common?

The earliest of Christian baptisms required a person be completely submerged in a body of water. The immersion was symbolic as well as metaphoric. When the baptism was completed, there was no doubt about the commitment.

When we commit to a goal, there should be no doubt as well. We should be all-in, completely immersed. We cannot simply put our toe in the water and declare, "I'm in." A toe is not enough. Even going in up to our waist only demonstrates a 50% commitment. Both imply we are hedging our bet. We need to go all-in.

How far are you in? Is it just your toe? Are you in up to your waist? What fear is holding you back from jumping in with both feet? Can you stop thinking about what might go wrong and think about what might go right? Can you walk through the fear and go all-in? When you are all-in, real change can begin to take place.

———

ACTION STEP: Today is a journaling day. Take one goal that you know you can commit 100% to doing and journal about it. Do you know why 99% is hard? Because you gave yourself a 1% out. 100% is all-in.

Headlights

—ᴡ—

Have you ever travelled by car at night? The headlights only illuminate about 160 feet of the road ahead, which is not very far at all. They certainly do not light up the whole journey, just very short distances in little fragments. Nevertheless, no one would refrain from traveling forward simply because the entire route was not visible.

Life operates in a very similar way. The entire journey will never be completely "visible." If we choose to move forward (into the darkness and the unknown), we will do so based on two things. We will move forward based on an educated decision and faith. That is it. It will never be the right time, the end will not be in sight, and we will not be completely certain. The only way to get from here to there is to move forward, regardless of the fear.

What are you afraid to move forward on? What would seem a lot less daunting if you viewed it in short distances and little fragments of time? Would that vision propel you to move forward? You don't need the whole journey to be illuminated for you to move forward because the truth is, there are detours and adjustments that you are going to have to make along the way. You just need to commit to making the journey; everything else will take care of itself.

———

ACTION STEP: What have you refrained from moving forward on because the journey seemed too daunting? Are you willing to take the first couple of steps? Put it down in writing with a few minutes of journaling.

Leave Your Mark

—∞—

Recently, I was on vacation in Paris, visiting my daughter. What a fabulous city! We learned about so many people and so many events. I love history.

What struck me the most about the trip was how so many people left behind their mark. Some intentional, some not so much. Gustav Eiffel designed the Eiffel Tower for the Universal Exposition in 1889. The tower was first described as "hideously modern and useless." Claude Monet painted "Impression, soleil levant" in 1874, which is where Impressionism got its name, although it was not well-received at first. And then there was Dwight D. Eisenhower, supreme commander of the Allied Expeditionary Forces in World War II, who gave the go-ahead for a massive invasion of Normandy, France (also known as D-Day), which was two years in the planning and was still seen as an enormous risk.

These were everyday people. They were not kings or queens, they were not gifted with riches, but they were passionate. They did not know they were making history, nor did they set out to change it (ok, maybe Dwight did), but they followed their heart.

Have you ever asked yourself, "How do I want to leave my mark?" What are you passionate about? Our *mark* does not need to be as big as Eiffel, Monet, or Eisenhower, but I believe we need to give it some thought. Maybe our mark is not tied to our job. Maybe it is our volunteer work.

The world is richer when we share our talents. Maybe one-hundred years from now, someone will be writing about us, studying us, or simply profoundly grateful for our gift to this world. Do not think, for one second, you do not have a gift to share. Not *one* second!

———

ACTION STEP: Simply write about your giftedness. What gifts do you have that you could share with the world?

Happiness Manifesto

—◊—

Can you really find happiness on the back of a business card?

Norman Vincent Peale writes about a friend, H.C. Mattern, who travelled the country sharing his very unique business card. The philosophy printed on the back of the card has brought happiness to him, his wife, and to hundreds of others who have had the pleasure of being in the company of Mr. Mattern's infectious happiness.

The card reads as follows: "The way to happiness: keep your heart free from hate, your mind from worry. Live simply, expect little, give much. Fill your life with love. Scatter sunshine. Forget self, think of others. Do as you would be done by." I would only add one thing to this Happiness Manifesto: Forgive quickly.

———

ACTION STEP: Look at all eleven ways to happiness (include forgiveness). Highlight the one or two you struggle with and write them down somewhere you will be sure to read. You are in charge of your own happiness and the Happiness Manifesto is a formula for creating the good life we all want!

Afraid of Heights? Me, Too!

—〰—

"Fear kills more dreams than failure ever will."
—SUZY KASSEM

If you have ever been faced with fear, any kind of fear, but especially the kind that paralyzes you, then please read on. Part of our recent trip to Paris was to celebrate our 25th wedding anniversary. We agreed on one romantic dinner, which Doug was planning as a surprise. Spoiler Alert: I am terrified of heights.

On day one in Paris, after valiantly getting to the first level of the Eiffel Tower (58 meters high), I found out that our romantic dinner would be on the 2nd level of the Tower (115 meters). Immediately, my body had a visceral response, a panic attack of sorts, and I told Doug, "I really don't think I can do it." That is when I found out he had been required to pay for this spectacular dinner in advance. My thoughts raced, "Oh no, I can't back out, but I am already paralyzed with fear. I'll never make it up there. Never!"

So I spent the next 24 hours in complete fear. I barely slept and every thought had me perseverating on the daunting task ahead of me. The morning of, I did a few rounds of energy work and begged a few friends to pray for me. Lastly, I told Doug, "If I am truly paralyzed with fear when we step out of the elevator, you are going to have to drag me the remaining distance to the restaurant."

As we were walking toward the Eiffel Tower, I started to cry; I was so fearful. But when we finally got inside the "leg" of the Tower dedicated to The Jules Verne Restaurant, I started to relax. It was not how I had pictured it in my mind. It was closed in and beautifully decorated. At this point, I knew I could do it. Ironically, **every** fearful thought I had **never** came true. My mind should have thought about the magnificent view, the exquisite restaurant, and the priceless night spent with my husband. I will never forget this night for as long as I live.

What are you afraid of? I am glad he paid for the dinner in advance; it forced me to face my fear. I wish more things in my life were "paid in advance" so I could not back out. Imagine all that we are missing out on because of fear!

———

ACTION STEP: Join me today in picking something you are afraid of moving forward on, either with your career or personal life. Now face it head on like it is paid in advance!

Receiving a Compliment

—⚊—

Here is the truth about me, I cannot accept a compliment. A compliment directed at me triggers something in my mind that causes me to immediately deflect it. Apparently, I am not alone in this knee-jerk response.

The instantaneous thought process in most people goes something like this: I am not thin enough, I am not good enough or I am not worthy enough to take the compliment so I will downgrade it.

We deflect for three main reasons:

1. We deny the compliment could possibly be true.
2. We reject the compliment to remain humble and modest.
3. We dismiss the compliment because of low self-esteem.

When we deflect a compliment, we diminish ourselves by responding as though we are not worthy of such a compliment. Today is the day we put an end to diminishing our worthiness.

———

ACTION STEP: Today, I am giving you two choices with which to respond to a compliment and they are,

1. Thank you for noticing.
2. Thank you.

After you say those words, say nothing! Regardless of what goes on in your mind, and your mind will try to downplay, diminish, and reject what was just thoughtfully and affectionately sent your way, remain steadfast and graciously accept.

The Great Imposter

—⚭—

I hate this word: *hate.* That is the word I hate. I genuinely do not remember who told me not to use the word, but it stuck. I do not allow my children to use it either. The word *hate* has such intense meaning and power and all of that *hate* sits in the heart of the hater, not the hated. I make my children come up with another word because rarely do they really mean *hate.* If the English language has over 470,000 words, there has to be a better word to describe our feelings than *hate.*

When my children use it, I say, "Nope. You don't hate them/her/it. Tell me exactly what it is you *hate.* This is where it gets good. This is where we find out exactly what the ugly blanket of *hate* is hiding. We get answers like, "She's talking about us behind our backs," or "I thought we were friends, but now she hangs with the popular group."

Hate is the great imposter. It allows us to circumvent our true feelings. When we force ourselves to eliminate the word *hate,* we get to the heart of what truly is upsetting us and then the healing can begin.

So you hate Brussel sprouts? No, you do not care for the taste. You hate your co-worker? No, her malicious ways infuriate you (dig deeper, why does she believe she has to behave this way?) You hate your ex? No, you do not. Identify his actions that upset you and how they make you feel.

Let us stop hating. It sits in **our** heart, not theirs. If we can determine what it is we hate, then we can either have compassion for them or, better yet, us.

———

ACTION STEP: Simply eliminate the word hate. When you do use it (accidentally, of course), take the time to:

a. Select a better word.
b. If it was toward a person, delve into why you used the word hate. The question to ask is, "What exactly do I hate about them?"

I Am Not Perfect.

—⚊—

O.K., I said it. I am coming clean. I am not perfect.

I was rereading one of my Facebook posts and realized I had a typo. It was nothing major, maybe it was a "you" that should have been a "your" or something similar, but it was a typo nonetheless. This was not the first time I had found a typo and I really got mad at myself for what I called at the time, carelessness.

I continued down this path, allowing the *troll* inside my head to continue this relentless mental attack. I said to myself, with the help of this *troll*, "You must be more careful. People will think you don't know how to write and you don't check your work. You need to be flawless. There is no room for error. This is a huge mistake and you must not make it again."

Here is the truth. No *troll* this time. I am not careless. I spend a lot of time on my writing and I deeply care about the content I send out. I write and rewrite. I delete and start again. I check and recheck. I labor over word choices. I use a dictionary and a thesaurus. I proof read repeatedly. And, I am not perfect. There will be typos occasionally. But the *troll* needs to go.

Not once did I recognize the good. Not once did I pat myself on the back. Too much precious mental space is given to the *troll*. No More. Do you have a *troll* too? I imagine you do. Today, we evict the *troll*. I know it will find its way back but as long as I am aware of the *troll*, I can evict it again and again. I am not perfect. I am human for sure, but my heart is in the right place. Good-bye *troll*.

———

ACTION STEP: Do you have a troll? Today, journal about the troll and how cruel, unkind and unhelpful it is in your life. Spend your journal time discrediting the troll. Remember the fabulous quote, "If I said to others what I say to myself, I would have no friends."

"I See," Said the Blind Man

—m—

Our priest gave a wonderful homily regarding Jesus healing the blind man. I know, don't talk about, money, politics, or religion, but hear me out. Ultimately, at the end of the passage, there is an ironic twist where the lesson is made that perhaps even those who can see are essentially blind.

Those words really struck a chord with me. We all obviously see what we see, but what are we missing? What is right in front of us in plain sight that we are completely blind to? Have you ever played the game where you have to guess what was taken from the room while your eyes were shut? As I sat next to my daughter in church and asked myself, "What am I blind to?" A few things popped up instantly.

It is not easy to identify where we are blind, but I believe if we never take a moment to think about it, then that is a blind spot in itself. We can ask questions like, "What are my priorities and am I giving them my utmost attention?" or the one I asked myself in church, "What am I trying to justify in my own mind, but I know is wrong?" Initially, this is not a feel good exercise, but I assure you, when we shed light on anything we have been blind to, it can generate some really good feelings. We are all blind to something. Find it. Change it. We will all feel a lot better when we do. I certainly did.

———

ACTION STEP: It is really difficult to see exactly where we are blind, but a great first step is to spend a few minutes thinking about possible blind spots. Here are some prompts:

1. Who might you be turning a blind eye to? Family? Staff?
2. What role of yours might you be blind to? Parent? Work?
3. Where are you blind within work? Home?

"Houston, We Have Lift Off!"

———∞———

I have read that when a rocket is launched into space, it expends more energy in the first few minutes of lift off than it uses over the next several days to travel almost half a million miles.

I can really relate to the rocket and maybe you can, too. In anything I have ever done, it has been the launch which has been the most difficult part. I tend to procrastinate, dawdle, and even dodge getting started, but why? There are always a few simple reasons; like a tremendous fear of the unknown and not knowing how, followed closely by the fear of failure.

NASA never said, "We will not be sending up the rocket because it expends too much energy." The rocket literally went straight into the unknown on its first flight. No one at NASA said, "It wasn't worth it. Let's just stay on the ground from now on. Telescopes are fine, really." I do not know about you, but I do not want to stay "on the ground"; I feel like I would be missing the good stuff.

Join me in picking one idea you would like to launch, something you have thought about forever, and commit to giving it all the energy necessary to get past that initial liftoff. Once we get past the launch, it will be a lot easier; but just sitting on the launching pad with no plans to ever lift off seems like a big waste of time and talent. They call it a launching pad for a reason. Let's go. The countdown begins: 10, 9, 8, 7, 6 . . . !

———

ACTION STEP: What would you like to launch? Journal about your idea. Journaling is still on the ground and safe. If you have a few extra minutes, write about all of those fears that are keeping you on the ground. How real are they?

Double-Edged Sword

—∭—

"Before criticizing your spouse's faults, you must remember it may have been these very defects which prevented him/her from getting a better spouse than the one he/she married!"
—ANONYMOUS

Now that should make us all pause and reflect! It is a very humbling statement. I heard this joke about marriage on the radio and it made me laugh out loud as I felt the sting of its truth. The joke also reminded me of the Bible verse, "He who is without sin can cast the first stone," which can surely be repeated with an ample amount of sarcasm or mockery.

When we gaze at our partner, what do we see? Faults? Mistakes? Shortcomings? Or do we see their beauty? Their strengths? The reason we married them in the first place? No one is perfect, not even you or me! Looking for perfection will always disappoint. Only we can decide what we see when we gaze at our significant other. Decide wisely and with compassion. Remember, he or she is gazing at us, too.

———

ACTION STEP: Spend a few minutes writing about both the anonymous quote as well as the Bible verse. Visualize your spouse/significant other and write about their beauty and their strengths. Begin speaking words of affirmation, gratitude, and love toward your partner. Fault-finding will never be the bedrock of any relationship.

A Lesson from My Dad

—◊—

When I was a little girl, one of my fondest memories was the Saturday before Easter. On this day, regardless of how busy we were, my brother and I knew we had plans with my dad (my sisters were already grown).

Back then, all the fire stations sold Easter flowers. They would open up the garage doors, exposing the bright red fire trucks for all to see, and the entire pavement in front of the firehouse was covered in a sea of color from blue hyacinths to yellow tulips. The smell wafting from these fragrant flowers was magnificent.

The best part of this day was that I was allowed to pick any flower I wanted for my mom. I always felt a bit overwhelmed. I was drawn to the smell of the hyacinth but pulled to the beauty of the hydrangea.

And then, it got even better; we were all going to keep this a secret from my mom until Easter morning! Having this annual Easter ritual with my Dad was beyond special. He could have simply gone out and bought the flowers himself, but he always made sure we went with him and that we chose our own flower.

I am not sure which I loved more, his love for my mom or that he made sure we were a part of this ritual. I loved that day. I still love the ritual as my husband has taken it on. I do not love the flowers nearly as much as I love the ritual. There was something about the clandestine trip with my dad that I will always treasure.

Create memories!

———

ACTION STEP: It is never too late to start a ritual. Children (and adults) love rituals; it has an anchoring effect that puts a unique fingerprint on our families. Spend 5 minutes journaling about a ritual you would like to start. The goal is to make it something the family looks forward to each year. Pick one idea today and put it in your calendar so you will not forget. Rituals are memory makers.

Can You Hear Me?

—⟋⟍—

"One of the most sincere forms of respect is actually listening to what another has to say," Bryant H. McGill once said. Another great quote about listening is by Eugene O'Neill, "God gave us a mouth that shuts and ears that don't. That should tell us something." I recently read a great book by John Maxwell, *Becoming A Person Of Influence,* and one of my favorite chapters was on listening. I am known far more for my chatting than I am for my listening, so it is ironic that *Listening* was my favorite chapter.

John tells a great story of a man named Rodney. Rodney is currently re-married, but he had previously been married and has two daughters with his first wife. He had been having problems with his ex-wife constantly asking for more money for herself and the girls, which lead to many arguments. After Rodney heard Maxwell speak about listening, he called his ex-wife and asked if they could meet.

They met at a coffee shop and Rodney said, "Charlotte, I want to listen to you. Tell me what your life is like. I care deeply about you and the kids." Charlotte started to cry as she shared her struggles. Rodney said, "I've only been thinking of myself and I want to make things right. I've been angry for so long, I wasn't seeing straight." They talked for hours and a new foundation of mutual respect was formed.

It is never too late to become a good listener. Everyone wants to be heard.

———

ACTION STEP: Can we all think of at least one person we have not been listening to lately? Maybe it is not a spouse, maybe it is a parent, a sibling, or even our own child. Practice listening; it is a tremendously enlightening exercise.

Rocky Road or a Bump in the Road

—⚏—

"What would you attempt to do if you knew you could not fail?"
　　　　　　　　　　　　　　　　—ROBERT SCHULLER

We, most likely, have all heard this quote and yes, it is inspirational—to a point. If I were to give you the more realistic *Beth* version of this quote, I would say: "What would you attempt to do if you knew there would be stumbling blocks, obstacles, setbacks, snags, complications, and barriers all along the way, but every single one of these that you overcome will make you so proud of yourself. You will essentially be grateful they were there in the first place!"

Not exactly the same quote, but I like it. It tells the real story. The road will not be smooth, the plan will change often, but the goal remains the same and it will be incredibly sweet when we attain it. Do not be afraid of the journey. If it were all a smooth road, we would never grow. The snafus along the way, although challenging, determine our grit. I am never proud of the simple tasks; it is the tasks that show what I am made of that are the most gratifying.

Do not wait for the "I cannot fail" road; I am rather certain it does not exist anyway. Get started knowing that my view of the road is spot-on. The obstacles are the Universe's way of saying, "How badly do you want this?" When you are done, you will look back on those obstacles with gratitude. They will have made you who you have become.

————

ACTION STEPS: What thoughts did this post conjure up for you as you read about the road? Journal for a few minutes on what surfaced for you.

The "Show Me" State

—∞—

We all want our children to succeed and be better off than we are now. Quite frankly, almost everything we do is toward that end. But do we forget to allow ourselves to strive for the same?

> "Are you the adult that you want your child to grow up to be?"
> —BRENÉ BROWN

We tell our children to "take risks, and be more aggressive." We encourage them to "reach for their dreams and do not let anything stand in their way." "The world is their oyster, and the sky is the limit." "They can be anything they want to be in life." These are all great adages, but saying them and modeling them are not the same thing.

We are role models, and our children will model the role we demonstrate to them. Are we reaching for *our* dreams? Are *we* taking risks? We cannot tell our children who to become, we must **show** them! Regardless of how old our children are, we need to continue to show them so they know anything is possible at any age. So, let's reach big, grow, stumble, fall even, get up, reach further. The state of Missouri certainly gets it —they are the *Show Me* state!

> "What we *are* speaks so loudly that our children may not hear what we say."
> —QUENTIN L. COOK

———

ACTION STEP: Spend a few minutes writing about the fear you are willing to face right now so that your child will not be hindered by the same fear?

Child's Play

—m—

Yesterday, we celebrated Easter. I was hosting my family, which turned out to be twelve people: six adults and six "kids." I put kids in quotation marks because four of the six kids were in their mid- twenties. The youngest of all was fifteen-years old.

I decided to have an Easter egg hunt even though we did not have any little ones running around. I figured, who doesn't like a good Easter egg hunt? We upped the ante by making one big egg for each kid that was much harder to find and the treasure inside had some money. I borrowed this idea from my son's friend, Griffin.

It was so much fun to see these big kids running around searching for eggs! I wished I had made the hunt for the adults, too. As I watched, I said to myself, "It's so much fun being a kid." Youth is a mindset, really. I used to pine for the day I no longer was forced to sit at the kids' table. Why? Being an adult can be really overrated and even heavy.

The Easter egg hunt reminded me that I should be finding a way to be a kid every day. Skip, play hopscotch, or red light-green light, but whatever we do, do not sit on the porch and watch! Being an adult is **way** overrated!

ACTION STEP: What could you do today that would be kid-like? Can you lighten up home or work with your new mindset? Journal for a few minutes about all the ideas you come up with, but don't just be kid-like today—keep it going!

Criticism

—∞—

I have certainly doled out my fair share of criticism as well as taken it on the chin and perhaps you have too. When delivering criticism, it is usually done so with the intent of changing behavior, whether that be for a spouse, a co-worker, or even our own children. Unfortunately the statistics don't support that assertion. So if our intent was to change behavior, **and** 99% of people will not see themselves as wrong, how effective was the criticism?

The answer is—*not very effective.* It will not create lasting change and, more often than not, it has the capacity to create resentment. Our belief that we are going to correct someone will often result in them condemning and resenting us in return, which will make matters worse.

If we cannot correct behavior through criticism, then how do we affect change? First, remember we are dealing with creatures of emotion more so than logic. People are motivated by pride, and criticism is the antithesis of pride. Second, when we want to criticize another, perhaps we should take a moment to look at ourselves first.

Instead of criticism, let's try understanding. Why did they do what they did? Understanding breeds sympathy, kindness, and tolerance. Maybe it is a teachable moment? Couple all that with Dale Carnegie's wisdom, "But it takes character and self-control to be understanding and forgiving."

> "Any fool can criticize, condemn and complain—and most fools do."
> —BEN FRANKLIN

ACTION STEP: Jot down the names of a few people you are certain you have been criticizing. Is it your spouse? child? employee? Can you achieve the same result through kindness, compassion, and forgiveness? Now, decide if there is still time to go back and reverse the damage. I am rather certain sincere apologies are timeless, right?

Do You Want to Be Happier?

—⚊—

I know I do. Here is an interesting fact about happiness: most people think it comes from outside ourselves. For example, I will be happier when I get a new car or I will be happier when I can go on a real vacation. What is unfortunate about this thought process is that we decide we will remain unhappy (perhaps marginally so) until this big thing comes along and sometimes this *thing* is not even in the planning stages yet. Ugh!

Here is the truth: happiness comes from within. "What?" you say. We get to determine whether or not we are happy **and** we can proactively make ourselves happy with the simple desire (and thoughts) to actually be so. We have been in control of our own happiness all along but we have been waiting for the car/vacation/boyfriend/boss to make us happy!

Today, take advantage of the fact that we control our happiness. Here is a simple trick to not only make us happier but someone else as well: each day, let's make it our mission to make someone else smile. Let's really go out of our way. We can start with strangers. They are the best because they don't know us. Proactively choosing to try to make someone else happy will, invariably and without a doubt, make us *so* happy! I promise!

————

ACTION STEP: Here are two ways to be happier right now: First, see if you can make someone smile today or make yourself smile. Smiles are contagious and have so many wonderful health benefits. Second, write down all the things that you are happy about in your life right now. I believe everyone not only wants to be happy, but deserves to be happy.

Beware

—∞—

What I am about to tell you might not surprise you, you are most likely well aware on a subconscious level, but it will affect how you view those closest to you from this point on.

When we start to dream big, what invariably happens is all the people around us (family and close friends especially) offer their well-intentioned opinions to "help" us along. Their advice, while well meaning, is likely to deflate our dreams and dismantle our entire plan if we entertain their guidance.

Those that do not offer advice will usually take the mocking approach which is also an attempt to derail our dream. They make fun of our idea, but they will follow the ridicule with, "You know I am only teasing you?" Neither guidance nor ridicule is helping to champion our dream.

As we move forward with our dream, we need to be cognizant of these well-meaning people. We need to recognize them instantly as they have the potential to destroy our confidence. Mentally, I make every effort to dismiss people like this as soon as I spot them. Sometimes, it may even be necessary for me to tell those that ridicule to please stop.

Do not be discouraged, there is sage advice and guidance coming our way as well. It will be relatively simple to see and feel the difference. When someone is supportive, it will be undeniable. Be keenly aware of when it is important to listen up and when you need to shut it down.

———

ACTION STEP: I truly believe people mean well. If you have a great idea, do not be afraid to speak about it, but keep this advice close by. Use it to toughen up your skin for all the naysayers. Now that you know this, you will actually chuckle when you hear someone try to quash your idea.

Time Is Precious

—∞—

"My favorite things in life don't cost any money. It's really clear that the most precious resource we all have is time."

—STEVE JOBS

Time is precious, it is valuable, and it passes quickly. Once it passes, we cannot get it back. Make every second count. Progress into life full of intention. Do not let a second pass without enjoying those around you. Do not get distracted by that which does not matter. Put the phone and the laptop away and suggest others do the same. Engage. Listen. Laugh. Enjoy.

Time passes and we cannot get it back. Safeguard this time. Make it count. Like Steve Jobs said, "My favorite things don't cost any money."

———

ACTION STEP: Answer this question, "Am I getting distracted by that which does not matter?" Or the converse, "What is most important in my life?" Journal for a few minutes on either or both questions.

Someday

—⚬—

"When I . . ." is a close family member with "Someday . . .". Last week I was reminded of this fact when I interviewed three young adults from Trenton, NJ about their own success stories for the Urban Promise Trenton (an international non-profit empowering urban youth toward academic success) fundraiser.

After sitting with them for hours, I was blown away by their stories and the odds they overcame in order to be in the positions they are in today. To one of the young men I said, "I am sitting next to you and I know you made it, but if someone had told me just the beginning of your story, I would have never believed you would have survived." Not only have these three young adults successfully beaten the odds, but they are giving back to their community by speaking to all the schools in Trenton to inspire other youth to follow their personal paths to success.

They did not put off their responsibilities for reaching back to help other Trenton students for a "When I . . ." of their choice. They did not say, "Someday, when I am financially successful, I will help." They reminded me that I have to act *now*; I can give of my time and talent now. My responsibilities for those less fortunate than myself cannot wait for someday. I am wasting precious time waiting for someday. Someday is never. Who or what are **you** passionate about? Someone out there is counting on us. We cannot let them down. Someday has to be today!

———

ACTION STEP: Are you giving of your talents? Spend a few minutes journaling on how you can add value and to whom.

The Language of Emojis

—⁓—

I am a big fan of communication. I am also well aware that some things are better off left unsaid. Nowadays, we seem to use words less often. We use emojis a lot, which are defined as, "small digital images or icons used to express an idea or emotion." But do they?

Is the kissy-face the same as I love you? Does a sad face really convey our sympathy? Conversely, does the happy face really convey our joy or excitement? Although I love the simplicity of emojis, I do not think an emoji will ever adequately replace the multitude of fabulous words that capture the complete essence of an emotion.

Try this experiment for the next few days, let's replace our emojis with words. Yes, it will take longer, but it will be worth it if we really want to have an impact on those we text with regularly. Here is how impactful we can be:

HAPPY FACE: "You made my day!!!"
PRAYING HANDS: "Be certain of my prayers for you and your family"
THUMBS UP: "You're the BEST! What would I do without you?"
SAD FACE: "My heart is broken for you. How can I help?"

Do not be ordinary. Mark Twain said it best, "Whenever you find yourself on the side of the majority, it is time to reflect." Every place we want to put an emoji is an opportunity for us to truly connect with another human being at a deeper level. Don't be ordinary—be extraordinary!

———

ACTION STEP: Do not use emojis for three days, only use words. See if it makes a difference for you or those you text.

Keeping Up with the Joneses

—⁊⁊—

No one in my family has ever run track before, until this year. I attended my daughter's first ever track meet the other day, and the whole experience was completely foreign to me.

Katie is a hurdler and ended up coming in fourth in her meet after she caught her foot on the last hurdle. She wasn't really disappointed because she is so new to the sport. When we were leaving the meet, a teacher from her school saw her and hollered, "Hey Katie, how'd you do?" She explained what happened and he responded, "But was it your PB (personal best)? Did you beat your last time?" Katie giggled and said, "I don't even know what my last time was, I'm really new at this!" He advised her to keep track of her times and every race try to do better than she did the previous time.

As we walked away from her teacher, I thought about his words, "PB, Personal Best." Often, I get caught up in, "keeping up with the Joneses" or where I rank with others in my field and I take my eye off the ball. The distraction is my own demise; it eats away at my self-confidence and makes me unhappy. The only thing that matters is that I am better today than I was yesterday. Otherwise, I could stay caught up in a vicious cycle because someone will always be better. I simply need to stay focused on my PB.

In running, they tell you to never look at the other runners. Experts advise: "By definition, the full-out explosion of power occurs when your eyes are focused straight ahead, otherwise you are wasting critical energy." Yup, looking at the other "runners" in life is just wasting critical energy. I thought I knew that, but I am benefitting from a much-needed reminder!

———

ACTION STEP: Today, spend a few minutes journaling about how you have been looking at the other runners in life. More importantly, with your new insight, spend this time thinking about how you can focus on your *personal best.*

Winning Isn't Everything

—⁂—

I watched a video the other day about Roger Federer. He spoke candidly, not about his fabulous career filled with a record number of wins, but about losing. He said (and I am paraphrasing), "Losing makes you stronger. It allows you to become a better player. It motivates you to work harder, and you can focus on what you need to improve. You need the criticism so you know what you need to improve."

Whether it is in sports, business or life, it is not the wins that make us better, it is most definitely the losses. Sure they sting; no one hates losing more than I do, but the lesson only comes if we stop to take a really good look at what just happened. The lesson is lost completely if we blame the refs, our boss, or our ex. The questions Roger asks himself after a loss, I would guess, sound something like this, "What do I need to work on? How can I get better?"

These are not questions we generally ask ourselves after a win, but maybe we should. Or maybe we should look at a "loss" in a new light. Jim Rohn poignantly stated, "Don't wish it were easier, wish you were better." Wins are fun, don't get me wrong, but it is in the losses where true growth can occur. Beating ourselves up after a loss is not the answer either; we just need to ask, "How can I improve?" And be grateful for the lesson and the insight the loss provided.

———

ACTION STEP: Spend a few minutes journaling about a recent loss and how that can motivate you to work harder and focus on what you need to improve. This is not a beat yourself up moment. It is simply a "What did I learn" moment. Treat it as a gift.

Magical Eyes

—⁂—

Who is getting on your nerves? It would be great if the answer was, "No one. Everyone I cross paths with is pleasant and helpful." If that is your life, I want to move into your world. If that is not your life, then you must live in mine, and I have a quick tip to make things just a little bit better.

Life can be heavy. Rarely do people walk around and dump their heavy load on everyone they see (thank goodness); as a result though, they continue to carry the heavy load silently. In an effort to hide this heavy load from the world, the burden comes out in other ways. Maybe they cut us off, maybe they are mean to us, or maybe they simply say nothing. Regardless, the burden is there.

If we all had *magical eyes* and could see the burdens that everyone carries, would we become more compassionate? Just because we cannot see it does not mean it is not there. Oh, it's there alright, I am 100% certain. We all tend to want to right the wrong, an eye for an eye, but maybe it is best if we just see, with our *magical eyes,* the heavy burden and hold a space of compassion for them. It will make life a lot lighter. I do not know about you, but I could use life to be a little lighter.

———

ACTION STEP: All day, do your best to use your *magical eyes* and give **everyone** a pass. Your children get a pass, your co-workers get a pass, your spouse gets a pass, and every sales clerk you encounter gets a pass. See if you feel lighter when you turn the other cheek.

Are You a Success?

—⚊—

The perceived meaning of *success* has changed over time and, unfortunately, not to our benefit. Success, by definition, is a noun that means: the accomplishment of an aim or purpose. We have altered the definition of success to take on a much larger, more grandiose meaning. Today, when success is mentioned, we have visions of high-powered and high-paying jobs, magnificent homes, and exotic vacations.

As a result of the new definition, we have pushed success so far out into the future, the thought of actually achieving success has become profoundly disheartening. The pressure we put on ourselves to attain the "new" success causes us to overlook all the little successes along the way. Therefore, we become discouraged by our lack of accomplishments instead of proud of what we did accomplish.

I am not encouraging any of us to sell ourselves short or rest on our laurels. But, if we have not celebrated our successes along the way, then it is time. Beating ourselves up repeatedly for what we have not accomplished is pointless.

Today, we need to stop and recognize our successes. Breathe them in deeply. Use the strength that comes from them to propel us forward to our next success. Success is not an ending point far off in the future, success actually happens all along the way. If we do not stop to digest the sweet taste of success as it happens, then we have nothing to fuel the odyssey. Ironically, one of my greatest successes and proudest moments was hosting my first retreat. Although it operated at a financial loss, it was an amazing success in every other way.

ACTION STEP: Think about something you have been successful at doing. Be generous and kind with yourself on this one. Is it work, parenting, volunteering, or something else? Journal for a few minutes on all parts of this success—be as prolific and as complimentary as possible.

What Would We Do with an Extra 60 Hours?

—⟋⟍—

If we miraculously found an extra 60 hours in our life, how would we use it? Would we learn a new language? Would we dabble in painting or some other art medium? Would we write a book? Would we create our own business?

Sixty hours accumulates when we take ten minutes a day, for one year. Ten minutes! Undoubtedly, we all have ten minutes a day to invest in something.

If I had a dollar for every person who has said to me, "I just don't have the time for that right now," I would be rich and no longer frustrated. "I don't have the time," is an excuse. Start by carving out ten minutes a day; we can wake up earlier if we have to, but we must seize those ten minutes as if our life depended on it. Imagine what we could accomplish in sixty hours!

———

ACTION STEP: Make your ten minutes an early morning priority. Step #1 is to pick the thing you will be able to accomplish with your newly-found sixty hours and write it down here! Step #2, carve out ten minutes every day. It needs to be a set calendar item in your planner that is non-negotiable with you. I believe early morning is the best and most productive time. The items that are left for later in the day often have to compete with two killers, fatigue and lack of motivation.

Don't Believe Everything You Think.

—∿—

Seriously, do not believe everything you think.

ACTION STEP: For every negative thought you think about yourself, your work, your abilities, your health, your finances, etc., I want you to create a better, more positive, and more realistic thought. Take the time to write down a few of these more positive thoughts now.

Past, Present, and Future

—∞—

I have suggested living in the present to find happiness. It is not easy to live in the present because the past and the future are always wrestling for our attention and we usually succumb to their clever moves.

When we capitulate to the grip of the past and the future, we find ourselves knee deep in fear, doubt, and worry, among other profoundly negative emotions. Today, I have a short exercise that might help with living in the present:

Ask yourself, "Where is the past?" The answer is—only in your mind. "Where is the future?" Again, the answer is—only in your mind. It is only the present that you can physically be in and take pleasure in tasting, touching, feeling, seeing, hearing, laughing, and loving. So here's to the present! May we enjoy every single second!

———

ACTION STEP: Today, begin noticing how often you find yourself *traveling* to the past or the future in your mind. Think of which one you tend to go to more often. The past can bring us to a place of regret and sadness, whereas the future is more about increasing our anxiety and worry. Practice staying present.

Honest Abe

—∽—

April 15, 2015 was the 150th anniversary of the death of Abraham Lincoln. He died at 7:22 in the morning.

I am a tremendous admirer of Abraham Lincoln. I most recently read *Team of Rivals* by Doris Kearns Goodwin, but the book that really hooked me on Lincoln was *Lincoln on Leadership* by Donald T. Phillips. I read that book approximately 20 years ago and I still cite it regularly.

In *Lincoln on Leadership,* Phillips explained how angry Lincoln would get at his generals for their lack of progress toward the Confederate Army. General McClellan, in particular, gave Lincoln a great deal of angst. Lincoln's response to this insubordination was to write a letter to him. It is hard to think back one-hundred-fifty plus years but there were not a lot of other options!

The ingenuity of Lincoln's well thought out, well written, and profoundly frank letter was he **never** sent it. By choosing to never send the letter, he was able to rid himself of all the anger that was festering inside. Once the anger was neatly tucked away in an envelope inside his desk, he was able to regain his level head and proceed from a place of complete composure.

As a result of Lincoln's wisdom, I, too, have written a few letters that I never sent. The process of writing the letter was remarkably cathartic. I wrote one of these letters over two years ago and I am still grateful I wrote it and equally grateful I never sent it.

NOTE: This can definitely apply to emails that can be saved in your draft folder, but be very careful not to populate the "to" line.

———

ACTION STEP: Put this brilliant and sage discipline from Lincoln in your toolbox, and pull it out as needed. Although I have only used it three times in my life, it made all the difference in how I handled the situation.

I'm Coming Out

—✺—

I am coming out of the closet today. Before my husband reads this and spits his coffee across his desk, I guess I should explain. I am not gay. I do not believe gay people are the only people living in "closets." Life is very difficult and, as a result, most of us have a closet we have hunkered down into and are afraid to come out for fear of judgment or simply because we think it is safer if we do not talk about our tough road.

If you know anyone who has come out, you have heard their story of liberation. They are finally free. It was not better or safer in the closet. The closet is no place for anyone to live their life. The closet might be a failing marriage or drug-addicted child. Maybe you are stuck in a job you hate or your family life has deteriorated recently. All of us have a closet we are living in, and although it seems safer in there, it really is not.

Today, come out of your closet. Choose to be vulnerable with someone. Share your story. Be authentic. The best version of you is the authentic, genuine, and real you. None of us is perfect. I am living proof of that fact. Sharing our story with a trusted friend will bring us freedom we have not felt in, well, maybe ever.

———

ACTION STEP: This may be beyond your comfort zone. You may have kept this secret for a long time. If you cannot reach out to a trusted family member or friend, would you consider sitting down with a pen and paper and writing a letter? The letter could be to yourself, a cherished family member who has passed away, or God. You can burn the letter when you are done if you wish, I just want the burden of carrying this heavy load to be a little lighter. Closets are no place for anyone to live.

"Snap Out of It!"

—⟋⟍—

Let us look back over the last couple of years and take a moment to identify the most significant changes that have occurred in our life. Now, for each meaningful change I want us to identify whether it was the result of accident, destiny, circumstance, or personal decision?

Change occurs in two ways. It either occurs as a result of something outside of us and therefore the change happens **to** us or as a result of something within ourselves that affected the change. External versus internal.

The consequence of external change is that we gradually and unknowingly change—not to thrive, but simply to survive. We do as well as we can. We play our roles, we do our jobs, we save for the future, and we hope for the best. We abandon those dreams we had as a child, and we are stuck in the mundane routine of adult life.

If we relinquish control and allow the external world to take the lead on changes in our life, it will. Conversely, internal change, which is created by personal choice, positions us firmly in the driver's seat. What we do and become is entirely within our grasp if we choose to take hold. Do we want to be guided by the thoughts, ideas, demands, and influences of others or of ourselves? Who has our best interest at heart?

If most of our change has been external, then this is a wake-up call. We **all** inadvertently submit to auto-pilot, but sometimes in life we can all benefit from a quick dose of Cher in Moonstruck, "Snap out of it!"

It is time for us to grab the wheel of life. The only thing that stands between us and self-directed change is us! For the journey ahead we will need a strong will, belief, a good attitude, positive emotion, and the commitment to act. We are all set. Let's go!

———————

ACTION STEP: Look back over the last couple of years and take a moment to identify the most significant changes that have occurred in your life. Now determine whether it was the result of accident, destiny, circumstance, or personal decision?

Circus Act

—∞—

Recently, I attended an event for the Princeton Chamber of Commerce. The speaker had all of us enthralled with first-hand tales of Presidents and First Ladies. I was already captivated by her storytelling, hanging onto her every word, when she described one particular politician as "walking a tightrope daily for over 40 years." That visual dominated my every thought.

I do not know if the word "tightrope" struck everyone else like it did me, but I instantly felt exposed and vulnerable. I wondered how many people feel like they are walking the tightrope of life. Not only is it a constant balancing act (publicly and perhaps privately), but it is also exhausting. There is definitely a point of no return (or so it seems), when turning around does not seem like an option. And all along the way, there is the unrelenting fear of one misstep. Her word, "tightrope" weighed so heavily on me that night.

If "tightrope walker" resonates with you or someone you love, it is time to take action. Acknowledging the tightrope is the first step. Turning around is almost always an option; there is rarely a point of no return. But, most importantly, we need to help secure the safety net. There is nothing scary about a tightrope **when** the safety net is firmly in place. Do you need a safety net or can you serve as one?

———

ACTION STEP: Are you the tightrope walker or is someone you love? If it is someone you love, then can you help create a safety net on their behalf? It is amazing how much less scary tightrope walking is with a safety net. If it is you that is the tightrope walker, can you create a safety net? Who will you reach out to for support? Journal about either right now; this is really important. The safety net allows us to exhale. Exhaling feels so good.

Happiness Is Worth the Fight

—w—

Recent statistics show, year after year, that 70% of Americans hate their jobs. Of that 70%, at least 20% are actively disengaged and the other 50% are simply disengaged.

That blows my mind! Why would someone repeatedly go to a job they hate? I know someone will say, "Beth, you don't understand. I have no other choice. I have to pay my bills and my healthcare costs, etc." We *always* have a choice! Always! We may not be able to make an immediate change, but we are kidding ourselves if we think we don't have a choice.

I get so intense and passionate about this because, as a coach, I watch people surrender their happiness without even looking at all the viable options and it makes me incensed. If you are one of the 70% (approximately eighty-five million people) who are unhappy at their job, then do something about it! Email me, hire another coach, or talk to a mentor, but stop believing you are stuck in this job you hate.

Never surrender your happiness. Never! Fight as if everything depends on it, because it does. Life is too short to relinquish our happiness to a bad boss or a beat job.

———

ACTION STEP:

"Never surrender your happiness"   —BETH FITZGERALD.

Consider posting this quote somewhere you will read it every day. Journal about happiness and where it is being leached from your soul. Then make a plan to get out of any and all situations that are draining you of your happiness. It is *that* important!

The Dream Team

—m—

What do all these people have in common: Oprah Winfrey, Anthony Robbins, Richard Branson, Ted Turner, Abraham Lincoln, Anna Wintour (Editor of Vogue), Bill Gates, John Mackey (Whole Foods' founder), Ralph Lauren, Ben Franklin, and Coco Chanel?

They never graduated from college! My point is not to dismiss the value of a college degree, but to question how much weight we are attributing to it. Whether we have a degree or not, is that what defines who we are? Does the degree, or lack thereof, put us in a box? Are we making an agreement with the limiting belief that only those with a college degree become successful?

The eleven people I mentioned above chased a dream. So did the very young billionaire founders of Dropbox, Tumblr, Mashable, Spotify, and WordPress, all without a degree. I believe we need to ask ourselves, "Have I put myself in a box?" **Are we defining ourselves and therefore putting limits on our potential?** Look at those eleven names again. They were all ordinary people with a huge dream and no box. These kinds of boxes are pretty easy to get out of; we are actually just one thought away. What is your dream?

———

ACTION STEP: Today, we think. Think about your answer to each statement below. Are you in agreement with a limiting belief? If you are, then think of another answer that dispels the limiting belief.

- Only those people with a college degree become successful.
- The people that are successful always come from money.
- You have to start young to make a lot of money.

- Successful people are extraordinary in some way, they have a special talent.
- Can you think of your own limiting belief sentence?

Note: If you have a college degree or even an advanced degree—don't dismiss this post as not applying to you. The highlighted sentence above applies to all of us!

Who Knew?

—⟋⟋—

It is spring so it is quite possible that you too are seeing all of the daffodils in bloom everywhere! They are such a joyful flower for me and they confirm spring has arrived in New Jersey—finally! But there are some things you might not know about this colorful little beauty.

Daffodils are a sign of good luck in Wales and China. Daffodil sap is toxic so they can't be mixed with other flowers. A natural compound in daffodil bulbs, called narciclasine, is being researched to combat aggressive forms of brain cancer. And daffodils contain a compound, galantamine, which is used to treat the symptoms of Alzheimer's. Who knew, right?

Did you have daffodils in a box? I did. I had completely underestimated this welcome sign of spring. How can we apply this to all the people around us that we, without thought, put in a box? Are they white or black, rich or poor, smart or dumb? People are just like daffodils—multifaceted. There is one box we all fit into—the desire to be loved. So how would your day change if you put everyone in *that* box?

———

ACTION STEP: Throughout the course of the day and the days to come, every time you mentally put someone in a box, think of how we underestimated the daffodil. Think about how many facets these people must have. But unlike the daffodil, remember everyone's innate desire to be loved. If *we* change, everything changes.

A Lesson from Kindergarten

—⚏—

How does the public speaker stand up in front of thousands of people and deliver a flawless speech without vomiting, passing out, or simply stuttering and stammering through the whole thing? How does a surgeon perform open heart surgery perfectly? You might even be saying, "I could never do that!" Public speaking alone has most people fearing death far less.

So how do they do it? The answer is practice. The speech we saw, was not her first. No surgeon goes from the textbook to the operating room. And the same is true for you and me. Whatever it is we think, "I could never do that!"—yes we can. What stops us is not the lack of money, or lack of talent, or that we are not smart enough, or good looking enough. The only thing stopping us is our mindset. If we say "I could never do that," then guess what? We will continue to be right until we change that thought.

Part of that thought might be fear or lack of belief, but none of it is true. Remember, "You can be anything you want to be as long as you put your mind to it." Ah, when did we last hear that sentence, in Kindergarten? No truer words have ever been said, and it is likely we all have said them to our own kids. The speaker or the surgeon is successful because she put her mind to it and practiced a lot! What do you want? You can be anything you want to be. It is just a thought away, so start practicing!

———

ACTION STEP: Journal for a few minutes on the statement below.

You can be anything you want to be as long as you put your mind to it.

What have you abandoned because you felt it was out of reach? Really dig deeply into what this one sentence means to you.

I've Got Everything I Need and Nothing That I Don't

—◊—

I know it is grammatically incorrect but I didn't write the song lyrics. *Homegrown* by the Zac Brown Band is where those lyrics originated and I believe the words have so much truth, I wish everyone was singing it. Actually, I wish everyone believed it.

There are needs and wants in life. Our needs are basic. Our wants, however, elicit an emotionally charged feeling of lack. Once we recognize the lack, then we feel insufficient, inferior, and jealous, just to name a few. Here are some examples. I have a car, but I want a nicer one. I have a house, but I want a bigger one. I have a job, but I want a better one.

I am not asking any of us to play a smaller game by accepting our current situation. I do not want any of us to stop striving for bigger and better. Not at all. Reaching for the stars is a great way to be, but we want to reach for the stars from a place of thankfulness and gratitude, not resentment and jealousy. Let's go back to the *Homegrown* lyrics. The song ends with these words:

"It's the weight that you carry from the things you think you want."

"I want" is a considerable weight to be saddled with, and we single-handedly carry that weight as we walk right past "I am grateful for" to set our sights on "I want."

Today, let's grant ourselves permission to let go of the baggage. We have been hauling this heavy load for too long and it has done nothing but weigh us down. "I am grateful for" places us in the present, which is not only where joy is found, but also it's a lot lighter.

———

ACTION STEP: Spend 5 minutes journaling on either of the lyrics from the The Zac Brown Band song *Homegrown*.

"I've got everything I need and nothing that I don't."
"It's the weight that you carry from the things you think you want."

Bull's Eye

—⫴—

What is your target? Most people do not think about targets. Adding a target changes everything. The bulls eye was created for a reason. It was to determine how close someone came to what they were really shooting at. That is why, in life, a target is crucial.

What is the target for your job? What about your marriage? Do you have a target for your family? And the most neglected of all may sometimes be ourselves; do you have a target for your own personal growth or even self-care? Our targets should be put in writing for two reasons: first, so that it is out of our head and well thought out, and second, so it is visible like any other target. We cannot hit a target we cannot see.

Once we have determined the target and we know what we are shooting for, only then can we truly get dialed-in to what we want. The target gives us focus and clarity, and it eliminates all the aimless drifting. Whether it is darts, arrows, or life, having a clearly defined target and aiming for the bulls eye is what it is all about. That is where success lies.

———

ACTION STEP: Today's action can go as far as you would like to take it. As you read the post, did a particular target come up in your thoughts? If so, that is likely the one your intuition is guiding you toward, so write it down here. How much time and commitment can you give toward hitting this target? Can you commit five minutes a day? Make sure this target is visible to you daily and take daily strides toward attaining it. You can do this!!

My GPS Stinks!

—⚉—

Yesterday, I used my GPS to help me get to somewhere that I essentially knew how to get to on my own. As much as I love my GPS, I truly believe it is very often a crutch I do not need and it stops me from thinking on my own.

First, the GPS is not always right. I override it a lot. Second, especially when I am in a rush, I do not even stop to look at where I am going on a map; I relinquish all the power to the GPS, foregoing me actually thinking. And third, I never get lost anymore; she is always recalculating—again waiving my right to actually use my brain.

The GPS crutch is real, but it is also a metaphor for life. We do not get lost anymore because we play everything so safely. We do not think as much anymore either; we follow what society tells us is acceptable. Driving home yesterday, I turned off my GPS. I do not want the crutch anymore. She is still there should I get really lost, but I am OK with being a little lost sometimes and having to use my brain to get un-lost.

Safe is not necessarily how I want to live my life. Adventurous, yes. Risk-taking, yes. But most importantly, I want to make sure I am thinking for myself at all times. I can do this!

———

ACTION STEP: Are you playing this game of life too safely? Journal for a few minutes on ways you are or you want to be more adventurous in life. Think outside the box. We are just journaling, not quitting our job, so be brave and take some risks.

A Rough Patch

—⁂—

Do you play golf? Have you ever had to hit out of the rough? Why do you think they call it the rough? What do you think happens to us mentally when we know our ball is in the rough?

The rough is obviously a literal place in golf, but it also has a metaphorical place in our lives. Who hasn't been in the rough? The key is to be aware of where our mind goes when we see we are in this difficult spot.

Immediately, a few things happen. It is likely we actually verbalize an, "Ugh" or some other heavy sigh. Our mind might even say, "This is bad!" Our physical body will slump and we will experience various emotions like disappointment, defeat, and discouragement. We just allowed our mind to make the rough bigger than it truly is. After all, it is just grass, right? Our five-iron will rip right through it.

Don't get me wrong, I understand the obstacle in front of you is real. But maybe, just maybe your mind made it bigger than it truly is. Your attitude is **everything**! We need to stop calling it the rough! Our ball is in the grass, that's it! We need to change our mental dialogue to, "My ball is in the grass, I love a little challenge, and I can do this."

I think the inventor of golf called it the rough just to get in our heads. He succeeded—until now. Now we know it is how our mind perceives the challenge which determines our approach. Will we be a warrior and conquer both our mindset and the challenge at hand, or will we allow ourselves to be a victim and therefore become mentally defeated? It is our choice every time.

———

ACTION STEP: Today, think about all the ways you have allowed your mindset to get, stay, and set up residency in the rough. Now, spend 5 minutes journaling all the ways you can change your mindset to have a better and more optimistic view. Take a minute to experience how these words make you feel: fairway, sand-trap, on the green, and in the rough. Interesting, huh?

Thank You, Mikayla

My dear friend, Scott, sent me an article yesterday about an extraordinary eight-year-old New Jersey girl named Mikayla. She was out to dinner with her mom and insisted on picking up the tab for a police officer who came into the restaurant to grab a bite to eat. As the story unfolded, the officer found out this young girl's father was also a police officer who had been killed by a drunk driver while Mikayla's mom was pregnant with her. She never met her father.

Scott's wife, Kerri and I are reading the story simultaneously in different locations and both of us are crying. Kerri texts, "People are more good than bad. The world needs more stories like this." Amen, right?

Well, at that moment, I was sitting in a doctor's office thinking about how annoyed I was by the staff. Kerri's words are running through my head as I picture Mikayla and the police officer. Mikayla added more love into this world, and now I had a choice to add to her love or negate it with my own "justified" negativity about this so-called incompetent staff.

What happened next was amazing. I went to check out, with Mikayla on my mind. I engaged the receptionist with love in my heart. We talked about her son and her concerns about him serving in the armed forces. We both filled up with tears as we discussed her very real fear. I realized then that people are more good than bad, and the world does need more stories like this, **but** somehow we have to participate in creating them. We are Mikayla. We have to be Mikayla. What a great lead she took at eight years old, and I am happy to follow her.

ACTION STEP: Can you be Mikayla too? Think of all the places where you might be able to add joy and happiness today. It could be at your own breakfast table, on your way to work, or within the office. Have fun with this; you might be amazed at the results you get. Journal the results here after the day is complete.

Deadline

———⚭———

Here is a quick tip. Do you want to get something done? Set a deadline.

We use the word deadline all the time but, historically, it had a very different meaning. A deadline referred to the boundary around prisons during the Civil War which, if prisoners crossed, they would be shot by the guards. Fortunately, this definition is not very applicable these days.

Today, I am not talking about real work on your plate that needs to get done, but a self-inflicted deadline will work for that, too. I want all of us to pick something else that has been burning in our hearts to do, but we keep procrastinating with words like, "I'll do it when I. . . ." Fill in the blank. Did you say, "Have more time" or "Have more money" or my favorite, "When the kids are grown". Pick **one** baby step and give it a **deadline.** FYI, the first deadline for this step has to be less than a week from today. It is just a baby step. We can do this!

————

ACTION STEP: Today, you have two questions to answer.

1. What is it that has been burning in my heart to do, be, or have?
2. When is my deadline to take the first step? 7 days or less!

"We Have Nothing to Fear but Fear Itself."

FRANKLIN D. ROOSEVELT

—⁂—

Fear is the enemy. Sometimes fear is so present we literally feel the physical ramifications of it, like a racing heart or sweaty palms. But, more often than not, fear sits silently in the background, awaiting its turn to whisper, "Don't do that, do you know how risky that is? You could lose everything. Do you know what people will say? What if you fail?" We do not even think about this ever-present fear, yet this is the one we should fear most as it resides unceasingly in our head.

If we allow it, fear will drive our every decision. Sometimes, that is a good thing. Most times though, it is not. So I am asking all of us to think about all the things fear is keeping us from, whether that be as personal as switching jobs or as global as terrorism. I want us to ask ourselves this question, "I have allowed fear to permeate my life. At what cost?"

The opposite of fear is not bravery; it is acceptance. Fear has no foothold if we accept what has the possibility of coming. When we accept the fear, fear has nowhere left to embed its tentacles.

Here is a real example. I face my fear every day when I post on Facebook. My internal whisperer says, "What if your post is awful? What if no one likes it? What if it offends? What judgement happens on the other side of every post?" I have taught myself to post anyway. I walk into that fear daily. There is another whisperer too, and she says, "What if your post helps just one person? What if one person needed your post to make it through the day?" For that, I will risk failure and judgement every day of the week.

ACTION STEP: Spend a few minutes journaling about fear. Fear is built into our system and it is *never* going away, so it is best we learn how to accept it and live with it. One idea is to jot down some fears and then give each one a rating of 1–10. The number does not indicate how afraid you are, but how valid it is as a fear. A lion in front of you is a 10, but switching jobs may be more like a 5. Does numbering the fear help in offering you a new perspective?

Have You Ever Heard of the Pygmalion Effect?

—◊—

By definition, it is the phenomenon whereby the greater the expectation placed upon a person, the better he performs. The effect is named after the Greek myth of Pygmalion, a sculptor who fell in love with a statue he had carved.

Here is the truly interesting part of this effect: In an experiment, teachers were told a particular student was especially gifted (actually she was simply an average student). The student was treated differently by all of her teachers. The expectations were raised exponentially and the student rose to meet them. The student became a leader in the class and her grades were commensurate with the expectations.

Who in your life could use a little Pygmalion Effect? If you are a teacher or a coach, then you can really take this and run with it. The effect will remain long after your season with this child. If you are a parent, then which one of your children could benefit from the Pygmalion Effect? There is usually one in the family that needs a self-esteem boost. Finally, if you are a manager, which one of your staff members needs you to surreptitiously implement the Pygmalion effect to further their growth?

Remember, the effect is achieved when the student fully grasps we have a much higher belief in their ability then they have in themselves. Ultimately, that is when they begin to believe it too. I hope you have earmarked someone in your life to believe in. They will forever be changed by your actions, and so will you.

———

ACTION STEP: Who were you thinking of as you read about the Pygmalion Effect? It is all about raising the bar. Take 5 minutes to create your secret plan to help this person overachieve.

How Powerful Are You?

—⚭—

On Sunday, Doug and I were finishing up our 3.5 mile walk/run. We were near the end and we decided to run the last fifty yards or so. It was uphill, the sun had been slow-cooking us for most of the journey and was going to continue to do so for these last few yards. Our target was the two big shade trees up ahead.

As we started to run, I became acutely aware of my mind's "internal roommate." I was tired and I heard the roommate say, "I don't think I can make this distance." The competitor in me decided to challenge the "roommate." I said to myself, "Do not agree with that! Put your head down and just go. Listen to your body, not that voice. You can do this."

I did it! I could have run farther, too. That was just a fifty-yard dash. What is your "internal roommate" keeping you from accomplishing? We hear her talking to us every day. "Don't leave your job, it's safe. I know you hate it, but safe is better than unemployed," or "It's just one bowl of ice cream. You deserve it! Just go back on the diet tomorrow." This "roommate" thinks she is helping, but she is very often holding us back. Can you listen for this voice today? Will you be brave enough to challenge the "roommate?" Ironically, I will bet she is talking to you right now.

———

ACTION STEPS: Today is an awareness day. First, be aware that there is an internal roommate talking to you at all times and she is not necessarily helpful. Second, know that you always have an override button called free choice to shut her down. The roommate is always present, but listening to her is optional. Sadly, eviction is not truly possible. Move forward, firmly knowing that you can challenge, override, or opt-out of listening to this voice whenever you wish! Sometimes, I laugh at her and say, "Nope, not today!"

Start Dating

—⟋⟍—

I am strongly encouraging you to date, especially if you are married!

Let me explain. While attending a public speaking course in Florida, I had to give a speech every day for three consecutive days. I could choose any topic, but it was best if I felt really comfortable with the material since I had very little time to craft and memorize. For one of the speeches, I chose to talk about a cornerstone Doug and I rely on to strengthen our marriage.

I inadvertently learned this fabulous gem from my parents. The cornerstone is: always continue to date your spouse. My mom and dad always referred to each other as "boyfriend" or "girlfriend". I adopted that little nuance after I got married. When I think I have heard Doug enter the house, I will say, "Is that my boyfriend?" It is not so much the vernacular that matters, but it does constantly remind me to continue to date Doug because marriage has a way of changing everything.

When you are dating, it is **all** about the other person. Everything is done to please the other. Marriage sends us off in different directions but dating is all about building the strong connection. Today, I am reminding all of us to date our spouse. Doug and I plan at least one outing a month that is just the two of us. It is all about reconnecting, catching up, solidifying the bond. We plan it well in advance. We all know how hard it is to carve out time, but we make it our priority. We get dressed up. It is a date! We covet that night. We are highly intentional about planning it and we look to make it special in some way. Not expensive, but special. They are different.

Today, tell your spouse you want to start dating!

––––––––––

ACTION STEP: If you are not already dating your spouse, then grab a pen. Journal today for 5 minutes on ways to begin dating your spouse. You can be far more creative than we have been. What would you plan if you were in the very beginning stages of dating? Let your mind travel back there, the really good ideas reside there.

The Litmus Test

—∞—

When it comes to your job, have you ever thought about whether you are pushed or pulled? This is the Litmus Test for whether or not you are doing something you truly love.

If we are "pulled" to work every day, we are energized at the thought of getting started. It takes no effort to get ready for work because we are chomping at the bit to engage in this activity. The emotions surrounding this pull might be excitement, anticipation, and joy. When we are pulled, it feels almost effortless, as if there is a huge magnet pulling us in and we are offering no resistance. We never tire of doing this work.

On the other hand, if we are "pushed" to work, there is inherent friction. Pushed does not imply the opposite of pulled as there are varying degrees of pushed. If we are feeling pushed to work, it takes a little bit more to get us out of bed and out the door. We may be feeling preoccupied, yanked in different directions, unsettled, and lacking focus.

Neither is necessarily good or bad but we should be aware. If we are pulled to work, we are in a great pace, a slipstream of sorts. On the other hand, if we are pushed, it may be time to take inventory. Why do we feel this way? What is making us feel pushed. As always, it is in our conscious awareness that we can make changes and grow. Autopilot is not an effective strategy, especially if we are feeling pushed.

ACTION STEP: Pulled or pushed? Which is it? Spend 5 minutes journaling on whether you are pushed or pulled to work. I have been both. Pulled is much better.

Good Is the Enemy of Great

—⚡—

"I would love to be average; I want to fall right in the middle of the pack," said no one ever. Most of us, unfortunately, do fall right in the middle, not because we want to, but because good is the enemy of great.

Let's repeat that phrase to ourselves, "Good is the enemy of great." Is our marriage good? Is our job good? Is our health good? If I swapped out the word "good" and replaced it with the word "mediocre", would we still be happy? When I realized good was equivalent to fine or mediocre, I was no longer happy with good. I wanted great!

I want the word "good" to make us all feel unsettled now, maybe even perturbed. I want us to say, "I don't want a good marriage, I want a great marriage! I want my job to be incredible! I want my health to be exceptional." When we hear ourselves say, "good," I want us to follow it up with, "Maybe for the pack, but not for me!"

Please note, great is not even near good; it is in another country! It is going to take dedication, commitment, and maybe all our heart has to give, but with all of this effort will come success, fulfillment, pride, and genuine happiness from a job done not just well, but *great*. Here's to great!!

———

ACTION STEP: What in your life is good? How can it become great? Journal about each topic below:

Faith?
Family?
Marriage?

Parenting?
Volunteer work?
Job?
Health?
Friendships?
Extracurricular?
Fun?
Fill in your own -

The Hard Road

—⚮—

Have you ever heard of the expression, "The hard road"? I hear it a lot when I am talking with clients. "I always wanted to be/do/have X, but that would be a hard road now."

Hmm. Sometimes I think the road we are already on is the actual *hard road*. Isn't doing a job you hate the hard road? Isn't being unhappy in a marriage the hard road? Isn't feeling unhealthy and out of shape the hard road? So which is it? Are we on the hard road already or is the change where the hard road really begins?

If you are not happy, then I am going to offer up the possibility that you are already on the hard road and it's likely you have been on it for a while. Change is scary, I agree. But do not cloud your judgement by predicting a hard road ahead, because you have been handling the hard road, perhaps unknowingly, for some time now. Take a moment to recognize how strong and powerful you are. You have been on the hard road and were not even giving yourself credit for tackling that challenge. You can do anything! You are a lot tougher than you think.

ACTION STEP: Spend 5 minutes journaling your answer to the question, "Am I already on the *hard road* now?" Exactly where is the *hard road?*

Love Heals

—◦◦◦—

Love heals! I have said those two words before and I am certain to say them again. Love is not just a feeling, it is a noun *and* a verb. Love is something we do. It is an action word requiring our enthusiastic and engaged involvement as well as our active participation. It does not simply come to us, we must put in the effort.

Love, the feeling, comes from love, the verb. If we find ourselves drifting off into love, the feeling, but forget love is a verb, then we should go out and love, affirm, listen, sacrifice, empathize, serve, appreciate, and any other action we know will demonstrate our deepest love to others.

Proactively moving forward in love (v), is how love grows exponentially. I have yet to hear anyone say, "I have enough love, thanks. I'm good."

———

ACTION STEP: Today is not a journaling day or a thinking day, it is an *action* day!! Go actively love anyone and everyone. Surely you can start with family, but that is the easiest one. Call a friend who could use some love. Love a stranger with your kindness. Reach out to either your church/synagogue/temple and see if anyone needs a home visit. Call a non-profit organization and volunteer. Go out and love and I promise you this with 100% certainty, you will receive so much more love in return than you could ever possibly give.

On the Fence

—◊◊◊—

Yesterday a friend of mine shared a quote with me I had heard before, but had not thought about for a while.

"Indecision is a decision."   —UNKNOWN

She really made me think. Life is filled with making and avoiding decisions daily. Hindsight is definitely 20/20 and it would be a lot easier to make decisions if the outcome was guaranteed, but it is not. When we fail to make decisions, we find ourselves making a decision anyway.

Here is what is most important: it is a known fact that most successful people have a common trait— they make decisions quickly. It does not mean every decision made is correct, it just means they decided. Gordon Graham also has a great quote, "Decision is a sharp knife that cuts straight and clean; indecision a dull one that hacks and tears and leaves jagged edges behind."

Usually, indecision means, up until now, the answer was "no." Rip off the band-aid. Do not listen to the fear, listen to your gut. Your gut is always right.

———————

ACTION STEP: What are you waffling about? Stop sitting on the fence. You have thought about this for a while (some of you for years!). Today, decide. Yes or no? In or out? Journal for 5 minutes on your decision.

With Mother's Day Approaching

—∞—

I remember when my eldest daughter Devon was first born. She was just days old when I went to visit my mom and dad. I gazed adoringly at Devon, then I turned to my mom and asked, "Am I going to worry like this forever?" My mom smiled and with the warmest empathetic look she replied, "Yes. I still worry about you." (I was almost 31 years old at the time)

As many know, motherhood never ends. Today, let's toast all of the mothers who paved the way before us. I am so grateful for the example my mother gave me. This job is not always easy, but I would not change it for the world!

Enjoy your day!

ACTION STEP: Below is a poem of sorts about motherhood that was shared with me. I love this poem and I hope you do, too. It is equally applicable to fatherhood. Your only action step today is to read this beautiful poem!

My promise to my children—As long as I live—
I am your parent 1st—your friend 2nd. I will
stalk you, flip out on you, lecture you, drive
you insane, be your worst nightmare & hunt
you down like a bloodhound when needed
because **I LOVE YOU**! When you understand
that, I will know you are a responsible adult.
You will never find someone who loves, prays,
cares, & worries about you more than I do! If
you don't hate me once in your life—
I am not doing my job properly!

I Just Want to Ask One Quick Question . . .

—⚎—

Are you diminishing yourself by the words you choose? I certainly was, but I will no longer do that to myself now that I am aware.

Do you use these words: just, brief(ly), hope(fully) kinda/sorta, and lil' bit? If you do, please stop! You are minimizing your worth with every use.

How many of us have started an email with this line, "I'll be brief" or "I just want to ask one quick question and hopefully not take up too much of your time!" You are telling the other person their time is more valuable than your time and you are not worthy of anything other than a brief moment. "Kind of/Sort of" and "Lil' bit" are used more in our speech than they are in our written work, but they also reduce our worth and represent us in a small, unimportant way.

Imagine a president, any president, whether it be of a country or a corporation, saying, "I will be brief, I just want a moment of your time," or "Hopefully, we will be able to win this war/campaign." You cannot imagine it because it would **never** happen. They command our attention, own the space, and deliver their message. We can and should do the same.

Stop hoping, hope is not a strategy for success. We can **hope** the Phillies win the World Series because that is out of our control, but in our life, we must stop hoping, and start making a plan, and doing. Today, I am asking all of us to declare our worth. We must stop using these words. If you choose to be brief in an email, then be brief, but do not diminish yourself by saying so or qualifying.

So, hopefully you kinda sorta understood what I briefly wrote. I just wanted a little bit of your time, I hope that was ok? **Never again** will we diminish ourselves in any way, especially with the words we choose. We are **important**, we are **worthy**, and we are **valuable**. Own it!

––––––––

ACTION STEP: Write these words down so you remember to never use them again: just, brief(ly), hope(fully) kinda/sorta, and lil' bit. I have done this for years and I am still deleting the word *just* with some regularity. But when I delete *just,* I feel incredible powerful. Deleting that word is equivalent to me saying, "Your time is not more valuable than mine!"

Names and Labels

—⚮—

I am not a fan of humiliation. I guess no one would say they are a fan of it, but it happens. Intentionally and unintentionally, people are humiliated every day. On the vibrational scale of emotions, shame and humiliation are the lowest possible vibrations we can experience and no one wants to feel this way—ever.

On April 28, 2016, the NFL draft began. That year, the last pick was #253 and it went to a young man from University of Southern Mississippi, defensive back Kalan Reed. What you might not know about the NFL draft is that since 1976, the last pick gets bestowed the title, "Mr. Irrelevant." The humiliation does not stop there, a jersey is presented with #253 with "Mr. Irrelevant" on the back and the player and his family are invited to spend a week in Newport Beach, California, culminating in a ceremony awarding him the Lowsman Trophy (think Heisman, only this player is fumbling a football).

At first, I thought this was hilarious, but after I gave it some serious thought, I decided that deliberate and intentional public humiliation is not okay. If a high school decided to give out such a jersey, the nation would go berserk. He was chosen 253rd in the NFL draft, so let me explain the odds on his accomplishment: 8% of high school football players will play at the college level; there are almost 73,000 college football players, about 16,000 of whom will be eligible for the draft; 1.6% are drafted.

So is "irrelevant" the best term to describe Kalan Reed? I don't think so! His success up to this point is far from irrelevant. He beat the odds! He had a better chance of being struck by lightning than being picked in the NFL draft. I have a better name for the 253rd NFL pick: impressive, or remarkable, maybe unbelievable, even extraordinary, or incredible, but not irrelevant. I did not even mention all the work this young man has put in over the last eight years or more, as well as how long he has been dreaming of becoming an NFL player, and then to be cast as Mr. Irrelevant? NFL, I must respectfully disagree with you.

Sometimes I get on my righteous bandwagon and I am unapologetically there right now.

ACTION STEP: Words really matter. Labels can be inaccurate and just plain wrong. Today, think about labels you innocently use to describe family, coworkers, and friends. In revisiting these labels, are there any that need to be eliminated from your vocabulary? Are there any that sounded funny at first, but now, after further examination, need to be retracted? Today is simply a check-in day.

Red, Red Robin

—⚭—

For the past couple days I have been watching a robin outside on my porch. She keeps flying into the ceiling fan and staying there until I make a sudden movement that scares her off. I really could not figure out why she kept flying in until yesterday.

Finally, I noticed a twig in her mouth. One twig at a time, she has been building a nest. As I watched, my first reaction was how torturous it must be to make something that slowly. But as I continued to watch her progress, I thought of how many things I could accomplish if I just chipped away at them like this bird. Baby steps, many and continuous, ultimately add up to success.

What could we accomplish if we followed this robin's lead, one twig at a time? I have a few things written down now, thanks to her. What could we accomplish if we took one step every day? Who knew a robin could provide such inspiration? Can you take her lead too? And, do you know what the robin symbolizes?

Robin: A symbol of growth and renewal. The energy of this bird will teach you how to move forward with grace, tenacity, perseverance and assertion.

———

ACTION STEP: For today, simply write about the word, *growth*. Don't make it bigger than it has to be. Spend 5 minutes writing about what *growth* means to you and for you.

Pulling Back the Curtain

—∽—

Why do we believe that everyone else has it all pulled together? We all seem to believe that we are the only ones with faults, so to speak. You know the faults of which I speak. We lose it with our child and then we beat ourselves up because we think of Mary, our friend, who we are certain has never raised her voice. Or we look enviously at our very successful colleague Bob, who dresses sharp, has the perfect family, goes on great vacations, and never seems to deviate from perfection.

Today, I am pulling back the curtain. Mary and Bob have *stuff* too. Trust me when I tell you, **everyone** has *stuff* and those that tell you they do not have anything going on in their life that is not perfect, are lying. Actually, the ones that play the perfect card, are usually the ones that have the most *stuff*.

I am pulling back the curtain today because so many people are living a life weighed down by their *stuff* and feeling alone. They are carrying shame, humiliation, sadness, guilt, and other extremely unhealthy emotions because they long to be *perfect* like those around them. No one is perfect. Please trust me when I tell you, you are not the only one with *stuff*. I have *stuff*, too. And do not make your *perfect* neighbor your aspiration. You are **awesome** just the way you are!

———

ACTION STEP: I believe reading this page was the action step, as long as you can now breathe easier. We all have *stuff*. Let out a big exhale on that one and repeat after me, "We all have *stuff!*"

Mount Everest

—∿—

"Mt. Everest, you have defeated me once and you might defeat me again. But I'm coming back again and again, and I'm going to win because you can't get any bigger, Mt. Everest, and I can." —SIR EDMUND HILARY

Sir Edmund Hilary spoke those words when he was asked to address an audience that recognized his first attempt at summiting Mt. Everest. There was a photograph of Mount Everest behind him on the stage, he turned to face the picture of his nemesis, and spoke those words of conviction, throwing the gauntlet down.

What is the mountain in your life you are facing right now? Does it seem insurmountable? Can we use Sir Edmund Hilary's words to empower us? It is important to note, Hilary conquered Mt. Everest in his mind first. The famous explorer has another famous quote that is arguably even more powerful than the first; "It is not the mountain we conquer but ourselves."

Whatever our mountain, know it is not the mountain we are battling, it is our own fortitude. We need to look our mountain in the face and say, "I am going to win," and then go make it happen. We cannot and will not accept no as an answer.

On May 29th, 1953, Hillary and Nepalese Sherpa mountaineer Tenzing Norgay became the first climbers to reach the summit of Mount Everest.

———

ACTION STEP: What is your mountain? What seems insurmountable? Take a moment to write it down. Now, think about what first step you could take toward conquering this self-proclaimed beast? One step at a time.

What Is Your Modus Operandi?

—∾—

When you have an incredibly brilliant and inspirational thought like, "I am going to go back to school" or "I am finally going to switch careers" or "I am going to open my own business"—what stops you? What is the modus operandi (M.O.) that operates in your thought process that prevents you from moving forward yet again? Is it procrastination, fear of failure, what will others think, or "other"?

Our mind is ferociously cunning. Today, we need to identify our M.O. As a general rule, people are usually consistent with the negative M.O. they tend to fall back on. For instance, if we are a procrastinator, that will be our Achilles heel repeatedly.

Once we have isolated our vulnerability pattern, only then can we dismantle it. Isolate the pattern. You know it, but it is likely you have never owned it until now. Today, you (and I) will own it.

———

ACTION STEP: Think about and isolate your self-sabotaging pattern. Use the examples in the first paragraph to help determine how you sabotage your success then journal about ways to overcome this Achilles heel.

The Gold Standard

—⚏—

Nobody says to themselves, "Let me lower my standards." Unfortunately, it happens over time unless we are consciously aware and ruthlessly diligent about maintaining our standards.

Most people would say they have not lowered their personal standards, but before we say that, let's answer a few questions about ourselves. We will use five years ago as an arbitrary time frame:

Where is my weight in relation to five years ago?
What professional growth has occurred?
Is my marriage/relationship stronger?
Is my faith/spirituality stronger?
Is my physical condition better or worse?
Are my friendships stronger?
Am I eating healthier?
Am I happier than I was five years ago?

If any of our answers do not indicate improvement, then it is likely we have lowered our standards. My wake-up call to standards happened very innocently when one of my teenagers cursed in front of me. This was not the first time, but I had to pause and say to myself, "That was not tolerated before, why am I OK with it now?"

It took me a few seconds and then I told my teenager, "I understand you curse now with your friends, but it is not OK for you to do that in front of me." I know this seems trivial, but all standards are an indication of self-respect.

Our personal standards are reflected in how we treat ourselves as well as how we treat other people. Standards are also mirrored in how we expect to be treated by other people. When we have high standards we expect to be treated with the highest of regard. However, when our standards are low, it suggests that we allow ourselves to fall prey to other people's influence.

———

ACTION STEP: Today, scrutinize just one of your personal standards. What standard has inadvertently been lowered over time? Can you say out loud, "I won't tolerate that anymore! I respect myself too much to allow that to continue."

I Did the Best I Could at the Time

—m—

I read a quote the other day that was life changing. The author was talking about past mistakes and regrets and she suggested using a sentence that has been very helpful to her during those times: "I did the best I could at the time."

I love that quote! When we slip into the space of regret, we have left the present and are choosing to live in the past. Since we cannot change the past, there is nothing healthy or productive about going there. Regret is a form of self-punishment. Life is stressful enough, we do not need to add self-punishment.

For me, "I did the best I could at the time," has a comforting and forgiving feel and tone. The only reason regret even surfaces is because we know better now. So why are we punishing ourselves if we did not have all the information from the start? Our argument for regret is flawed so we need to consider letting it go. "I did the best I could at the time."

P.S. We have grown since then. Instead of regret, let us focus on how much stronger we are now because of it.

———

ACTION STEP: Where in your life would you like to apply this sentence? Spend 5 minutes journaling about how you feel now that this sentence has been applied to that time. Do you feel comforted and forgiven?

Parenting: 101

—〜—

Parenting. Wow! By far, the toughest job I have ever held. I have four children, all between the ages of seventeen and twenty-three. There have been times recently when I really doubted whether I was going to make the duration. I have definitely searched to see if there was a clause in my parenting contract that allowed for a leave of absence, a sabbatical, or maybe I was eligible for an early release program.

Do not get me wrong, I adore my children, but in a moment of complete transparency, there are days I am not sure I have the stamina for this job. I regularly question whether I am truly qualified for this role. I think I am in over my head. I am certain I am making wrong decisions at times and I wish we had been invited to a mandatory training program, or a workshop, or at least been given a user's manual, for goodness sake!

For all of you out there who occasionally question your role as parents, I am right there with you, my friend! This is the hardest job on the planet. Ironically, I believe it is the hardest job because we love our kids so much. Everything we do is toward that end; parental love is the deepest love we can have for a human being. I get weary and question my ability to fulfill my role as a parent but then, out of the blue, comes a, "Thanks Mom." That off-the-cuff remark fills my tank and I can continue the journey. This job is the most difficult and the most rewarding; occasionally we experience glimpses of the purest pleasure we have ever known. Stay strong parents! We can do this!

ACTION STEP: In all good consciousness, I cannot go on about how tough parenting is and then give homework! I am simply sending loving thoughts your way, regardless of whether or not you are a parent. We all have times we feel weary, so I am sending you my love and support from afar.

Eureka!

—⋘—

I hear it all the time, and I have certainly said it myself. Maybe you are different, but I've heard or said that *the problem* with my current situation is due to the economy, the industry, the company, my financials, my predicament, my (ex) husband (wife), my lack of education, my race, my sex, my lack of time, my kids, my lack of experience, my age, my weight, my circumstances, my location, my hair color, my shoe size, and my dog.

Nope! I am not buying it for me and I am not buying it for you. I will quote the late Jim Rohn, "For things to change, you have to change." That quote is worth chewing on for a while.

If we are open to the possibility that all the excuses I listed above are exactly that, excuses, then the problem must lie elsewhere. If the problem is within us, and the only solution is for us to change, then we would have the answer to what is holding us back! EUREKA!! For things to change, we have to change–and in doing so, we reclaim our power. This thought is deep, but it is the panacea for all that ails us. We can take any reason we have for not moving forward and create this sentence, **"I used to think _____ was holding me back, but now I know it's been me all along. When I change, everything changes!"**

———

ACTION STEP: Today is a journaling day. Use this highlighted sentence above as your prompt. Fill in the blank but don't stop there; keep writing. Reclaim your power!

Something You May Not Know about Me . . .

——∞——

I did stand-up comedy in New York City. It was probably about ten years ago. I decided I wanted to take a comedy class. I read the description of the class and learned the final exam would be performing live at The Gotham Comedy Club which is where Jerry Seinfeld started his career.

With nothing but complete **fear** running through my body, I signed up for the class. I wanted to take this enormous risk because I was not sure if I could actually perform live stand-up, I love to tell jokes, and I wanted the challenge.

The eight or so weeks of class were so much fun. Crafting jokes, listening to others tell jokes, stumbling, bombing, succeeding, all were a part of this journey. I met great people. The teacher was hilarious! But all along, we knew what loomed on the horizon—The Gotham Comedy Club live performance. Fear pervaded. Lots and lots of fear.

The night finally arrived and we were all there, ready to perform. I was given the second to last spot which was a huge compliment. The last spot is reserved for the very best. They finally introduce me and up I went. The fear was present in every part of my being, but I said to myself, "You are prepared! You are ready! Just say the first joke and the rest will roll off your tongue." I was almost right.

The first few jokes were great! The laughter was really motivational. And then it happened. I blanked. I could not remember the next joke. It took me a second or two, but it felt like an eternity. The entire audience was staring at me, waiting for me to not only speak but to be funny, all the while I was feeling the intense heat of the spotlight pointed straight in my eyes. It felt like the walls and the ceiling were slowly closing in on me. I cannot remember exactly how I recovered, but I did. Phew! I hit the ground running again! I finished strong. The crowd went wild (or at least that is how I remember it!)

I will never forget that night at The Gotham Comedy Club, not because of any part of the successful joke telling, or the laughs, but because I took the risk. I faced the fear and I lived to tell about it.

What risk are you afraid to take, because I assure you there are not many risks that are scarier than doing stand-up comedy live in New York City! Take the risk. You may find that one of your proudest moments will be the risk you took, regardless of the outcome. I know mine is. Take the **risk**!

———

ACTION STEP: Today, journal about all the possible risks you have been interested in taking for years. When you are done journaling, circle one you are willing to commit to doing. Now, pick a deadline to get it done! Come on, I did stand-up, you can do this!

Poverty of the Soul

—◊—

What brings you joy? What fills your heart? What makes you happy? Now go do it! Get off your phone, get off your computer, and create happiness. It is that simple. We live in a world where we **allow** endless demands on our time. Stop allowing the phone or emails to dictate your day. Take a few moments to answer these questions now: What brings you joy? What fills your heart? What makes you happy? Set the wheels in motion to pursue these things or spend time with these special people.

We are rushing through life, which is a huge mistake. If we are spending a day with someone we love, let's give them our undivided attention. Let's turn **off** the cell phone. There is no tombstone that says, "I wish I had spent more time on my phone."

Ironically, I am required to turn my phone off before a tennis match, but I do not require the same of myself during our family dinners. Please help me understand my own logic here! Well, that will not be the case at our dinner table anymore.

My phone/computer/email do not fill my soul. People fill my soul. Laughter fills my soul. Nature fills my soul. Balance is important and multitasking is the kiss of death. We need to choose, actively and consciously, to fill our soul.

ACTION STEP:
STEP #1, answer these questions:
   What brings you joy?
   What fills your heart?
   What makes you happy?

STEP #2, shut off the electronics! Tomorrow is never guaranteed. Enjoy everything about today!

Are You an MVP?

—⊸⊸—

I attended my son's high school spring sports varsity dinner last night. For over an hour, coach after coach came up to the podium chronicling their season, telling tales of highs and lows along the way, and revealing the coveted MVP. Although every coach explained that a team is a team and the MVP could not be the MVP without their very important teammates, not one coach verbalized having any difficulty in coming to a conclusion on the individual they picked as the MVP.

Here is what struck me the most about every MVP—it was not their amazing athletic ability alone that was highlighted. As a matter of fact, their athletic ability was easily overshadowed by many other amazing character traits. Each chosen athlete had qualities that made me want to know them well beyond their statistics. They were described as compassionate, smart, fun, hard-working, selfless, caring, etc. They had many amazing qualities in addition to being very gifted athletes. These teenagers changed the team not only because of their talent but because of their character.

You may be very good at what you do, but would your "coach" or your "team" select you as the MVP? Have you ever thought about what it takes to be the MVP? Would you behave differently if you thought an MVP award would be handed out at year's end? Today, I am going to give that some serious thought, starting with my role as a mom.

ACTION STEP: Journal for 5 minutes today on the role under which you would like to receive the MVP. You can choose multiple roles if you want. What do you need to improve upon for MVP to be an option?

Fun and Games

—◊◊◊—

I had the good fortune of turning fifty in 2014. I do not know why I waited until fifty, but as fifty approached I decided to make some changes. One of the changes I decided to make was that life needed to be a bit more fun! I had chosen *responsible* before but now I was choosing *fun!*

One of the first fun choices I made was to purchase a fun car. My last three cars have been Yukon Denalis. Essentially the Denali is a school bus. It is enormous, but with four children and two large dogs, it was a practical car. Now I wanted a fun car. I deserved a fun car. I was fifty, if not now, when? So we went to our local Jeep dealer and purchased what I would describe as a very fun Jeep Wrangler!

The car had paid for itself by weeks end! The entire family was grinning from ear to ear! The top had been off and at least one bird "christened" it; we froze with the roof off because it was so cold and we didn't know how to put the roof on yet. Regardless, the ear-to-ear grins remained. Honestly, they all piled in the car to go to the supermarket with me! The happiness in my house was palpable! It was a great purchase. Had I known, I would have bought this Jeep ten years sooner!

My point, as summer is about to begin, is when are you going to choose fun? I waited until fifty. Do not wait that long! Trust me, it was a big mistake. Where in your life are you being way to responsible and practical? Is it time for you to cut loose? I believe so! Choose fun! Create fun! You will not regret it, I promise you.

———

ACTION STEP: Spend 5 minutes journaling all the ways you could add more fun into your life. I have yet to meet anyone who has said, "I already have way too much fun in my life; I really need to scale it back." It does not have to involve buying a car. If you are struggling to think of ways to add fun, then try Googling it.

Do Your Best

—ɷ—

"Do your best, that is all anyone can ask of you."

Have you heard that phrase before? I heard someone say something similar yesterday and it really made me think. I was stuck on the word "best." What is my best? It sounded so nebulous. Of course I will do my best, but what is my best and how do I know if I'm doing it?

Here is the truth; if we are trying to get the best out of someone (or ourselves), the worst thing we can say is, "Do your best." We don't even know our best because we haven't accomplished our best yet. Our best is still inside of us. To accomplish our best, we need to set a goal which is more challenging than anything we have already attained.

It has been statistically proven that specific hard goals produce a higher level of output then a general, "do your best." I could ask you to jump as high as you can or I could say you need to jump over a three-foot bar. Your best on the former might not be your best on the latter. So how do we make sure we are doing our best? How do we make sure our best does not remain inside of us? What we believe our best is is based on our previous *best,* but if we want our very, very best, it is going to require that we set a bar that we have never attained before. Scary, right? It's OK. Do your best, that is all anyone can ask of you.

———

ACTION STEP: Where in your life could you add a challenging goal so you would produce a higher level of output? Journal for 5 minutes on this challenging goal because I'll bet your best is still inside you.

The Other Self

—⚊—

Every day we get to choose who we want to be. Maybe we have not looked at it this way before, but the choice is available to us each and every day. Today, I want us to choose the gutsy, confident, fearless version of us!

We have chosen him or her before, maybe not with any regularity, but we have chosen to be that person in the past. We can tap into that bountiful resource today. Our gutsy, confident, fearless self is just as available to us as is our cautious, uncertain, play-it-safe self; it is simply a matter of choosing.

There is something in your life that has been waiting for the gutsy, confident, fearless you to show up and today is the day. Make it happen. Be brave. Go for it.

———

ACTION STEP: Identify, in just a few words, that *something* in your life that you want. Write it down! Now go do it! Take a step, just one baby step. The momentum will start, but it requires you to take that first step. It is **Newton's First Law of Motion:** An object at rest stays at rest and an object in motion stays in motion. Get moving!!!!

Oh Horse, Please Drink!

—⚮—

"You can lead a horse to water but you can't make him drink."

Why? As a life coach, this may be the most frustrating part of my job. Everyone loves quick fixes and tips they have never heard before, but when push comes to shove, they dig their feet into the ground and it would be easier for me to push an elephant a mile than to make this horse drink.

The truth is, the "water" is outside our comfort zone. Getting things done within our comfort zone is certainly productive and helpful, but outside our comfort zone is where real growth happens.

How can we say yes to the scary stuff? First, assess the risk. Most things outside our comfort zone are just outside, not a mile away. Say yes to little risks. I find most of the horses that say, no, haven't really given it some thought—it was more of a knee-jerk reaction. What could we say, yes to that definitely scares us but is worth the risk? You have something in mind right now, don't you? **Do it**! Don't be the horse that wouldn't drink. If drinking horses could talk, they would say, "I can't even begin to tell you how amazing the water tasted. I am so glad I took the drink!"

———

ACTION STEP: Is it possible that you, too, are standing right next to the water? Journal for 5 minutes on something you would like to move forward on but you are just a tiny bit scared. Spend part of your 5 minutes assessing the risk.

"You Are in My Thoughts and Prayers."

—∞—

I am not a fan of this statement. I know people mean well when they say it, but it feels overused and can lack its true and deepest meaning. If we are going to say these words, presumably the person we are saying them to could really use our thoughts and prayers. So from an integrity standpoint, it cannot be treated lightly, like a to-do list item that we may or may not get around to doing.

To toss this platitude out there, which can be untrue and insincere, despite the encouraging tone with which it is often said, falls flat in my book. My thought when I hear it is always, "Are you really going to pray?" If not, please don't say you will. It is important to say what we mean and mean what we say. The person in need could really use to be comforted and platitudes are not the *warm hug* they need right now.

So what are some alternatives?
- I cannot comprehend how difficult this time must be for you.
- Know we are all thinking of you, and wishing you strength.
- My heart breaks for you, and I am sending my love your way.
- I hope you will feel the strength and love from the many people who care deeply about you and your family.
- Please know that I'm here for you.
- Be certain of my prayers. (If you feel strongly you are going to pray)

Life is tough enough. When someone is going through a rough time, we need to stop long enough to create a sentence that conveys the love we truly wish to send to them. I am not suggesting that anyone using this phrase does not mean it from the deepest part of their soul; what I am suggesting is that it has become overused and there may be a better alternative.

———

ACTION STEP: Simply bookmark this page for the next time you need to send out words of sympathy or caring. I hope the six suggestions above offer a more accurate and sincere alternative to convey your deepest sentiments.

Summer Kick-Off

—✳—

Finally, as we near Memorial Day, the unofficial start of summer has arrived! As we prepare to head into this weekend, maybe you are already transitioning into your *summer-mode* as everything begins to wind down. One thing is certain, we will all be spending a lot more time outside, which is a really good thing for both our mind and our body.

I am going to suggest exploring the possibility of meditation, but I believe I can hear the groans already, so give me one minute to explain. Can we start by trying a walking meditation? Download an app from iTunes or Google some walking meditations. In this practice, we are using the physical and mental experiences of walking as the basis of developing greater awareness—killing two birds with one stone, so to speak.

The benefits of meditation are amazing. Stress reduction alone is reason enough to meditate, but add the chance to increase gray matter, focus more, raise our level of calm and various other health benefits, makes it a no-brainer (pardon the pun). A walking meditation takes all those benefits and gets us up and out of the house, which makes it even more powerful. If you add this to your summer routine, you will not regret it.

———

ACTION STEP: Download the app! I use the Walking Meditations app. The variations include Being Present (16-minute walk), Body (17-minute walk), and The Senses (18-minute walk). You will need ear buds as well. This practice has been so wonderful for me, I hope it will be for you as well

Talk with your doctor before engaging in any exercise.

Channel Your Inner Turtle

—ᗰ—

Sometimes we simply don't have the time to commit a random act of kindness. We need to catch a train or a plane, and although we want to help, we simply don't have the time. Or do we?

The other day, I was arriving home from Florida. My plane landed in Newark. The journey ahead of me looked a bit like *Planes, Trains, and Automobiles* and I was Steve Martin. If all of my timing was perfect, after I landed in Newark Airport, I would take the shuttle from the airport to New Jersey Transit. I would travel on NJ Transit for an hour to Princeton Junction where I would get in my car to drive home. Everything hinged on that first shuttle. If I did not get to NJ Transit in time, I had to wait an hour for the next train, but I was optimistic.

I got off the plane, grabbed all my bags, and started sprinting through the airport. With the shuttle just a flight of stairs away, I stopped at the machine to purchase my train ticket. I am so familiar with these machines, I could do this task blindfolded if need be, so it took me less than a minute to purchase my tickets. I was definitely going to make this train. I knew it. And then it happened!

The elderly couple next to me asked for help. Internally, I was screaming, 'Nooooooo!' But they were the sweetest little couple and they could not figure out the machine. I felt compelled to help them and I knew I was going to miss my train as a result. I did for them what I had just done for myself, at record speed I purchased two senior citizen train ticket to New York City. This couple was from the San Francisco Bay area celebrating their fiftieth wedding anniversary. They were adorable, it was like helping two little kids.

We travelled on the shuttle together chatting non-stop about all of their anniversary plans for this momentous occasion. When we arrived at NJ Transit train station, I helped them navigate there as well but then we needed to part ways since we were headed in two different directions. I will likely never see these two sweet people ever again. I hope they enjoyed their anniversary in New York City. I hope others helped them along the way, too, even if it was not convenient for them to do so.

I struggled with my decision to help them, but after I made the commitment, I was so glad I did. They needed help and a lot of it. Even if I did miss the train (which miraculously I did not), was spending an hour in Newark really going to change my day dramatically? No, but helping them did. I felt useful. It made me happy. Apparently these feelings aren't uncommon. It's called The Helper's High.

Lesson learned Beth Fitzgerald. Slow down. Help others. I believe I rush to gain more, but more of what, I don't know. In reality, I lose way more than I ever gain by rushing. As my husband said over the weekend, "Is there any way for you to channel your inner turtle? Never mind, you don't have an inner turtle!"

ACTION STEP: Are you in a position to help others on a daily basis? If you leave the house, it is safe to assume the answer is, "Yes". Take the time, from now on, to lend a helping hand. The Helper's High awaits!

In Honor of Memorial Day . . .

—⚉—

Shortly after the Japanese bombed Pearl Harbor, my father and all his teenage friends went to the local Army recruitment office to enlist. They were enraged with Japan and felt compelled to serve their country. Initially, my father was rejected by the Army. Here is a strange fact, to qualify for the Army in 1941, each candidate had to be able to close only the left eye (for a right handed shooter). My dad could only close his right eye, therefore, the Army was forced to reject his application.

My father would not be deterred and rejection was not an acceptable answer. He was committed to fight for his country. He proceeded on to the Navy Recruitment center where he found success. They accepted him and he went off to defend his country. I am always moved by his and many other servicemen's or women's resolute determination to serve their country.

About 20 years ago, I took my parents to NYC. When my father laid eyes on the Statue of Liberty, he was overcome with emotion and declared, "I have not seen her since I was the first boat returning from WWII into the NY Harbor." Then he looked at Doug and me and proclaimed, "You will never be able to appreciate the American flag unless you have served your country. It is an unbelievable sight!"

To this day, as I look at the American flag, I replay my father's words and desperately try to search for that feeling that only a person who has served America can feel when they see the stars and stripes. Memorial Day is a federal holiday in the United States, meant for remembering the people who died while serving in the country's armed forces. I believe we should all take a moment to honor those courageous people in some way. I will be remembering my dad and all of my uncles who served.

ACTION STEP: If you know someone who served, please take a moment to thank them for their service even if they are no longer with us. Go one step further, and say thank you all year round, if and when it seems appropriate.

With tremendous gratitude to all of those who have served, past and present.

HARRY 1943

Don't Be Fooled by the Data

—⚏—

I received a Fitbit as a gift for my birthday and I loved it. But now that I have had it for a few months, I am realizing it does not tell the whole story. It gives me a lot of stats likes steps, heart rate, sleep overview, etc., but what it captures in data, it misses in depth.

My goal is 10,000 steps a day which my faithful band will capture even if I spend a leisurely day shopping. But if I run 3 miles, I will fall short of that goal. Which one was better for my health? I feel like life is similar: sometimes we get caught up in the stats but overlook our soul. We live in a nice house, get paid a wonderful salary, have a great family, so the stats look good but the stats do not pick up on how unhappy we are at the job we hate or our relationships are suffering.

Do not be fooled by the data, it does not tell the whole story. We need to look past the data to measure, monitor, and improve our story based on intangible information we get from our heart and our soul. We need to ask the tough questions like, "Am I happy?" "Am I living a purpose-filled life?" "Am I doing what I love?" The true "Fitbit" has been with us all along; it is not on our wrist, it is in our heart. Check out *that* data!

—————

ACTION STEP: Today is a journaling day. Take some time to answer the questions above like, "Am I happy?", "Am I living a purpose-filled life?", and "Am I doing what I love?"

Check in with your heart.

The Basis of My Entire Marriage Rests On . . .

—⚭—

Pigs in a blanket! I guess that warrants an explanation. Twenty six years ago, I was blissfully engaged to Doug. We were running about making every kind of marriage decision known to mankind. You might remember those decisions: china pattern, crystal pattern, linens, venue, band, etc. The decisions were endless, but all along the way, Doug simply deferred to whatever I wanted. At the time, I thought his compliance was fabulous.

As the big day approached and the stress began to ramp up, we arrived at the venue to finalize the menu for the reception. We were analyzing the hors d'oeuvre options when Doug declared his desire to have pigs in a blanket. It only took me a millisecond to shoot down that absurd idea. My reasoning was simple, "Cocktail weenies" are not sophisticated enough for a wedding." I was completely unprepared for Doug's reaction. He dug his heels in deeply and refused to budge. His argument was simple, "Everyone loves pigs in a blanket!" I, then, dug in deeper with, "They are **not** what you serve at a wedding!"

My memory gets hazy as to when and where this argument was settled, but I am certain it was settled within 24 hours. I was wrong, and not just wrong about *cocktail weenies!* This is when I realized marriage is all about concessions, meeting half-way, and never needing to prove you are right. I wanted to impress others and, in doing so, I did not want to hear Doug's thoughts or ideas. Not a good basis for a marriage.

You will all be happy to hear, not only did we have pigs in a blanket at our wedding but we have served them at almost every function since. Doug taught me a huge lesson that day. I love to be *right* and to win any argument, but at what cost? If cocktail weenies are the concession

I make for a happy marriage, then so be it. It is a small cost. And truthfully, can anyone be *right* about cocktail weenies?

————

ACTION STEP: Do you have a "pigs in a blanket" story? If you do, let it go. Winning that argument is not winning at all. I smile every time I serve or see this life changing hors d'oeuvre!

The Lemonade Stand Rule

—⚍—

I do not know when, where, how, or why I adopted this rule about ten years ago, but here is my rule:

Never, ever, ever drive by a lemonade stand without stopping.

I never thought about it before adopting the rule, but imagine for a moment you are the child selling lemonade. You finally convinced your mom it was a good idea. You made a huge mess in your mom's kitchen making potentially the "best" lemonade of all time, and you dragged everything in the garage to the curb to begin your first entrepreneurial venture. You have images of all the things you are going to buy with your profits: A new bike, that expensive video game, and maybe even a new car (for your mom, of course)! This day is going to be epic!

Strategically positioned by the curb, you are ready to sell lemonade and then it happens. You see the first car coming up the road, you jump out of your little lawn chair, grab the homemade poster-board sign and hold it as high as you can, waving it to and fro. Your first sale is almost here. You cannot wait to pocket the cash. Wait! No! Stop! They did not just drive right by you? Yes, they did. Your heart is broken, maybe even crushed.

Repeat rule: Never, ever, ever drive by a lemonade stand without stopping!

I had the pleasure of stopping at my first lemonade stand this season. It was run by an adorable little boy near the local seminary. I think he was a little afraid of me, but he handed me my cup of lemonade anyway and I gave him a dollar. I should have given him five dollars just so I could see his face really light up. I hope his first business venture was profitable; I loved his entrepreneurial spirit.

––––––––––

ACTION STEP: Lemonade stand season is upon us. It might be best if we all prepare by hiding some dollar bills strategically inside our car. Stopping at any lemonade stand is a huge win-win; everyone ends up happy! Stop even if you don't have any money; explain and wish them well!

The Lesson of Love

—⚭—

I was reminded of a famous quote by Maya Angelou this weekend when I attended the funeral of an incredibly dear family friend: "People will forget what you said, people will forget what you did, but people will never forget how you made them feel."

I met Mr. Benoff as a small child; my parents were best friends with Sam and his wife, Joyce. As I sat at his funeral listening to all the fabulous stories as well as reflecting on my own fond memories, I realized that Mr. Benoff always made me feel loved. He was really fun to be around and he was always smiling and laughing but the feeling he left me with consistently was loved. It is a warm feeling that has not faded one iota over the years.

Have you ever thought about how you make people feel? Go well beyond your inner circle. My memory of how loved I felt by Mr. Benoff is at least 44 years old, so if you don't think it matters or that people won't remember—I am evidence to the contrary. Take the day and ask yourself, "Do those around me feel loved?" It's a really important question to ask yourself.

With gratitude to Mr. Benoff for the lesson and the love.

ACTION STEP: Today, ask yourself "How do I make people feel?" If *loved* is not the answer, what is? And would you like to make some changes?

Congratulations Graduate!

—⚂—

For all my graduates out there, high school or college, this one's for you. Congratulations! You did it!! It was not easy, but you achieved an amazing milestone as a result of all your hard work and commitment. We are so very proud of you!

You thought it was going to feel amazing to be done and it does but somehow there is this gnawing angst that is sitting in the pit of your stomach desperately yelling, "What now? This is so scary. I'm not even certain I know what I want to do. I'm not sure if this is the right place for me? What if all my choices were wrong?"

I feel your pain like it was yesterday and it was *so* not yesterday! I have a few valuable pieces of advice I hope you will find helpful.

1. AMAZING YOU: You are doing your best to please your parents (and yourself), impressing them with grades and honors, and choosing a responsible career path. But learn this fact quickly, your parents already believe you are amazing! You do not need to do anything more. The "trophies" are wonderful, but all parents truly desire for you is health and happiness! Earning a "B" is fine, especially when the "A" was going to give you a stomach ulcer, or worse. Exhale my friend, you are applying too much unnecessary pressure on yourself. It is not healthy and you are going to burn out if you keep up this pace.

2. PURSUE PASSION: Honor what you are good at and passionate about, not what you believe everyone thinks you should be doing. If you do not honor it now, it will gnaw at you forever. It will never go away because it is your giftedness and it is why you are here. Your passion will always answer from your gut or your heart, but rarely from your head. When you compromise your desire, you compromise your strengths.

3. STOP WORRYING: Don't worry about picking the wrong major. You are at college to learn, to have fun, and to get a degree. Rarely does your major turn out to be your occupation. I graduated with an economics degree and I went into finance. They sound similar but, trust me, they are not. My friend was a modern dance major who ultimately ran a hedge fund. Worrying is a waste of time. Your work ethic is far more important than your major.

4. FIND A MENTOR: Choose someone in your life and ask them to be your mentor. A name should have popped into your head as soon as you read, "Find a mentor." This person is someone you respect, admire, and enjoy being around. Get as much knowledge as you can from their years of experience. They will be honored to share their wisdom with you. Also, take the time to mentor someone yourself. Looking forward is important but so is reaching back.

5. ACT: This is not a race to the finish, it is a journey. The "winner" is essentially the person who discovers why they are here, what their passion is, and then pursues it with all of their being. Do not worry about failing, take as many risks as you can. Every action, regardless of success or failure, grows you as an individual.

6. FAITH: There is a power higher than you. Explore it now while you are open to all possibilities. Somewhere along your journey, you will need this, especially if you have not already tapped into this source of peace and comfort.

You are amazing and the world needs your giftedness! Do not second guess all of your talent! Your cup runneth over! If I can borrow your vernacular, we need you to "BRING IT"!!

ACTION STEP: If you are a recent graduate, reread this, and this time let it let it sink in to the amazing, passion-pursuing, and worry-free you! If you are not a recent high school or college graduate, please make a copy and pass this along to someone who is. Consider adding your own words of wisdom before sending.

Falling off the Wagon

—⟋⟍—

I fell off the wagon big time, so to speak. Although this post is about faith for me, keep reading as you can *fill in the blank* for whatever it means for you.

We regularly attend a local Episcopalian church in Princeton. We used to be heavily involved and attended services weekly. For a myriad of reasons, about a year or so ago, I essentially stopped going. My attendance was spotty at best. While I still remained faith-filled at home with prayer, it bothered me that I was not motivated or engaged to go on Sundays. Unfortunately, I did nothing to change this, until last week.

I decided to visit my priest to express where I was spiritually and to see if he had any ideas to help me. His advice was simple, "Just come". He elaborated on what it means when we show up and engage. I knew then that I had subconsciously met with him because I needed some accountability. I was really glad we spoke.

After that meeting I started attending Sunday services again. I engaged. I arrived with intention, which is a bit more than showing up. It was, literally a step in the right direction for me. Have you fallen off the wagon with anything in your life? Do you have a disconnect with someone or something? Maybe it's as simple as your exercise regimen or as important as your relationship with your parents. Maybe you know it, but like me, were a bit unwilling to own it? I'm encouraging you to talk to someone who will get you back on track, especially someone who will hold you accountable in some way. It may seem too far gone, but it's definitely not. Trust me. It might be as simple as, "Just come!"

———

ACTION STEP: Spend 5 minutes journaling about an area in your life in which you feel you have fallen off the wagon. Use these 5 minutes to simply become aware. Don't judge. Awareness is kind, judgement is not. Be kind.

Fiesta!

—ᴍ—

I was in New York City one night to meet a client. Doug met me afterword at an outdoor cafe for a bite to eat. We could not stay long because we had promised our daughter we would be home in time to quiz her for her history final which was the next day. Before taking the train home, we stopped at Pret-a-Manger in Penn Station to grab a hot tea.

The cashier could not believe we were ordering a hot beverage given that the day was still stiflingly hot and humid. We explained we needed to be *on our game* when we got home so we could quiz our daughter. "We are too tired to quiz you" was not going to float. He laughed at our story and then he did something completely unexpected; he treated us to our drinks. He said he was *touched* by our commitment to our daughter. We were floored! We thanked him profusely and I promised to call the store when she received her grade. The name on his tag read, "Fiesta." We will not forget him for a long time.

Fiesta made our day and I am still talking about him. If you are in New York City, you might even stop by this Pret-a-Manger and I hope you do. Energetically, he raised my *happy* to a lot happier. It was not the free tea, it was the kindness. What if we all tried to do this daily? I am going to pull a "Fiesta" today and I hope you will too. He made my day!

———

ACTION STEP: Will you buy a stranger a cup of tea? Can you think of other ways for you to spread kindness? We may not see the repercussions of our actions, but that does not mean there is not a ripple effect.

Nobody Cares What You Think!

—⁓—

This sounds harsh, doesn't it? I learned this lesson twenty-five years ago while I was working in the World Trade Center at The Oppenheimer-Funds. I was taking an in-house public speaking class which was being taught by our head of sales. This class was, to this today, one of the most valuable classes I have ever taken. I still use much of what I learned in that class.

Very early on in this class, one of the fifteen or so students must have said, "I think . . .". Jim, our instructor, quickly and forcefully blurted out, "Nobody cares what you think!" If he had left it there, I may have been scarred for life, but he went on to explain why—"Your audience wants to know what you **believe**."

For all of us who are leaders, managers, public speakers, or anyone else who will speak in front of 2 people or 2000, no one cares what we think but they will always care about what we believe. If we want to know the impact of *think* versus *believe,* imagine yourself in front of a crowd of thousands. They are all there to see you deliver a powerful keynote address. As they wait on the edge of their seats, will you begin with, "I think" or will you choose, "I believe"? Word choice is incredibly important as well as powerful.

Thank you, Jim, for many wonderful lessons. I am extremely grateful.

———

ACTION STEP: Today, begin to remove *thinking* from your vocabulary and start *believing.*

Thank You Margie!!!

—⁂—

As you may have gleaned by now, I have many rules I live my life by. The other day, my friend Margie shared one of her rules and I adopted it immediately. It is a brilliant rule if you have children (or adults) with cell phones.

Margie's rule is, "If there are 2 or more people in the car, put your cell phone away—we are going to talk." Before learning Margie's ingenious rule, I was driving my children everywhere while they unremittingly went through Snapchat, Instagram, and texting without coming up for air or engaging in even the slightest bit of conversation with me. I was, by definition, a chauffeur.

This morning's drive to school with my teenage son reminded me what a gift Margie had given me with her very simple rule. If you have ever driven with a teenage boy, you understand how painful a ride it can be. The silence is deafening. As a parent, I reach for any topic that I believe might result in a conversation but, invariably, it almost always fails. What I likely receive is an almost inaudible grunt or one word answers.

But not this morning! The phones were away. I cannot remember who started the conversation, but it was meaningful. He told me stories of one particular kid at school that everyone loves. The stories were hilarious. We laughed a lot. The ride was about 20 minutes long and it was a joyful start to my day!! I am still smiling.

———

ACTION STEP: If you would like to adopt this rule from Margie, I am sure she wouldn't mind. It is a great rule. Take control of the car and the communication you have with your children while you can. We all spend a lot of time in the car, we might as well make it count!

Our First Family Wedding!!

—⚮—

The Fitzgerald family has a big celebration coming soon, as one of our nieces will be getting married! As the excitement mounts, I was wondering what piece of advice I would want them to know about marriage. My mind was like a video game, barraged with thoughts like rapid fire, so much so that I could not grab on to any one thought. There are so many *words of wisdom* that could and should be shared with a couple entering into such a lifelong commitment.

I finally landed on the least obvious one of all. Like most of my lessons, I learned it from Doug and I learned it the hard way. Doug and I were having a conversation one day, early on in our marriage. Doug casually said, "You know I never say a bad word about you to others. I listen to men say some unbelievable things about their wives, but I just want you to know I never do that!" I sat there in disbelief. That statement turned my world upside down for many reasons, and changed me forever.

My first reaction was appreciation that he would hold me in such high regard as to never bad-mouth me in any way. My second reaction was shock, wondering what all the men were actually saying about their wives! My third and final reaction was the one that changed me forever and it was shame. I had been bad-mouthing Doug in front of my friends. Simple stuff like, "And he leaves his wet towel on the bed," or, "he forgot the recycling again!" Enveloped in shame is not a place anyone wants to be, trust me on this one.

Am I perfect now? No. I am deeply aware of what I say about Doug and I do my best to never speak ill of him even over simple stuff like wet towels. I admire and adore Doug beyond words.

As painful as that lesson was, I am glad I learned it. I looked up "bad-mouth" today to see its synonyms; decide for yourself if this is what you want to do to the person you love: belittle, criticize, disparage, demean, slander, diminish, malign.

ACTION STEP: I am certainly not trying to shame anyone, that was too awful of a feeling. I'm just raising awareness from my own learning experience. Your action step today is to never bad-mouth your partner behind his/her back, regardless of how innocuous you believe it to be. Instead, always have each other's back.

Face Your Fears

—◆◆—

We all have heard the expression, "Face your fears," and it is likely we have shared such advice with our family and friends, but do we adhere to this sage advice ourselves? The answer is, "Probably not." Most people will not elect to face their fear unless their back is against the wall. Growth only occurs when we face our fears; otherwise we are living within our comfort zone and it is called so for a reason.

Recently, I chose to face one of my fears. I realized I had never driven into New York City. I have been the passenger, but never the driver. With tremendous trepidation, I drove into New York City in the rain. All went well until I made a wrong turn, went through a scary tunnel and ended up in Brooklyn! The visceral response of the fear of being lost in Brooklyn was overwhelming. I was beyond scared. The toll-taker in Brooklyn was my savior! I think we are best friends now. She gave me all the right answers to get back into Manhattan and I told her, "I love you!" We laughed and off I went, still petrified.

I ultimately arrived at my mid-town destination, with the fear still palpable in my chest. I attended a class, ironically titled, "A Course in Miracles." When I departed, the most amazing thing happened, the fear subsided. I actually enjoyed the ride home. I cruised up 42nd street, I flew down 5th avenue like I owned it, I jockeyed my way through 7th avenue near Madison Square Garden to pick up my daughter, and finally, I inched my way through Soho and into the Holland Tunnel in a torrential downpour. I thoroughly enjoyed driving in the city on the way home. The fear was gone.

Here is the revelation: as we get older, we are less likely to elect to face any fear which means we will not grow. What is a fear you know you have, that you are willing to face head-on? Just do it! Face it. You will not be disappointed, I certainly was not. I feel like I am standing just a bit taller now from pride in my own accomplishment. If I can do it, you can too!

———

ACTION STEP: Pick a fear like I did, one that is simple. Maybe it is dogs, heights, snakes or even bridges. Now make a plan to face it head-on. You can do this!

Valedictorian

—ɯ—

I had the pleasure of attending my daughter Katie's high school graduation recently. As I sat in the audience, I was struck by all the awards. Many were for academics, some were for athletics, service was another, and the list went on. It made me think not so much about who won the awards but who didn't.

If you are not the valedictorian, who are you? And what category did you put yourself in? What I was afraid of as I watched 300 high school students get their diploma, very few of whom were awarded a distinction, was would they now categorize themselves as average? I was worried because I know they are anything but average!

What I have learned in the five years or so I have been coaching is that everyone has this special something inside of them. It's beyond a gift, it's far more special than that. Yet somehow it gets buried so deeply, they no longer see it or are afraid to use it. Maybe it's because at some graduation years ago when they didn't win an award for the smartest student or the best athlete, they decided they must be just average. They are anything *but* average and so are you! Find your gift and start using it; trust me when I tell you, it's like being your own valedictorian!

———

ACTION STEP: Today spend 5 minutes journaling about that special something that is buried deep inside of you. What is it? You are *not* average!

Contrary to Popular Belief

—∽—

If you can truly absorb and apply these words, you will be able to change anything in your life. I am making a big claim here but I intend to deliver.

Our life is defined by our beliefs and our convictions of who we are as a person. Many of these beliefs became ingrained in our subconscious when we were a child and there are others we adopted as an adult. Regardless of when they became our beliefs, they are very hard to change. Our subconscious is very powerful.

The reason beliefs are so difficult to change is because we usually forge ahead to change a particular behavior but we do not change the belief. Beliefs drive behavior. Research shows that if we commit to something for twenty-one days, we can change a behavior, but that is not necessarily true. Let me share an example.

Have you ever witnessed people who have lost a lot of weight, only to gain it all back again? They changed their behavior, but not their belief. They ate healthy and exercised and the weight fell off, but deep down in their subconscious there was always the belief that would sabotage the success. The belief could have been many things like, "I have been overweight my whole life," or "I hate the gym," or "I'm not disciplined enough to continue this healthy lifestyle long term." If we do not change our belief, we will always revert back.

What would you like to change? Is it losing weight or your self-sabotaging procrastination? Do you believe you are not good enough or that you are too disorganized? Beliefs run the gamut. Only the negative beliefs are the ones that should be targeted for change. If you are currently identifying with a negative belief, ask yourself this question:

"Is that who I am or how I used to behave in the past?" The answer is almost always, "how I behaved in the past" because we are in complete control of our future. Now, let's put a toe in the water by giving our subconscious a story it can believe.

"I don't love the gym! But that is ok. I really like to walk. I always feel great when I finish walking. Exercise is the key to my success, not the gym. I can enjoy the health benefits of low-impact walking for a long time and that thought motivates me!"

Different belief, different behavior. We are in total control.

————————

ACTION STEP: What limiting belief is holding you back? Spend 5 minutes journaling on what new story you can tell your subconscious that it can believe. The subconscious is shrewd, so do not try to trick it. If you remember the "lowest common denominator" in math, that is what we are shooting for here. What is the very first baby step you can agree on with the subconscious. Turn to your gut to find out if you are both in agreement. The gut never lies.

The One Sentence That Changes Everything

—◊◊◊—

Life is funny. Everything seems to be going along fine, then one person or situation completely derails everything, leaving us spiraling down to an emotional place we have no desire to visit, let alone take up long-term residency. The worst part is, it is likely we have been here before. It is definitely an, "Ugh, not again" moment.

If you, too, are currently experiencing one of those moments, I have one powerful sentence for you to say to yourself: "I am determined to see things differently."

As we explore this idea, let us allow love to lead our thoughts. How can we view this person differently? Maybe it is not the person, but the *specific actions* or *attributes* of this person. How can we view those differently? How can we view this *whole situation* differently?

Unfortunately, we see the world the way we *want* to see it. We have given everything in our life all the meaning it has for us. But we always have access to a more loving interpretation, it is just a matter of having the courage and determination to see things differently. Seeing it differently can bring us peace and joy, if we let it.

————

ACTION STEP: Whose name popped into your mind when you read the question, "How can I see things differently?" Can you be **open to the possibility** of seeing things differently? If you refuse to release your grasp on, "I'm right" (and you may very well be right), then essentially you will be doing as Buddha said, "Holding on to anger is like drinking poison and expecting the other person to die."

A Powerful Lesson at Miniature Golf

—m—

I had the pleasure of taking my daughter and three of her friends minia-ture golfing the other day. I told Clare we could do anything, but it had to be outside since it was such a beautiful day. Clare chose miniature golf. It was a summer bucket list item for her, if one can have a bucket list at the age of thirteen!

On the fifth hole, which backed up to a big pond, Clare asked, "What happens if I hit it in the water?" I shrugged my shoulders and responded, "Well, it will cost you a stroke and we will have to fish your ball out of the water." Sure enough, with one mighty swing of her putter, the little pink golf ball went flying into the pond! Her head whipped around toward me as she blurted out, "Did I just make that happen because I thought about it?" Classic words from the daughter of a life coach. I could not help but laugh and nod, affirming what she had just said. She quickly followed up her statement with, "So, I should have thought hole-in-one?" This was not really a question but an epiphany.

Fast forward to the fourteenth hole and what do you think happened? Sure enough, Clare sank a hole-in-one! She told her friends, "See, you just need to think it, just think it!" Clare is still on top of the world because of her hole-in-one and even more so because she knows she cre-ated her own reality.

I know many of you will read this and think, all of that was luck or coin-cidence. Thoughts are powerful things. Do not say them or even think them if you do not want them to be so. Ask any athlete who has ever said, "I hope I don't strike out," or "I hope I don't miss this shot." The "don't" does not help you. You have just filled your mind with the words "strike out" when you could have offered up "base hit!" The mind is so powerful! Use it to get what you want, not what you don't want. If you want to test my theory, go play miniature golf!

———————

ACTION STEP: Spend 5 minutes thinking and journaling about thoughts you say either out loud or to yourself that have a negative slant. It could be as simple as, "I am not a good cook" to as egregious as, "I will never get promoted." Spend time creating new thoughts that have a positive twist, and definitely ones that don't start with the word "don't." Some alternatives are "I am", "I will", "I can", and "I am determined to".

Today Is *You Are Awesome* Day!

—⚋⚋—

Yup, *You Are Awesome* in every sense of the word! Now be honest, how uncomfortable was it to hear those words? I know that voice inside your head said, "No I'm not." I really hate that voice. I hear it, too, and I do my best to shut it down in me as well as in you!

I know the voice told you all the things you are not awesome at, but the voice is wrong! Please trust me when I tell you the voice is very wrong! Instantly, I know you compared yourself to others by saying, "I'm not as good a mom as Kerri," or "I'm not as nice as Jen." That voice only picks up on the "you could do better" moments and we need to celebrate the "wow, you are incredible" moments.

For today, I want you to trust *my voice.* I am telling you without a doubt, "You are awesome!" I want you to quiet the negative voice in your head and think of three really amazing things you have done. Maybe it was a big work project or maybe it was simply an awesome home-cooked meal. Write it down. When you complete the list, I want you to write, "I AM AWESOME!" Spend the day (at least) bathing in that thought. "I am awesome! I am!"

P.S. I would really like you to continue this every day. It is an extremely powerful ritual. "I am" is the most powerful statement a person can make. You can pair it with any complimentary adjective you are feeling or want to feel.

———

ACTION STEP: Your work has been spelled out for you above. Remember, three is the minimum, but you can add more. Regardless of how many you write, do not forget to add, *I AM AWESOME!*

My Facebook Experiment

—ɯɯ—

On June 28th, my sister-in-law Amy posted a quote on her Facebook page that went something like this, "This summer, put your phone away for a few days and make some memories that no one knows about. Make some memories that are just yours." That quote really made me think about how I use Facebook.

I love Facebook for so many reasons. I love catching up with old friends. I love being more connected to those I do not see very often. I love all the things that make me laugh, and I love all the things that make me cry. One thing I really struggle with in regard to Facebook though, is the fine line I feel that exists between sharing and bragging. So I took Amy's quote to heart and challenged myself to remain off Facebook with all my summer *memory making*. For me, that meant anything that might even remotely appear to be boastful. This quote heightened my awareness of how I was using social media.

Overall, I did well, but fell off the wagon once. This experiment changed the way I viewed Facebook. The world does not need to see everything I do. Amy's quote made me pause and really think about why and what I am posting socially. Is it to share, to celebrate, or am I bragging. For me, sharing is awesome, bragging is not. Sometimes, the lines get blurred. I have joked for a while now that Facebook needed to add a button after Like, Share or Comment; they need to add "Please Stop!"

I learned a very big lesson during this experiment. My son said it best when he declared to our family "I don't document my life through my phone—I live it."

———

ACTION STEP: Spend 5 minutes thinking about what you post on Facebook and why. Look back on a few of your more recent posts and ascertain your intention. There is no blaming or judgement here, just reflection.

Why Do I Always Put Myself Last?

—∞—

If you are a mom or a dad, you know what I mean. I tend to put myself last. I realized this at a lacrosse tournament this weekend. Some of what we do as the selfless parent is good and honorable, but there is another part I now recognize as very unhealthy.

Why is it so hard for many of us to do things for ourselves before we do for others? Maybe we believe the good parent sacrifices herself for her family and, increasingly, for her work. Parents often feel they are responsible for everything. In doing so, we diminish our worth, we forego our dreams, and we postpone our life essentially until the kids are gone. Not only is there nothing healthy about this thought process, but living our life entirely for our children, although well-meaning now, is simply teaching them to do the same later in life.

My friend Jane, who has her masters in Psychology, said this:

> "The id is the childlike part of us that seeks pleasure.
> It is very important that we do not starve it."

Are you "starving" yourself? I was.

———

ACTION STEP: Make a list of ten things you like to do that make you happy. When is the last time you purposefully did any of them? Foregoing this short exercise is putting yourself last and who ever said, "I hope I'm last?" After you have your ten items, see how many of them you are currently doing on a regular basis. If the answer is less than three, please take the time to schedule at least one of them so you are not starving yourself of happiness. It is critical that we feed this part of our psyche.

"I Am Too Old for That."

—∿—

If I could stop everyone from saying that line, I would. It is, essentially, us throwing in the towel. Why would we sabotage ourselves, regardless of our age? The subconscious hears, "I am too old," and then does its best to makes it so! Age is a state of mind and I refuse to let my mind believe anything but, "I am young and plan on staying so for a very long time!"

Age does not define us. We can use our mind to cut through expectations and obliterate fake limits. Below are a few amazing people who did extraordinary things at an age that most would call old.

1. Diana Nyad, at age 63, swam from Cuba to Florida (103 miles) without a shark cage. It took her 53 hours. Google it. She is amazing!
2. John Andrews, (at age 84), had skied 528 of the 700 ski resorts in North America, and plans to finish the rest.
3. Francis Hesselbein, is 102. She is the CEO of Francis Hesselbein Leadership Institute.

I could go on. When did we accepted our numerical age as an indication of what we are capable of doing? If we could roll back the clock ten or fifteen years, what would we do? So what is stopping us now? Let's go do it! If our response is, "I can't do that now," then we need to change our mindset. Do you know how many people thought Diana Nyad could actually swim from Cuba to Florida at the age of sixty-three? Only one—her! Her whole team did not believe she could do it. The only person you need to believe is you! Nike is right, "just do it!"

———

ACTION STEP: Let the following question be your journaling prompt: If you could roll back the clock ten or fifteen years, what would you do?

"You Are So Much Better Than You Think You Are"

—⟋⟍⟍—

I can honestly say that to every single client I meet. I am truly amazed at people's propensity toward negative self-perception. The dumbfounding part is that they are not downplaying their ability in an effort to be humble and they are not underestimating themselves by a little— they are way off the mark. Not only can I say this about every client, but I can say it about almost every person I meet. The misalignment is staggering.

Now apply this observation beyond my little universe. If we are performing to our perceived ability versus our true potential, what are we not doing that could make all the difference in the world? If we are athletes, how many shots did we not take because we thought we might miss? At work, what are we holding back from doing because of that small seed of doubt that is festering in our mind?

Trust me when I tell you, the smaller game we are playing will in all probability never serve us, our company or our team in any true capacity. We need to play full-out. No one will ever remember what we did not do. We will never get a bonus or a raise for what we did not do either.

We need to put this quote somewhere we will read it every morning before we start our day. Let these words permeate our subconscious: "you are so much better than you think you are." Somehow, we believe playing it safe will save us from making an error or looking bad, but all it does is make us average. Ironically, we worry about the possible mistake, but we never take the time to envision the victory. Imagine Chris Berman, the famous sportscaster, shouting his famous phrase for you: "HE—COULD—GO—ALL—THE—WAY!" And the crowd goes wild! Let that thought fester in our minds instead.

———

ACTION STEP: Today is a journaling day. Spend 5 minutes or more writing about the gap between your perceived ability versus your true potential. Where are you playing is safe? What would *all-out* look like?

What Is Shinrin Yoku?

—⚊⚊—

Shinrin Yoku is the Japanese practice of "forest bathing." In the 1980's, Japanese scientists began studying the positive health effects of spending time in the forest and their results were staggering! Here is a compilation of just some of the amazing health benefits linked to Shinrin Yoku:

- Lowers stress
- Fights cancer
- Enhances mood
- Boosts immunity
- Increases relaxation
- Improves physical, emotional, and mental well being

So what does forest bathing entail?

- Go for a walk in the woods, leave the cell phone & ear buds behind.
- Engage the forest with all 5 senses (maybe skip tasting).
- Commit to a couple of hours, bring a book if you want.

Scientists took blood samples from a group of volunteers after a trip into the forest. The group simply strolled in a wooded area and their levels of cortisol (the stress hormone) plunged almost 16% more than when they walked in an urban environment. Their blood pressure showed improvement with just fifteen minutes of the practice. Women who walked two to four hours in a forest on two consecutive days saw a nearly 40% increase in the activity of cancer-fighting white blood cells, according to one study. The residual positive health benefits, after one 2–3 hour trip into the woods, lasted seven days.

One of the biggest benefits came from breathing in chemicals called phytoncides, which are emitted by trees and plants. "Phytoncide exposure reduces stress hormones, indirectly increasing the immune system's ability to kill tumor cells," says Tokyo-based researcher Qing Li, MD, PhD, who has studied Shinrin Yoku.

I am not a doctor, but a hike in the woods sounds like a good thing.

———————

ACTION STEP: Maybe a hike in the woods would be a good thing for you or someone you love. **See your doctor before performing any physical activity.** I have done many of these hikes and every time I have left the forest invigorated, and I usually come back with a few answers to questions I pondered while surrounded by nature and silence.

Breaking the Rules

—∞—

Yesterday, I broke all the rules. Essentially, I'm a rule follower, as long as the rule makes sense to me. I am definitely a rule follower when it comes to family, rituals, observances, holidays, etc. But yesterday, I broke all the rules and, ultimately, it felt great.

A while back, we were invited to see U2 with our dearest friends. We hemmed and hawed over our answer because the date of the concert was Father's Day. The "rules" are: we celebrate with Doug's dad on Father's Day, along with our own kids and all of Doug's family. Tugging at us was, "But it's U2, it will be so much fun, who knows if they'll go on tour again?" The rules weighed so heavily on us, but finally we decided to break the rules and accept the invitation.

Guilt is an awful emotion, but so is always doing what is right when it is at your own expense. Do you always do what's right and expected of you? There is a price for that, too. Foregoing your own joy all the time, regardless of who it is for (children, parents, co-workers, friends, etc.) is not healthy either. We wear it as a badge of honor, but in doing so, we drain our own tank. Today, I am encouraging you to break some rules! Don't be so dependable, put yourself first, shake things up. It feels really uncomfortable at first, but after the fact, it feels amazing! My battery is definitely recharged. And here is the funny thing, everyone survived without us for a day!

Side note: We did celebrate Father's Day with Doug's dad prior to Father's day. And Doug did celebrate with our children prior to the concert.

ACTION STEP: Are you a rule follower? Spend 5 minutes journaling about rules, rules that you follow and rules that could be broken. Become aware of how you feel as you write about breaking a rule. Please note: I am not suggesting you break the law or get yourself in trouble.

A Goalie's Guide to Life

—✺—

I feel like I start every post with, "I was at lacrosse tournament this week-end . . ." In fact, I was at a lacrosse tournament recently and I had a conversation with a goalie's mom. She was explaining how difficult it is to be a goalie. The mental toll is extraordinary. How quickly a goalie can recover from the mental and emotional lows determines, in part, how well he will perform the next time out.

The goalies with the shortest memories are the most successful. A goalie should spend about fifteen seconds after a goal processing what just happened. It should go something like this:

> Could I have made the save? Yes or no? If the answer is no, then *tip your hat* to the shooter and move on. If the answer is yes, then do a quick evaluation of why you missed the shot. Once you have your answer, file it away as a lesson learned, then put your stick up and get ready to play.

The minute the goalie feels responsible, loses self-confidence and begins to feel deflated, he is done. Nothing has changed about the goalie's ability to make saves **until** he gets in his own head. The key is to stay in the present moment, deal with it objectively, and move on. This is mental toughness at its best.

Now, to those of us who are not goalies, how does this apply? We, too, perseverate on the negative and when we do, we feel responsible, we lose self-confidence, and we become deflated. Unlike a good goalie, we often spend too much time rehashing the negative and far too little time acknowledging the successes in our life. What happens when the goalie makes a fantastic save? There is a very short mental celebration (like half a second) and then he is back in the game. The same is true for us. We have the tiniest celebration for a success, yet we rehash the purported failure for unnecessary lengths of time.

We need to adopt the mental toughness of a goalie. I am giving all of us fifteen seconds to process the negative events in our life. We must be massively objective. Why did it happen? Can we learn from it? Remember, opportunity is often disguised as misfortune. Rehashing the negative in our mind over and over again will **never** serve us. We all need to take a page from the Goalie's Guide to Life, "I'll give it fifteen seconds then I am moving on!" And, if we have extra time, let's go celebrate our successes—half a second is not nearly enough time.

ACTION STEP: We need to celebrate our successes! Journal about how you will celebrate successes going forward. As for the negative events in life, "Opportunity is often disguised as misfortune." Ask yourself, "What lessons did I learn?"

The Worry Wart

—∿—

Worrying is a big waste of time! Almost everyone worries about something and some more than others. Recently, I explored this topic in order to eliminate worry from my life. *Merriam Webster* defines worry as "to feel or show fear and concern because you think that something bad has happened or could happen."

In essence, we are wasting all our precious present moments tangled up in fear and anxiety about some future event that may or may not happen, rather than actually enjoying life and engaging in the here and now.

Money is a **very** popular worry. Is our worry about money doing anything to make our bank account increase in value? Did our worry pay a bill? Fund college? Increase our retirement account? No! All our worry did was waste that present moment. Now that moment of time is gone forever and we wasted it thinking about the future *and* it changed nothing.

Nothing ever changes as a result of our worry. We can all benefit from reading that sentence again and letting it sink into the depths of our being. **Nothing ever changes as a result of our worry!** Our child is not safer, our job is not more secure, and our bank accounts are not larger because we worried.

It makes no sense to worry about things over which we have no control. Worry is an enormous waste of time. When we realize we are wasting time that could be spent in peace, joy and happiness rather than in fear, anxiety and worry, why would we choose the latter?

———

ACTION STEP: I'm on this journey too. Being aware of how pointless worrying is, is the first step! Here are my worry rules...

Can I do something about it?

    a. If yes, then proceed to doing something about it.
    b. If no, then actively try to stay in the present.
    c. If I still find myself worrying, stop and pray. I love the adage, *pray or worry, but you can't do both!*

Where Is the Joy?

—ᴍ—

In June of 2016, I had a really big scare. I was playing tennis and I had pain shoot through my jaw and radiate down my left arm. This had actually happened the week before as well, but this time I realized how stupid I was being for not getting it checked out by a doctor.

My doctor encouraged me to see a cardiologist immediately. The cardiologist, after hearing what had transpired, handed me a bottle of water and an aspirin and proclaimed, "No activity at all and take an aspirin every day until we have test results." And thus began a barrage of tests which took about a week to complete.

To say, "I was scared," was an understatement. I felt like a ticking timebomb. I went right to my go-to resource, Louise Hay's book *You Can Heal Your Life*. Under "Heart," she professes that problems may result from lack of joy. Hmm. I had to really think about that one, as I consider myself a really happy person. Contemplating that thought, I realized I was myopically focused on work. I was not stopping to experience joy. I was missing all the moments that were presenting themselves to me. I absolutely needed this wake up call.

The affirmation Louise Hay associates with the heart is: I bring joy back to the center of my heart and I express love for all. Since my scare, I ask myself every day, "Where is the joy?" I write it in my planner as a task for me every day. This one sentence has changed my life. We can find joy in anything if we are looking for it. I ask myself this question all day long. I have found joy in traffic, joy in ironing, and joy in other mundane activities. Once we look for it, we can find it anywhere.

When I returned to the cardiologist, I found out that I had successfully passed all of my tests. My heart is fine. Actually my heart is better than fine now that I ask constantly, "Where is the joy?"

ACTION STEP: Consider asking this question of yourself daily. "Where is the joy?" Maybe it is a question for the dinner table or late night, before bed. But make sure you ask it of yourself daily. Your answer is food for the soul.

Where Are You on a Scale from 1–10?

—⚏—

I love the 1–10 scale; it puts everything in perspective for me. Today, we are going to do a simple exercise. Rate each of your important relationships. Where do these relationships stand currently, on a scale from 1–10? Write each one down on paper. If they are not at 10, why not? We already determined they are important to us, so presumably, we would want them to be at 10.

Now for all the relationships that are below a 10, figure out why. Excuses are not going to help us here. We can start with our perspective, but truthfully, if we want to get to a 10, we need to look at it from the other person's perspective. If we can see how they see us, then that gives us all the information we need to improve. The bottom line is always, "There is only one person I can change on this planet and that is me."

Regardless of whether we are starting at a 2 or an 8, let's get these relationships as close to a 10 as possible. You will be amazed at how quickly relationships can improve by simply focusing our attention and intention on this relationship.

————

ACTION STEP: Make a list of your important people. For each person on your list, write at least one powerful proactive action step you will take today to improve the relationship.

Why Do We Set Goals?

—⚊—

One reason we set goals is to finally conquer *this thing*, once and for all. Jim Rohn said it best, "The ultimate reason for setting goals is to entice you to become the person it takes to achieve them."

Part of what we accomplish when we set goals is that we develop habits, willpower, perseverance, grit, self-motivation, time-management skills, determination, etc. If we crush *this* goal, then we will have the motivation to propel us to accomplish the next goal and perhaps each subsequent goal thereafter.

The goal is secondary. Becoming a new powerful person is what we are targeting. We need to jot down some of the words we would use to describe who we are becoming. I have written down words, such as, committed, strong-willed, and determined. What words would you chose? Immerse your mind in those words and simply bathe in them for a bit. Who are we becoming? We are so much stronger than we think we are—we are just scratching the surface of our potential.

———

ACTION STEP: Set a timer for five minutes. Think of all of the words you would use to describe yourself as you work toward your goal and write them down. We very rarely (ok, maybe never) write down powerful words that describe us. Keep these words handy for when you need a boost. This is who you are becoming! Well done!!

Mind Your Q's

—∞—

You all know IQ (Intelligence Quotient), some of you may be familiar with EQ (Emotional Quotient), but have you heard of PQ (Physical) or SQ (Spiritual)? If we can tap into all four of these quotients for any goal, we will greatly increase our chances of success.

Here is how it works using weight-loss as our example. We decide we need to lose a few pounds which is our EQ talking to us. Our IQ will respond immediately, and say things like, "I know how to do this, we will only drink water, eat kale, and work out two times a day!" We all know how we get when we first start something, a bit overzealous. The PQ does not agree (we feel it in the pit of our stomach) but the IQ and EQ move forward regardless. We do ok for a little while but then it becomes too much and we quit. Does this sound familiar?

To get a diet (or any other goal) to be successful, we must make sure our PQ is in agreement. We need to reduce our plan until we hear our PQ say, "OK, I can totally agree to that plan!"

What about our SQ? The Spiritual Quotient is the whisperer. If we are aware of it and therefore listening for it, we will hear it. It whispers at the elevator, "Maybe we could take the stairs?" or in the parking lot it says softly, "Just park farther away and enjoy a brisk walk." The beautiful part of the SQ is that it is always gentle and always kind.

If things are not going well in relation to your goals, perhaps you do not have all your Q's in alignment. Give it another go and make sure you listen for that SQ, it is so reassuring.

ACTION STEP: What goal have you been struggling to attain? Do not pick the big lofty goal right now, choose a smaller one. Spend a few minutes journaling about each "Q" and how your mind-body feels about the task ahead.

IQ (Mind)
EQ (Emotion)
PQ (Gut)
SQ (Heart)

White Space

—✺—

I visited our home in Vermont with my son while we were touring some New England colleges. There is something about this state that is therapeutic to me. When I am there, my pace is slower and I am more relaxed. I jump off the merry-go-round for a while and settle into a place of calm. A big part of the serenity for me comes from the Green Mountain State's beauty, but another part comes from the laid back nature of the people who live there. Vermont is not New Jersey.

I never recognized how different New Jersey was until I visited Vermont; the dichotomy is glaring. As I became aware of the tranquility that comes over me there as if I had just turned the volume knob down on life, I also thought about how I operate in overdrive all the time-with the "volume" on full-blast. Even our vacations are jammed with activities and a to-do list. Blame it on the times, or where I live, or my DNA, but regardless of what I pin it on, it is unhealthy. Do you ever feel the same way?

This begs the question, "Where is the 'white space'?" White space is a reference to the free space on our calendars that is not scheduled, and hence, the white space. White space is the place where we rest, create, or think. The body and the mind **need** white space. Many people nowadays say, "I think I have ADD." It is more likely they are overbooked, overworked, and simply need white space in their life. People who have white space on their calendars can be viewed as underachieving or slacking off, when really the white space is what refills their tank. An empty tank serves no one; not us, our employer, our children or our friends. Squeezing one more thing in does not make you efficient, it makes you tired. You might want to repeat that sentence to yourself out loud: **Squeezing one more thing in does not make me efficient, it makes me tired.** That is not how we function at our best.

———

ACTION STEP: Take a look at your calendar today. How much white space is on it? You may need to make some tough decisions and say "No" to some things you would have otherwise said "Yes" to doing. The "No" will be difficult at first but it will benefit you exponentially when you are actually enjoying your newfound peacefulness. Spend 5 minutes putting white space into your calendar. Block off times and call it thinking time if you wish, but hold onto that space dearly.

Pizza Man

Last Friday night, I headed to our local pizza place to pick up our ritualistic Friday night dinner. Like every other Friday, I see all of the same men manning the counter. I should know them by name by now, but I don't. Every week, they acknowledge my familiar face and I acknowledge theirs, but we continue to be perfect strangers.

This Friday was just a little bit different. The one young man who is always pleasant, never unnerved by the chaos of the Friday night crowd, was outside cleaning the front windows. I subconsciously marvel at him each week because he maintains this extraordinary homeostasis amid the pandemonium. He has this genuine appreciation for the patronage. It is not over the top at all, it is subtle and understated, just like him.

As I got back in my car with the pizza and was about to back out of the parking lot, I realized it was time to tell him. I "rolled" down the window and said, "Excuse me. I just wanted to tell you how warm and welcoming you are, you really set the tone for this place!" He was immediately grateful and responded, "Thank you! Thank you very much. I really appreciate that!"

I am glad I finally told him that, although it took me years to do so. He deserved those accolades. He, alone, changes my experience at this pizza place. I really should have asked him his name! Next time I will.

ACTION STEP: Who is making your life more pleasant but remains a perfect stranger? Is it pizza or coffee? There is someone you see regularly that needs to be told, "Hey, you make my day more pleasant and I am grateful for you." Spend the next few minutes thinking about who it might be. It can be more than one person. Now make a commitment to telling them they make a difference.

Have You Ever Felt Lost?

—∞—

I mean metaphorically have you ever felt lost in your life. Have you wondered where you were headed and if there was any sense or meaning to your day-to-day activities or were you simply drifting through life?

I hated that feeling. I remember it all too well. It felt like I was on a treadmill; there was no way to get off and everything felt mundane, monotonous, and senseless. The big question I kept asking myself was, "There has to be more than this, right?" But the struggle continued because although I had the right question, I was not coming up with the right answer.

If you are feeling lost or stuck, here are a few tips that helped me when I found myself in that exact same place in my life:

1. Talk to someone you trust. I thought I was the only one who was lost, so I kept it to myself. Get it out of your head and brainstorm with someone. I promise it will be cathartic. Remember, you are not the only person who feels this way.
2. Accept this feeling of being lost as a gift. Once I realized I was lost, I knew I wanted something better. Knowing you are lost is actually the best wake-up call. Embrace it!
3. Carve out some time just for you, off the "treadmill," that will allow you to think about what you want and what you are passionate about. People tend to go at this from an all-or-nothing viewpoint. Do not get caught in this trap. If you like painting, paint! You do not have to quit your job to become a painter. Start small; make listening to your soul a priority and do everything you can to find a way to feed it. When the soul is fed, you will no longer feel lost. Far from it!

———

ACTION STEP: Follow steps 1–3 without judgement, i.e. let ***everything*** be a possibility. We tend to shut ideas down because they do not make financial sense, geographical sense, or any other kind of sense. You are just exploring, so allow yourself complete freedom. Remember, you are not quitting your job or selling your house, so have fun with this adventure.

Good Enough

—m—

Doug, Clare, and I went to visit Katie at college this weekend. While we waited for our table at a local restaurant, the woman next to us struck up a conversation—actually it was incessant bragging. Within minutes we heard about her alma maters Yale & Johns Hopkins, her great job, how smart she was, etc. It was PAINFUL!

Fortunately, our table opened up and we were saved, but she really got me thinking. Why do we brag? We all brag to some degree. Bragging is actually a way of compensating for low self-esteem. The most common survival-strategy for low self-esteem is to believe, "I am good enough and important if people think well of me." But his flawed thinking requires the approval of others.

What if we were simply good enough and important right now? What if we agree we are okay the way we are and we no longer need the approval of others to make us feel okay. I guess I prefer that others like me, but if I have to prove myself with accomplishments or pedigree, maybe them not liking me is okay? I don't want to have to do or say things to get their approval anymore. I am good enough and important. And so are you!!

———

ACTION STEP: Today, write down something you brag about. Is it your children, your golf game, or something else? Now journal for 5 minutes on why you brag about that. Does the journaling bring some insight?

Meet Me Halfway

—⚍—

182 down and 183 to go. 26 weeks. That's it.

Did you set goals on January 1st? Was there something you wanted to accomplish before year's end? If you did, you have 183 more days to make it happen.

I write a lot about drifting. Drifting is going through life on autopilot. Our life will happen regardless of whether or not we get involved, but it is a whole lot better when we take control and drive the decision-making process. When we do take the wheel, we are living a life by design not by default. Today, I am simply reminding us of the calendar.

For some people, it is very motivational to be made aware of the calendar. The sense of urgency acts as a kickstart for change. 183 days is a lot of days, but it is not 365. We need to make every day count if, on December 31st, we want to be able to say, "I DID IT!" Ask yourself what *has to be* accomplished on or before December 31st?

If you have not given it any thought, there are still 183 days at your disposal to make a significant change in your life. Do **not** wait until January 1st of next year to choose something. That date is arbitrary, culturally accepted, but arbitrary. Choose now. Act now. 183 days may not seem like a lot but it would if I said you could not use your car for 183 days or you can only eat kale for 183 days!

We need to revisit our goals or make a goal, but whatever we do, let's take complete advantage of the next 183 days. These days are a gift for us to use in any way we wish. How will we choose to use them? Be intentional.

———

ACTION STEP: The prompt for today is, "What do I *really* want to accomplish before year's end? Remember, on December 31st, we want to be able to say, "I DID IT!" Journal for 5 minutes.

I Love Love

—ɯ—

A weird sentence for sure, but I love love. On June 26, 2015, the Supreme Court approved gay marriage in all fifty states. I am not here to make a political stance in any way, but what happened after the decision was a deluge of Facebook postings and I was reminded that I love love. I do not care about anyone's sexual orientation at all. I do not care about religious preference. I do not care about political preference. And I do not care about nationality, race, or even one's favorite color. What I care about is LOVE.

There is nothing more beautiful to me than to witness love. Whether it be the love of a child, a spouse, a friend, a parent or even a perfect stranger. Nothing beats *love.* I recently saw a picture of two neighbors, an older man and a young boy, realizing they were both alive after a tornado touched down on their street. The love in this picture was so palpable. The way he held this child was that of a parent, not a neighbor. This picture warmed my soul. It reminded me to love my neighbor, and the definition of neighbor should truly be everyone with whom I come in contact with.

Love is universal. It is what **everyone** wants and needs. I will speak for myself when I say, I need to love more and judge less. I need to love more and argue less. I need to see everyone the way the man in the picture saw his little neighbor and friend. I need to work harder at being a loving presence in this world. The world needs more love.

Today, I will begin reminding myself daily how much I love love! It is perhaps the most powerful thing I can do. If you see me, expect a hug!! I am spreading the love!

ACTION STEP: Many horrific and unspeakable things have happened in this world. Now more than ever, we need love to be ever-present. Will you shine your light in this world and be a source of love to all who come in contact with you? We need everyone!

Where Is Your Spirit?

—⚍—

We spend so much time in our heads and so little time in our hearts. It should really be the opposite. The head lies. The heart never lies. So why do we spend so much time up there?

We believe our head is where all our intelligence comes from, but does it? I will let you decide, but I am challenging you to simply check in with your heart by asking, "Where is my spirit?" If your reaction is anything like mine, then life will instantly get peaceful, quiet, and slower as you answer that question.

Summer is supposed to be the time when we recharge our batteries. So here is a friendly reminder for all of us, but especially me, it is time to check in and ask ourselves, "Where is my spirit?"

———

ACTION STEP: Spend 5 minutes today checking in with your heart. What is your heart telling you about:

family?
work?
friends?
life?

July 4th

—◦◦◦—

Here is some history related to the 4th of July . . .

The American Revolutionary War lasted eight and one half years (1775–1783). The war had its origins in the resistance of many Americans to taxes, which they claimed were unconstitutional, imposed by the British Parliament. We probably would not have won had it not been for France stepping in to help. On July 2, 1776, the Continental Congress formally voted for independence, and issued its Declaration on July 4, 1776.

Freedom did not come without a price. Proportionate to the population of the colonies, the Revolutionary War was at least the second deadliest conflict in American history, ranking ahead of World War II and behind only the Civil War. Disease claimed far more lives than battle. At least 217,000 died during active military service. 2,500 alone died at Valley Forge in the winter of 1777–78.

Today, we will fire up the grill, play baseball, watch fireworks, and raise the Stars and Stripes. We will do so freely because fifty-six men signed the most revolutionary document the world had ever seen in 1776. They could not predict the outcome of what they set into motion, but they knew freedom was worth risking it all.

Remembering the sacrifices of so many some 240 years ago, as well as the sacrifices of our current military personnel, should help us all appreciate the 4th of July. Here's to all of us having the courage of our own convictions to do the most with the freedom we have been given.

———

ACTION STEP: What, in your life, do you feel so passionately about, that you would fight for it? Are you giving it your all now or could you crank it up a notch? Will you agree to increasing your commitment to this cause by just 1%? Just a 1% increase. Ben Franklin said it best, "Little strokes fell great oaks."

Neither Bad nor Good

—⟋⟍—

I had a cup of tea yesterday and there was a quote on the tag which read: *The difference between a flower and a weed is a judgment.* My mind immediately thought, "Right, who am I to decide? I generally accept social norms."

But then I started to think beyond flowers and weeds to major life experiences. One of the greatest sources of unhappiness in life can be the difficulty we have in accepting things as they are. When we see something we don't like, we wish it could be different. We've judged it as bad, rather than saying, "It's not bad or good, it just is."

Instead of judging something as bad, what if we simply accepted that this is the way the world works? Maybe we can try to better understand why. Embracing "why" may give us the clarity we are looking for and thereby eliminating some of the pain. What are we supposed to learn from every self-proclaimed weed we have in the garden of our life right now?

———————

ACTION STEP: Today, spend 5 minutes journaling about the "weed" that is in your garden right now. It just is. Why?

Penny for Your Thoughts

—∽—

Happiness. Who does not want more happiness in his or her life? There are many ways to increase one's happiness, but it has been scientifically proven that one of the simplest ways is to express gratitude. Just being grateful enhances our mood. If happiness improves with gratitude, then why not take the time to be grateful?

I recently read about a CEO who goes to work each day with ten pennies in his left pocket. Each time he expresses gratitude or says thank you, he moves a penny from his left pocket to his right. He will not leave work until all the pennies have been moved to the right pocket.

Well, that seems simple enough. I like simple. Ten pennies. I am *grateful* he made it so simple.

ACTION STEP: Grab 10 pennies (or dimes, they're smaller) and get started!

Four Words

—∾∽—

Criticism is probably not a favorite topic of conversation, but no matter how hard we try, it will always come our way. We receive criticism from our boss, our colleagues, our spouse, our friends, and our kids! Some of it is subtle and some of it can be rather harsh. Our knee-jerk reaction is to defend ourselves followed shortly by some form of anger and incredulity at the person who delivered the "good news."

Although criticism is tough to hear, and I have deflected my fair share of it, I have come to the conclusion recently that criticism is the best piece of information I can receive to make me better. If we only hear accolades, which are nectar to the ear and the ego, we will not improve ourselves. Criticism, on the other hand, is where growth and improvement can originate, if we let it. The criticizer may have intended to insult us or he or she may have just wanted to make us aware; regardless they are highlighting an area we need to address and then conquer.

So here is the most powerful sentence I can offer to help embrace criticism:

"You might be right!"

That one simple sentence changed everything for me. It is such a neutralizing statement. "You might be right," eliminates excuses, gets me out of 'fight-mode', and opens up all sorts of possibilities for self-awareness while still leaving me the option to determine, "are they right, or not?"

I believe that every criticism is based in some truth. Criticism usually opens me up to a revelation that allows me to grow. So, when the next criticism gets hurled your way, remember to respond with, "You might be right!"

———————

ACTION STEP: Has anyone given you some criticism recently? Take a good look at it today through the lens of, "You might be right." Be open to any and all possibilities of self-awareness; that is where personal growth lies.

Party Time

—◆—

About a month ago I was invited out to lunch by a friend. He and I met through business and we continue to meet periodically to talk shop and catch up. We bounce from topic to topic and always run out of time before we run out of conversation.

During this particular lunch he asked me, "When have you celebrated?" I truly didn't understand the question so I asked, "Celebrated what?" He chuckled and said, "Your business." I was still a bit perplexed so I asked, "For what?" He smiled and said, "Drive is not your problem, Beth. Pausing and celebrating is. When are you going to stop long enough to celebrate what you've accomplished so far?"

Wow. What a wake-up call that was for me! My whole life I had reserved celebrations for true and authentic wins that were *recognizable* like winning a championship or getting a promotion, but what about all the little wins along the way? There might never be a recognizable win, as I have narrowly defined it, so I decided to celebrate now! I am encouraging you to celebrate your wins too! The celebration recognizes all our hard work! Thank you, Greg!

———

ACTION STEP: Today, journal for 5 minutes about all the things you *haven't* celebrated but should have. Now plan a little celebration—or a big one! Mine was simply a toast while out to dinner with friends. I verbally recognized my win in front of my husband and my friends.

Life Is Hard

———✺———

"Life is hard." I hear that a lot. But is it? Is it possible that we are making life harder than it needs to be? Are we making it harder because we resist everything that is not easy, simple, or fun? What if the *hard* part was actually a gift? What if it was the universe redirecting us, sometimes with a gentle nudge and other times with a flagrant shove?

Today, let us take a look at all of our struggles and ask ourselves, "How am I being redirected? What is the universe trying to tell me that I am resisting or downright refusing to hear?" Our answer will be found in the silence. This technique never fails me.

———————

ACTION STEP: If life is feeling hard for you right now, I am truly sorry. I hope that by following these three steps you find some much-needed relief:

1. Pick one struggle that is really weighing heavy on your heart. Write it down.
2. Answer the following questions via journaling, "How am I being redirected? What is the universe trying to tell me that I am resisting or downright refusing to hear?" (The answer will come from your heart not your head).
3. What revelation did you receive?

Lessons from My Dad

—⁂—

My dad, Harry, taught me so many valuable lessons. One of my favorites came when he was older, maybe in his 60's or 70's. My parents were going to visit some friends in Florida and my dad said, "I don't always love visiting them, they are old!" I laughed out loud and said, "Dad, you are the exact same age as them!" He quickly replied, "Yes, but I'm not old!"

I was understandably confused and asked my dad to explain. He went on to tell me the many ways in which these friends were old. They dress old, they behave old, and they talk old. My dad said, "I know exactly how old I am, but I have no intention of behaving that old. I don't want to drive to dinner if I can walk. I don't want to listen to the music, I want to dance. There is a lot of life left in me. Maybe one day I'll be old, but not if I can help it."

I think of him every day. I choose *young* every day. I never take the escalator, I always take the stairs (usually racing all of my kids). I never mention getting old. I am conscious about remembering people's names and not falling back on "the memory isn't what it used to be." Do not be old. Old is no fun. Get up, get out, be young. Choose to do something younger than what is age appropriate. Listen to my dad, and refuse to act your age! Thanks Dad!

———

ACTION STEP: Step number one is to journal about all the ways you have become *old*. Step number two is to journal about all the ways you are going to change so that you begin to think, act and be young!

Broken Windows

—⚉—

Have you ever heard of *The Broken Windows Theory?*

In its most straightforward form, the theory states that once an urban area tolerates broken windows or vandalism or other smaller crimes, then the area has paved the way for subsequent occurrences of more serious crimes to occur.

How does that apply to all of us? What is the "broken window" in our life? The "broken window" is what we tolerate in our life that causes a chain of events that negatively impacts our day, whether that be in productivity, success, efficiency, effectiveness, etc. For example, maybe it starts with our alarm clock. Many of us have said, "If I could just get up a half hour earlier and . . ." Fill in the blank here with read, meditate, work out, etc., but we have hit the snooze button, either figuratively or literally, and therefore it is one of our "broken windows."

The domino effect of that one decision has a broad scope. Mentally, we will engage in a destructive internal chatter, criticizing ourselves for not getting up. We are less productive for not getting up and crossing that off our list early. We may or may not try to squeeze our intended activities in later in the day, making us less efficient and potentially harried.

What is your "broken window?" I have many. We cannot fix a broken window if we do not know it is broken. I believe I knew, deep down, I had a few "broken windows," but now I know for sure! Today I will fix at least one "broken window," permanently. Are you with me?

———

ACTION STEP: What is your "broken window?" Journal for 5 minutes on what your "broken window" is as well as how you will fix it.

To Be Honest . . .

—✺—

Ok, so I have a few pet peeves!

Most of my grievances are related to words or phrases. My biggest pet peeve is when someone says, "A whole nother." My hair stands on end, my eye twitches, and I use every amount of self-restraint within me to refrain from not correct them. Sadly, I have heard that phrase spewed out of the mouths of some highly intelligent people!

Today's pet peeve is not grammatically incorrect or, in the example of "whole nother," is it making up a word that does not exist. This one is more obscure. Today's pet peeve is the phrase, "to be honest." When we use a phrase like, "to be honest," it implies that perhaps when we have said other things we were not honest. Some of you may think I am splitting hairs, but think about when someone says that phrase; their head tilts, their tone changes and they often lean in when they are about to say it, as if it is some sort of secret.

Does it really matter? Yes, but only if we interact with people! This is especially true at work. It undermines the veracity of every other statement we make. If I am being honest with you now, then was I lying to you before? If we manage people, it is one of the worst phrases we can say.

ACTION STEP: Consider not using the phrase, "To be honest."

Why on Earth?

—∞—

Have you ever had a problem in your life that you just cannot seem to fix? Stubborn and recurrent problems are often symptoms of deeper issues so, although the quick fix may seem convenient, it is really just a temporary solution. To solve this problem we are going to need to dig down deeper.

Have you ever heard of the *Five Whys Technique* popularized by Toyota in the 1970's and still used today? Sakichi Toyoda, the founder of Toyota developed this technique in the 1930's. It was a *go and see* approach based upon an in-depth understanding of the processes and conditions on the shop floor, not the boardroom.

Their approach was as follows: when a problem occurred, they uncovered its nature and source by asking "Why" no fewer than five times. This helped to determine the root cause of the problem. We can use this approach in our life as well for questions like, "Why can't I seem to land that perfect job?" or "Why is my marriage still a struggle?" The first few *whys* will only scratch the surface, but as we continue to ask "Why?" we will really get to the core of the problem. This technique is amazingly effective and should be used for both personal and professional problems alike. It is a great tool for parents to use with teens.

P.S. It is also a great resource when you are struggling with a more esoteric question like, "Why am I feeling this way?"

———

ACTION STEP: What is the one problem that has been nagging at you this week? Now begin asking "Why?" *no fewer* than five times. After each answer, it is helpful to say, "OK, now dig deeper. Why?" Very often I will use this with my clients and we always seem to uncover some beautiful gems after about the fourth or fifth "Why." Give it a go! You will be glad you did.

We Just Need One

—∽—

As Wimbledon is in full swing now, I have my own tennis story to share. During a match, my partner and I were down in the second set, 5–1. The outlook, for sure, was bleak. But I went back to what another tennis partner, Helene, had taught me a few years back; she looked at me with full conviction and said, "We just need one!" When I first heard that line, I thought, "We need a lot more than one." But her point was powerful. The whole task was too overwhelming to process, so if we just got one point, then we could move on to the next point. One point at a time.

Her words of wisdom changed not only tennis for me, but life. Just get one. Just complete the next task. Do not get overwhelmed by the whole project; focus on the next step only. Being down 5–1 in the second set is daunting whether it be in tennis or in life, but focusing on winning the next point is not. *We just need one.*

My partner and I, point by point, rallied back to bring the match to a 6–6 tie and ended up winning in a tie-breaker. What part of life do we need to apply Helene's words of wisdom? What seems daunting? Overwhelming? Impossible even? Just say Helene's words over and over to yourself, "I just need one!" I can do this!

———

ACTION STEP: Today, journal for 5 minutes on where in your life, you might find it helpful to say, "I just need one little win here." Your answer will put you in the driver's seat to make things happen.

Are You Putting In or Taking Out?

—⚭—

The Marriage Box

Most people get married believing the myth that marriage is a beautiful box full of all the things they have longed for; companionship, intimacy, friendship, etc. The truth is that marriage at the start is an empty box. You must put something in before you can take something out. There is no love in marriage. There is no romance in marriage. You have to infuse it into your marriage. A couple must learn the art and form the habit of giving, loving, serving, praising, of keeping the box full. If you take out more than you put in, the box will be empty.

One of my dearest friends, Bonnie, sent me "The Marriage Box." I **love** it. After being married for twenty-six years, I believe "The Marriage Box" is a great visual to hold onto as we strengthen our marriages, whether you are married for twenty-six years or just engaged.

Marriage has also been equated to a car—if we do not consciously care for it and fill it with fuel, then the car will not operate at its full potential. Without care and attention, the car is guaranteed to ultimately break down and potentially be rendered useless.

"Marriage" is a word, a bond, and an agreement, but there is nothing magical about marriage. The magic comes from the couple. The romance has to be created, continuously, year after year. Romance does not just happen. It takes a conscious effort on both parties. It gets more difficult the longer the marriage, but that is exactly where the *magic* lies. The magic lies in the conscious desire to infuse the marriage with new life, repeatedly, " 'til death do us part."

In addition to giving, loving, serving, and praising, what amount of magic are you adding to your marriage? Sometimes we get so caught up in life (kids, work, bills, etc.), we forget that a little bit of magic goes a long way! Here's to creating some MAGIC!!

———

ACTION STEP: If you are in any relationship, "The Marriage Box" applies. Today, spend 5 minutes journaling ways in which you can fill the box with giving, loving, serving, and praising. Serving is the most misunderstood, but asking the question, "How can I make your life easier?" is a great place to start.

If I Could Change One Thing

—ᴍ—

Today, I want you to ask yourself that question. If you could change one thing, what would it be? Stay away from silly answers that are impossible like, "I would be taller." I would love to be taller too, but I am stuck with my towering 5'3" frame.

After you have arrived at the one thing you would **really** love to be different in your life, then follow it up with a second question. The second question is, "Why am I not pouring my energy into making it happen?"

If we know what we want to be different, then now is the time to change it. We cannot lose another day suppressing or ignoring this deep personal desire. Today is the day we will begin to make a significant change in our life. Commit to making it a priority. As I like to say, let's "slay this dragon." We deserve this!

If you are really committed to making this change in your life, then I am encouraging you to take consistent action. What result do you think you would achieve if you committed five minutes a day to this one thing for the next 90 days? Each action step that is achieved brings us closer to success.

P.S. For those of you who read this and said, "But you don't understand," I want you to know that is your comfort zone talking. Please do not listen to your comfort zone, it is infamous for keeping us small.

————

ACTION STEP: Journal for five minutes today on the thing you would like to change. I am always amazed at how much gets accomplished in just five minutes! I have used this powerful 5-minute tactic for many things—to plan my days, to write, to think, etc.

You Are Worthy

—m—

I didn't think I struggled with worthiness until I realized how many ways it can rear its ugly head. Most recently, I experienced feeling unworthy over a gift. Had it been my birthday or some other worthy occasion, I would have readily accepted this incredible gift. But it was not so I quickly went down the rabbit hole of unworthiness which apparently comes as a package deal with guilt. Good times!

So here sits this fabulous gift that I can't truly enjoy because I feel both guilty and unworthy! My thought process was, "I am worthy if it's my birthday but otherwise I am not." Why am I not worthy of a random gift? I get no say on a random gift, so shouldn't I always be worthy of that? Doesn't the word "gift" lose its meaning if I always have to be worthy of it?

I did some research on worthiness and I have some serious work to do. Brené Brown said it best, "There are no conditions attached to worthiness—it is unconditional." Martha Beck also wrote a great piece on worthiness for Oprah.com which begins with: *You'd be wholeheartedly thrilled with that gift, that compliment, that declaration of affection—if it weren't for the wary little voice in the back of your mind wondering how you'll ever be able to reciprocate . . . or did the giver really mean it . . . or what's the catch?* My big takeaway is that I am worthy—period. Wait, no, exclamation point!

———

ACTION STEP: Today, spend 5 minutes journaling about your worthiness. Attach worthiness to things like gifts and compliments—how are you at receiving them?

Freedom

—◊—

America: Land of the free and home of the brave! If I asked you to sell someone on America, it is likely you would discuss all the freedoms we have here, like personal freedom, freedom of speech, religious freedom, etc. We are free to engage in unique lifestyle choices and are free to pursue hobbies and beliefs much more broadly than other cultures would permit. This is why we have "The American Dream."

So, we have all this freedom but we do not exercise it. Most people have surrendered their freedom unknowingly. We have *followed the follower* instead of creating our own destiny. We are living lives based on fear. We keep the safe job instead of exploring our own entrepreneurial thought that has burned inside of us for years. We make excuses like, "I can't do that now," or "Maybe when I have more money/time/experience." We choose to remain "a small cog in the machine, well fed and well clothed, yet not a free man but an automation." (Erich Fromm)

There are 123 democratic countries in the world, and America ranks 20th for freedom. Do not surrender your freedom—go pursue it with all of your being! "Land of the free and home of the brave," that was meant for you. Maybe our forefathers added "home of the brave" for another reason, because they knew we would need a reminder that being free is one thing, but acting free will require some bravery and risk taking. If you are American or you live in any of the other 122 free countries, do not squander your freedom, someone fought valiantly for you and me to be able to do anything we want in life. Go for it!

———

ACTION STEP: Have you surrendered your freedom unknowingly? Are you following the follower? Are you playing it safe? Is there something burning inside of you entrepreneurially or otherwise? Set a timer for five minutes and journal about what all of this means to you.

The Art of Failing

——✦——

It has been estimated that only 2 out of every 100 people, after experiencing their second failure, will stay the course; 98% will quit and accept defeat. Let's direct our focus on explorers and scientists because they are the people who seem to see failure as only temporary. Alpinist Pete Athans learned how *not* to climb Mt. Everest the first four times, but has summited this beast seven times since. "Failure keeps you on your toes," says Athans.

Scientists and explorers take a much longer view. They recognize failure is part of the learning process. They know their negative results are part of the journey and can often lead to positive outcomes. So much can be learned from failure if we could readily accept it as a necessary part of the process and an essential part of growth.

ABN AMRO started an institute of Brilliant Failures to encourage entrepreneurship. Eli Lilly & Co. started throwing "Failure Parties" two decades ago to celebrate the data gleaned from drug trials that did not work (90% of all such trials fail). Historian Nancy Koehn, in an effort to teach her Harvard MBA students about leadership, lectures on the story of Ernest Shackleton's failed expedition to cross Antarctica on the ship Endurance. Through persistence, resilience, adaptability and crisis management, Shackleton brought the twenty-seven men on his team back home safely.

Has the fear of failure stopped you in the past? The word "success" is derived from the Latin word "succeeder" which mean "to come after". And what does success come after? Failure. We should not be afraid of failing; we should be afraid of not trying at all.

"Imperfect action trumps perfect inaction."
—HARRY S. TRUMAN

———

ACTION STEP: And now you know why we have so many action steps on these pages! Today, I would like you to follow ABN AMRO and journal for a few minutes about a Brilliant Failure. Afterword, you can have a failure party, just like Eli Lily.

It's Time to Celebrate!!

—꿍—

Most people approach a goal from a position of pain. They may nag themselves and demand perfection. The go-to "tools of the trade" are quite often guilt, doubt, and shame. Instead of celebrating the five pounds they lost, they see the ten they still have yet to lose. Does any of this sound familiar? Beating ourselves up may seem like the best way to get motivated. But consider this: if we attempted to motivate our employees with guilt, doubt, and shame, how long do you think they would stick around? How successful do you believe they would become?

Rewards create a feeling of doing something we want to do, not just what we are forcing ourselves to do. It is important to note, rewards have been proven to offer a huge psychological boost. When we give ourselves rewards, we feel energized, cared for, and contented, which boosts our confidence and self-control, which helps us maintain our new habits. When we do not get any rewards, we begin to feel burned-out, depleted, resentful and deprived, which is never motivating.

So, is it time to celebrate? Rewarding ourselves will increase our motivation, make us feel good, make us work harder, and it will remind us that hard work pays off. Try to make your reward meaningful. We are rewarding ourselves for whatever we have accomplished up to now. Look, if we do not reward ourselves, who will?

ACTION STEP: How will you celebrate? What will you do to tell your psyche, "Right on! Way to go! I'm so proud of me!"? I love when the gift fits the goal. If you are writing a book, buy yourself a new bestseller. If you are eating healthy, buy yourself a new workout top or even a great pair of athletic socks. New socks feel great! You choose, but whatever you do, do *not* skip over this celebration! You deserve this!

The Greatest Gifts

—▬—

*"The meaning of life is to find your gift. The purpose of life is
to give it away."*
—PABLO PICASSO

Those closest to me have heard me discuss the unique gifts that are
inherent in each one of us. Many of our gifts came at birth as if a blueprint was etched upon our soul; while others were simply added along
the way—seemingly accidental but surely serendipitous.

You may have inherently known about your giftedness as I am sure I
did. But everything changed years ago when I heard Lisa Nichols (if
my recollection serves me) say, "Your gifts are not for you! They are for
everyone *but* you. They are for the world." Definitely an aha moment
for me.

What are your unique gifts? Imagine buying the best present ever and
never giving it away. How disappointing is that?

"If you want happiness for a lifetime, help someone else."
—CHINESE PROVERB.

———

ACTION STEP: Today, spend 5 minutes writing down a few of your
greatest gifts. Now ask yourself: Am I giving them back to the world?
Am I giving them away for profit and/or not for profit?

A Vacation for Your Brain!

—⚊—

According to the New York Times, our brain is assaulted daily with facts, figures, newsfeeds, statistics, data and miscellany equal to one-hundred-seventy-four newspapers worth of information. And that stat is from 2011! It is no wonder our brains are overwhelmed. The active brain often seesaws between being engaged in a task and daydreaming. Both parts are critical because, although the task side allows us to build things like the iPhone, the daydreaming side came up with the iPhone idea in the first place.

With the constant flow of information from Facebook, Twitter, texts, email, Instagram and the like, we are not able to sustain our attention span on any one thing for very long. As a result, all this information is competing for the brain's attention and we can become overwhelmed and stressed.

If we want to be more productive, more creative, and have more energy, we need to consider truncating our day. Social media and even emails should **not** be allowed to constantly interrupt us; we should designate times to spend on these. Let's temper our multitasking so we will stay engaged in a single task for a solid 30–50 minutes.

Would you like to reset your brain and become happier, more creative, improve attention span, build self confidence and become less stressed? Me, too! Here are some neural resets:

- Dedicate times for social media, email, etc . . .
- Listen to music
- Take naps
- Take vacations (and unplug)

• Walk in nature (just looking at trees from a window lowers blood pressure)

Taking breaks is biologically restorative; we could all use a little break. Exhale. Don't worry; it will all still be there when you return.

———————

ACTION STEP: Our brains need a break. Today's task is all about not having your phone, email, social media at your fingertips all day long; I call them *The Great Interrupters.* Turn off your electronics for one-hour. Really off, not vibrate off or pop-up message off. Leave your phone behind at lunch and really engage with your co-workers. See how productive and attentive you can be without all of the distractions.

Adding Fuel to the Fire

—⚋—

A few years ago my daughter set a small tray of nachos on fire in our toaster oven. In an attempt to assess the situation, she opened the door, which made a small fire instantly much bigger. I came running into the kitchen to help. Fortunately, it was resolved quickly by closing the door to the toaster oven, unplugging the appliance, and starving it of oxygen. Crisis averted.

Where am I going with burnt nachos? I was thinking of fear this weekend and how it stops us from doing so much. There is a simple trick to extinguishing fear quickly. Fear feeds off of time just like fire feeds off of oxygen. The more time you give fear, the more powerful it becomes. It festers in your mind, getting bigger with time. So what is the trick?

Do not give fear the time it wants to scare and immobilize you. Action will suffocate fear but it will require bravery in the face of fear. I used to believe time would help, but now I know I am simply feeding the flames of fear. Think it over for sure, but don't ever believe that thinking will make the fear go away. We are going to have to act while we are still afraid. Oxygen is to fire as time is to fear. Act accordingly!

———

ACTION STEP: Spend a few minutes journaling about something you recently wanted to move forward on but fear held you back. Journal as if you did move forward and there was no fear. Where would you be today? This isn't about regret; it's about visualizing possibilities without the weight of fear.

Neutral Is Not a Gear

—◊◊◊—

Have you ever put your car in neutral? When you disengage the transmission, the car is completely void of its power. In addition, have you ever stepped on the gas when your car was in neutral? The engine races but the car goes nowhere. The noise sounds impressive, but the car stays exactly where it was before you stepped on the gas.

Where in life are we living in neutral? For a while now we have said we want something to be different, but we have yet to put our car into drive. The car will never move forward in neutral. We can step on the gas, but our car will never move forward. Please do not blame the car; this one is operator error. The car can move forward. It was built to move forward, but as the driver of this vehicle, we **must** engage the transmission by putting the car into drive.

If we continue to use the metaphor of driving a car to describe our life, there is one more thing we need to know; the car we own is not a clunker, it is the Maserati of cars. I am certain we cannot even comprehend the abilities of this car. It is a high-performance vehicle that has capabilities beyond our imagination, but it was not built to stay in neutral or, worse yet, park. It was built to drive. We are in the driver's seat. If we know we have been in neutral for a while now, then we must consider putting this amazing vehicle in **drive** and maybe even pressing on the gas. What do you think?

ACTION STEP: Are you in neutral? Spend a few minutes journal about where you might be idling, as well as possible steps you are willing to take. Have fun with this. Be silly. I have been in neutral about making yoga a weekly practice for about 2 full years now. I would write: Seriously Beth, you aren't in neutral, you're in park!

Loved and Appreciated

—⚉—

"There is more hunger for love and appreciation in this world than there is for bread."

—SAINT TERESA OF CALCUTTA (MOTHER TERESA)

This quote offers us the opportunity to view it from two different perspectives. Of course, we all love to be loved and appreciated—it kind of goes without saying, right? We might not consciously think about it or expect it, but when it's missing, we know it. Feeling unappreciated can evoke some very strong negative emotions and, as a result, it often causes us to change our behavior.

If we can recall a time that we felt unappreciated, then we can do a better job of appreciating others. Feeling unappreciated elicits in me a deep sense of hurt. What emotion does it evoke in you? Now, it's time to look around us—who have we overlooked? Who needs to hear how much we appreciate them? Who needs to be reminded of how much they are loved?

Dale Carnegie once said, "People work for money but go the extra mile for recognition, praise, and rewards." These quotes about love and appreciation are equally applicable at work as well as at home. Most people will wonder, "How did I do?"; recognition and appreciation are abundant resources at our disposal that eliminate any and all doubt.

———

ACTION STEP: Spend a few minutes journaling about whether or not you are truly appreciating those around you on a daily basis. Then choose two people, one from home and another from work, that you feel would benefit from some heartfelt words of recognition and praise. There are powerful benefits for both the giver and the receiver of appreciation.

My Not So Perfect Life

"When asked if my cup is half full or half empty, my only response is that I am thankful I have a cup."

—SAM LEFKOWITZ

The last two weeks have been a whirlwind. I have been preparing my house for a big graduation party, drove my daughter six hours to Virginia for orientation, met with a number of clients, gave a presentation to a local non-profit, hosted the graduation party (in the rain), spent the day on Long Island for a funeral, and drove to DC to move my daughter into her new apartment. Exhausted and spent are two great words to describe me right now.

But as I stood in my daughter's new apartment, surrounded by unpacked boxes, bags, and luggage, feeling completely depleted from not only two full days of packing and moving but also the last two weeks, I felt a smile come across my face. Amidst the clutter and disarray, and in dire need of a shower, I realized how blessed I am.

My thoughts about blessings ran the gamut in my mind; I thought of health, weather, safety, good kids, a big truck (with lots and lots of miles on it), food, family, friends, faith, etc. It was within the *chaos* that I accidentally took pause. Life is good not when everything is perfect, but when we are surrounded by the not so perfect. Life is good right now!

One extra quote for today: **"The things you take for granted, someone else is praying for."**

ACTION STEP: Journal about your not-so-perfect life, remembering that life is good right now!

True Grit

—〰—

Grit is defined by *Webster's Dictionary* as, "firmness of mind or spirit. Unyielding courage in the face of hardship or danger."

What is your level of grittiness? You may not have thought about grit before, but the Duckworth Lab at the University of Pennsylvania has researched it fully. They have developed a Grit Scale. If you would like to take the test to see how gritty you really are, check out: www.angeladuckworth.com/grit-scale/

When I think of grit, I think of people who lived during my parents era. They were gritty to the core. Perhaps it was living through The Great Depression that made them so. Our generation is softer and we seem to be creating a generation that is softer still. My children do not understand grit because I have made their lives easy. After analyzing Angela Duckworth's research, I realized what a disservice I have done to them.

The good news is that grit can be developed at any age. The answer is right in the definition, "firmness of mind or spirit." If we consciously want to improve our grit, then we must start with our mind. We must teach our mind to say things like, "I will **not** quit," and "I will **never** give up."

Grit is just as important in running a 5K as it is for a marathon. Grit can be applied to work as easily as it can be to a diet. Grit is important and if we are not actively developing it in ourselves and our children, then it will continually deteriorate.

———

ACTION STEP: Today, journal for a few minutes about what it means to be gritty and where can you be grittier in any area of your life?

Can You Create Happy?

—∞—

Yesterday I spent the day in New York City. When I arrived at Penn Station, I decided I was not going to be anonymous in a city of 8.4 million people. You know the anonymous I am talking about: it is head down, making no eye contact, and walking with conviction. The thought of trying to be anonymous felt like a lot of work and it gave me a very cold and robotic feeling.

I did not want that to define my day. I decided to make eye contact, smile as much as I could, and engage with people whenever possible. I cannot even begin to tell you what a *joyful* day it was. I met a wildly delightful woman named Lovely (cannot make this up) on 5th avenue, I had a fun conversation with a woman in the elevator at Lord and Taylor, and I laughed out loud with a gentleman at the Bryant Park Grille.

I could have chosen anonymous in a city so large, but to what end? Creating my own **happy** changed my whole day from anonymous and cold to engaged, light-hearted and fun. Imagine NYC, or any other city, if everyone decided to *create their own happy.*

If you have a minute, google the psychology of a smile. If you do not have a minute, then simply know this: a smile sets off a "feel-good" party in your brain, triggering all sorts of amazing side effects. Who would not want that?

———

ACTION STEP: Here are your new marching orders for today (and every day hereafter that you want to be happy): chin up, chest out, smile and engage! Create *happy* yourself. I guarantee you will have a great day!

The To-Do List's Alter Ego

—∿—

I love a written to-do list! Everything gets prioritized, nothing gets forgotten, and I feel a great sense of accomplishment, as well as relief, as I cross each item off the list. But have you ever written a not-to-do list?

The idea of the not-to-do list is to specify all the activities you are intentionally going to stop doing for the sake of greater productivity. Take a look at the activities that occupy most of your time. Look at the recurring things you have to do. Which ones are a waste of time or could be delegated or outsourced?

The only way for a super-productive person to continue to grow professionally, without burning out, is to periodically decide what he or she is not going to do. You will need some quiet time to reflect and create this new list. To-do lists have a tendency to grow; not-to-do lists help thwart that growth.

———

ACTION STEP: Today, spend 5 minutes creating a not-to-do list. Taking the time to create this list will be time well spent! Think big when you write this list. What meetings are a waste of your time? Which travel is truly worth your time? What items should be outsourced completely?

How Are You Like a Rubber Band?

—⚬—

Think of all the possible uses for a rubber band. Millions, right? Now think of its uses without stretching it? Not stretching a rubber band basically renders the rubber band useless.

Not many people like to stretch themselves because it means leaving their comfort zone and getting uncomfortable. But, and this is a very big but, we **cannot** grow if we stay within our comfort zone. We simply cannot.

Consider this:

- Not stretching is settling for the status quo.
- Stretching is not a genetic attribute; it is a conscious decision.
- Stretching requires change.
- Stretching is no longer playing it safe.
- Stretching sets you apart.

Going outside our comfort zone is uncomfortable, but we need to be brave and go anyway! When we feel uncomfortable—think acid rushing to our stomach, palms starting to sweat, and we are asking ourselves, "*How* am I going to do this?"—that is when we know we have officially left our comfort zone. And once we have left our comfort zone, it will never be that small again. Take a risk, it will be so worth it!

————

ACTION STEP: How can you stretch yourself beyond your current boundaries? Journal for a few minutes on all the possible ways you can stretch yourself. When you are done journaling, circle one you can agree to take on and set a deadline for its completion.

What Kind of Gift Will You Be?

—⚭—

I was wrapping a friend's birthday present this weekend and it got me thinking. Although I usually try to create a fantastically wrapped present, the wrapping paper covers up the gift, regardless of whether it is a serious heartfelt gift or a gag gift. It is just packaging. We can make anything look good if we wrap it beautifully enough.

"It's just packaging" is as equally true for people as it is for gifts. I can be dressed to the nines on the outside, but what's going on on the inside? It is what is on the inside that really matters. We take a lot of time to choose our outfit for the day, but if we do not take some time to make sure our heart is in the right place, then why bother with the new dress or the fancy tie? The new dress is not going to make anyone overlook how mean or unkind I may be.

I believe it is really important to dress for success, but if we are only concerned with the exterior, then we have skipped the most critical piece. Before we leave the house, it is not the one last look in the mirror that is most important—it is the time we take to check in with our heart. Will we be kind to the train conductor? Or the nasty barista? Or the colleague at work who could really use our help? Remember, it's just packaging. We do not want to be the gag gift, we want to be the Tiffany & Co. little blue box containing the most precious of gifts.

———

ACTION STEP: What kind of gift do you want to be? Spend 5 minutes journaling on how you can incorporate this thought into your daily routine. I know you want to be the little blue box!

Think, Think, Think

—⟋⟍—

Statistically, it has been proven, that we really do not think very much. You might be saying to yourself, "I think all the time, my mind never stops thinking!" Those thoughts you are talking about are not new thoughts, that is just your mind ruminating over old thoughts, worries, and anxieties. Real thinking is when we create, discover, invent, and shape new ideas. Studies show that we use our mind about 10% of the time for this kind of thinking. Only 10%!!!

So how do we create real thinking? I will give you a few topics today to put your mind in high gear. Have you ever questioned your own religion? I am not encouraging you to switch religions, but have you really thought about all the beliefs you have been taught and how they align with your own beliefs? What about work? Have you thought about what you do on a daily basis and why? Is there a better, faster, smarter way to get this done? Or are you simply operating on autopilot?

Sometimes in life we all need to think, and by sometimes I mean every day. Mindlessly following is so easy, but thinking takes time and energy. We tell our children from an early age, "Think for yourself," but by about age 30, we essentially do very little *new* thinking. Find ways to challenge your mind and sharpen your thinking skills. Today, ***think***!

———

ACTION STEP: We will be thinking today, just thinking. For it to be thinking, it has to be a new thought. I gave you a few topics to ignite the thought process, or grab the newspaper and head to a section you know nothing about. The Op-Ed section, I am sure, could spark a few new thoughts! Have fun with thinking!

You Be You

—∞—

Why do we always compare ourselves to others? We do it at work, we do it with friends, and somehow we manage to do it with total strangers!

I would almost be O.K. with the comparison if, in fact, we were impartial and equitable, but we rarely ever are. Our comparisons tend to find our own shortcomings without finding theirs. We highlight others strengths while focusing on our own weaknesses. And when we do touch on our strong points, we somehow manage to quickly acknowledge but then almost immediately minimize these strengths. We tend to see others as better than us, but I am certain they are not. Do you want to know why?

We should not truly believe other people are better than us because the comparison is faulty from the start! We can no more compare apples to oranges than we can a shortstop to a catcher. Everyone brings his or her own assets to the game. We have our own strengths, and when we look right past them we knock ourselves down a peg. Stop! Our colleague is not better, just different. Our friend is not better, just different. And the stranger is not better, just different. I want to be the best me. You should be the best you. But comparing us to each other is just silly. Pointless, really. We are wasting time that we could otherwise be using to be a better you and a better me!

———

ACTION STEP: How can we eliminate these damaging comparisons? Journal for 5 minutes on the ways you can focus on being the best you! Use Steve Jobs quote from his Stamford University Commencement speech: "Your time is limited so don't waste it living someone else's life. Don't let the noise of others' opinions drown out your own inner voice."

Today Is an Extraordinary Day

—⚶—

Make the decision today to be **extraordinary**. How can you be extraordinary at work? Go be that employee today. What do you need to do to be extraordinary at home or at the gym? Do that. What about becoming an extraordinary friend or spouse? Do not wait for them to be extraordinary first, beat them to the punch! Show them what extraordinary looks like.

The only difference between ordinary and extraordinary is choosing to be so. We got this! Now, go!

ACTION STEP: Today is all about action. Journal a few ideas that would make you extraordinary. Just a few. Pick your target. You can pick more than one, if you want. Why not? You're extraordinary!!

Winning Is Everything!

—⚭—

Wait, is winning everything? I consider myself a very competitive person. I really like to win. Who does not like to win? I like to win at cards and board games. I like to win at the grocery store by choosing the fastest line. And I like to win at work, as well.

This mindset has a negative energy tied to it because, for me to win, someone has to lose. I understand in a sporting event, there has to be a winner and a loser, but in a work environment, that is not the case. I decided not too long ago that this mindset could have some very negative ramifications, so I asked my life-coach how I could better channel my competitive spirit.

My coach explained that mutual support is competition's friendlier brother. Innately I knew that but was not practicing it. The energy tied to mutual support is extremely positive. This game plan means we both win. If I were a salesperson, my goal could still be to have the highest sales on the team, but I would also need to work toward helping raise sales for everyone else as well. It could be a win-win situation.

To be the brightest light does not mean I have to extinguish anyone else's. Energetically, by helping others, my light automatically gets brighter. It was difficult to make the crossover, but when I did, I felt lighter, happier, and less stressed. It was really powerful.

ACTION STEP: Do you have a mindset like me? Are you a competitive person who always likes to win? Spend a few minutes journaling about what it would be like to have a win-win mentality at work, at home, or elsewhere? Do not get lost in the word win. Look at some other words that mean the same thing. Do you need to be right? Is your word the *final* word at work or at home? If you are winning all the time, someone is losing. Look in that direction to find your answers.

Do We Speak the Same Language?

Many years ago, a friend of mine gave me a book that would forever change my marriage. She handed me *The Five Love Languages* by Gary Chapman. Although I love to read, I did not want to read this book. I already had a strong marriage and I felt that reading this book would be a waste of my time, but she suggested I read it, so I really felt like I had no other choice.

Feeling as though I was backed into a corner, I decided to read it as quickly as possible and get it over with. I dove into the book as a reluctant reader, but it became readily apparent that I did, indeed, need this book. Everyone needs this book!

Gary Chapman boils down a relationship to five basic languages. Every person speaks in one of them. It is how you receive the, "I love you." If you are not speaking the same language, it is very likely you and your spouse are not receiving the, "I love you." Below are the 5 languages:

1. Words of Affirmation
2. Acts of Service
3. Receiving Gifts
4. Quality Time
5. Physical Touch

Well, my husband and I were definitely speaking different languages. Although he was speaking my language, I was not speaking his at all. My love language is "words of affirmation." His love language is "quality time" and I was missing the mark completely! We had 4 small children at the time and all he wanted was to spend some time alone out of the house. I was focused entirely on the kids.

It is critically important for you to not only know your own love language, but that of your spouse or significant other. Since I had my revelation many years ago, I am very aware of making sure I say "Yes" to quality time with Doug. When I think of all the times I said "No" to going out, I get sad knowing I did not have this critical piece of information back then. Here's to love!

————

ACTION STEP: I invite you to read the book; it will be worth the time you sink into it. Or visit the website: www.5lovelanguages.com. It's important to learn each other's love language. You'll thank me. Well, thank Gary Chapman.

Target Practice

—ᴍ—

Recently, I started running again after a 10-year hiatus thanks to reading about Joel Runyon and his Impossible List. My goal was to be able to run the 5K Turkey Trot at our church in Princeton, New Jersey on Thanksgiving Day. I was only running a little over a mile when I left for vacation on Fripp Island, South Carolina.

On day two of vacation, I decided to go for a run. As I left the house, I noticed everything was different. At home, I was familiar with my one-mile loop, but here I didn't have a planned-out route. So I just started running but instantly my mind kicked in and fought me on everything. It told me all the reasons to stop: (a) I didn't have a planned route, (b) it was unbelievably hot and humid, and (c) it was too hard. "Just stop and walk," my mind told me. I tried to tune it out but I couldn't do it.

Ultimately, I spent almost the entire run battling my mind. I realized how important it is in life (or running) to always have a target and a plan. In an effort to stop all the thoughts of quitting, I arbitrarily chose the marina as my target turnaround point. That target gave me the goal I needed to focus solely on execution and to quiet my mind. Do you have a target you are shooting for? Do you have a plan to execute? Without a target and a plan you might find, like I did, the mind becomes your biggest adversary. Today, consider picking a target. You just might be pleasantly surprised! I was.

ACTION STEP: Spend a few minutes journaling about various different goals you might like to attain. Have fun with this list. When you're done, circle one. Make that your next target.

Attracting Abundance

—⚬—

Who does not want abundance? If you are like me, you have said something like this: "I want more money, better vacations, a fancier car, exceptional clothes, college paid for, weddings paid for, financial freedom, a new kitchen, more traveling, etc." This thought process runs through my mind daily, to one degree or another.

Abundance, like everything else, is energy and my thoughts are perpetuating the negative energy and stopping the flow. The way to change this negative energy is to recognize what we already have. This is not to put on rose colored glasses, but to find the place of gratitude and awareness. As parents, we may notice this need for change in our children as our parents saw it in us at the same age. They said, "You don't have any idea of how good you have it!"

To get in the habit of enjoying the remarkable array of abundance in my life, I am spending the next ninety days acknowledging my abundance in my journal. I hope you will join me. I have so many blessings that I look right past with my "anti-abundance" thinking and I bet you do, too. We need to stop focusing on what we don't have and focus on what we do have. Here is the coup de grace: What we focus on expands. If we want abundance, we must stop focusing on scarcity.

———

ACTION STEP: Start journaling about abundance!! You will see quickly how much abundance is in your life! Enjoy!

SIDE NOTE: I have been journaling on abundance now for about 10 days! "Wow," is all I can say! Here are a few things that came my way:

While on vacation, I held a baby kangaroo that happened to be at the place we had chosen to play mini-golf (can't make this stuff up); I had 3 hole-in-ones; I had a black butterfly land on my arm (black butterflies have a huge significance with me); we scored the last table of 6 for dinner outside watching The Band Perry perform, and more.

The best part of the journaling is how joyful it has made me. In realizing my abundance I found it is rarely anything material. Having my whole family together, hysterically laughing our way through 18 holes of mini-golf: Abundant!

"No Judgement"

—∞—

The blanket statement *no judgement* is generally followed by, well, judgement. We judge everything. And in judging everything, we have the potential to make life more painful for ourselves and others, than it has to be.

Starting today, let's give the real *no judgement* a try. Let's take on every experience, every person, every everything in the present, as if it is the first time we are experiencing it or them. Forget what happened last week, last month or last year. We have a clean slate. No judgement. Forget she was curt last time; give her a clean slate. Forget he asks a million annoying questions, be present and answer them all. This applies not only to those we know but also to those we don't know.

As always, it is our choice to judge or not. Giving someone a clean slate is as simple as choosing to do so. Our new actions may seem altruistic, but the beneficiary of *no judgement* is not them, it's us. We rarely tell others we are judging them, but our body and mind bears the brunt of this negativity. Ironic, huh? When we make an effort to find the good in people, we train your mind to be compassionate and caring.

ACTION STEP: Your action step for today is awareness. How often do you judge others? Not all of your judgements will verbally come out of your mouth, thank goodness. Be aware today of how many judgmental thoughts you have. You can even try to reverse your judgments in your mind. The more aware you become, the less you will judge.

Slay the Dragon

—m—

"Slay the Dragon" before breakfast! What does that mean? "Slaying the dragon" is overcoming the things we fear. Most of us have a "dragon" that we need to slay and the longer we wait in the day to slay him, the more unlikely it is that we will do so. "Slaying the dragon" is hard work and, more often than not, it is work we do not enjoy. Intuitively, we know our lives will be better once we "slay the dragon," yet we postpone this task or obligation, sometimes for very long periods of time.

"Slaying the dragon" will likely make us feel stronger, happier and more fulfilled. Not "slaying the dragon" may leave us with feelings of regret as well as disappointment in ourselves. Knowing all that, we still allow ourselves to postpone "slaying the dragon."

What is your dragon? It can be a daily routine or maybe it is a one-off item on your to-do list that you have postponed forever. It can be personal or professional. The dragon I need to slay is exercise (and meditation, if we are putting it all out there). I know exercise is not only good for my physical health but my mental health as well. When I finish exercising, I always have a strong feeling of accomplishment and pride. Everything I feel, both physically and emotionally, after exercise is amazingly positive, yet I still postpone "slaying the dragon." I make excuses why I cannot go to the gym first thing in the morning. I lie to myself and say I will go later, but I never do. Why do I sabotage myself? Perhaps because exercise for me is an unenjoyable task. It's a chore. It's a burden. And it's work.

Today, let us all agree that "slaying the dragon" before breakfast is a great way to accomplish very important (and sometimes unenjoyable) tasks. Knowing the dragon is still out there will ruin our day. Why have we let the dragon win for so long? Come on, we are stronger than this! "Slay the dragon"!

I must give credit to Michael Hyatt on this one! I believe he is the one who taught me the expression, "Slay the dragon!"

———

ACTION STEP: Spend a few minutes today journaling on your dragon. Name your dragon. Why have you been putting this thing off over and over again? Commit to slaying this thing before breakfast by populating your calendar with this new daily task.

What Makes You Happy?

—⁓—

This is a very good question. America ranks 108th out of 140 countries on the "Happiness Index," according to the Happy Planet Index. So my guess is that depending on where you call home, your answer to the question, "Are you happy?" might be, "Meh." Translation: not so much.

Here is the **Paradox of Happiness:** Wanting to be happy may actually make you unhappy. Happiness will come as a by-product of pursuing meaningful activities and relationships. It is a give-get relationship.

We all say we will be happy *when* we get the dream job, the higher salary, the great relationship, we lose the weight, etc. Our happiness tends to be laser-focused on getting but happiness is within our reach right now by giving. When we give, we receive. Happiness is always a by-product of a life that is meaningful and fulfilling.

————

ACTION STEP: Over the next week or two, practice giving. How many ways can you give? None of this has to be with money. You can give someone your spot in line, give away the good parking spot, give someone your time, volunteer, give a compliment, give away clothes or toys, give, give, give without one thought of getting anything in return. You are in control of your own energy, and giving has a completely different vibration than receiving.

The Golden Ball

—ന—

Have you ever read *Le Jongleur de Notre Dame* (The Juggler of Notre Dame)? It is a religious miracle story by the French author Anatole France, published in 1892 and based on an old medieval legend. It has also been retold by Tomie dePaola in a children's book titled *The Clown of God*.

This legend was told by our priest, who also happens to be a master storyteller, one Sunday in church. Everyone was captivated. As the story goes, the juggler juggles balls that are all the colors of the rainbow and one golden ball. The golden ball is a metaphor for that special something each and every one of us has, our giftedness. If you haven't given any thought recently to your "golden ball," it's time.

What is that one thing that only you do? You are better at it than anyone else. We all juggle a lot but we all have a "golden ball." Sometimes we are so busy with all the balls in the air, we forget one of the balls is different, it's special. Today, focus on the "golden ball." It is your giftedness. Make sure the rest of the world is experiencing this gift in some way. It's really important. This gift was never meant to be tucked away.

———

ACTION STEP: Today, spend 5 minutes journaling about your "golden ball." What makes you different? Everybody has a "golden ball." Take the time to know what yours is—it sets you apart.

Uncomfortable and Annoying

—∞—

My team and I had a fabulous time recently hosting our Finding Your Purpose Workshop. We implemented some changes for this workshop and we knew these changes would make our participants a little bit uncomfortable.

One of the changes was an art segment. I know art makes me uncomfortable. We added art because it engages the right-brain in us which is responsible for our creativity, intuition, imagination, empathy, etc., and we wanted to engage and activate that side of the brain before we dug deeper into the topic of purpose. But if you are a left-side of the brain person, like I am, this exercise is not only uncomfortable, it can be downright annoying.

Hmm. Uncomfortable and annoying. Why would we implement such a change? How could that be good? It is actually better than good; it is great. Being uncomfortable is great because it is our personal GPS indicating we have just exited our comfort zone! In the case of our art segment, our participants were forced to create art. In real life, we *rarely* choose the things that feel prickly because we love to remain in our comfort zone.

———

ACTION STEP: What is that one thing you always say no to? Is it bowling, yoga, hiking, cold-calling, cocktail parties, dancing, public speaking, or eating ethnic cuisine? Specifically and consciously do something that gets you out of your comfort zone and uncomfortable.

The Bucket List

———✺———

Have you ever said, "Yeah, I forgot all about that. I really need to start doing that again"? Sometimes, we simply need a reminder. I got such a reminder recently from my fifteen-year-old daughter, Clare.

Clare is my youngest child and she is an organizer and a planner. Every summer she makes a *Summer Bucket List,* and she attacks this list, item by item, until it is all checked off. This morning's item was to see the sunrise over the mountains of Vermont. Our whole family obliged, some reluctantly because we were on vacation. We rose to the 5:15 a.m. wake up call to see perhaps one of the prettiest sunrises I have ever seen (due to a fog hanging heavily over the valley). I am really grateful she pushed us to check off this item from her bucket list.

Do you have a bucket list? I do, but I have not revisited it in quite some time. I believe it's in a file in our home office and it's not doing me any good there. So here is a reminder to all of us: Create a bucket list and begin checking things off. Don't hide it in a file. Look at it regularly. Revise it. Think big and small. Take action. The only way to make sure it happens is to start by putting it on the list. Time has a way of quickly slipping away from us. Make this list a priority. Once our bucket list items are written down, they are a lot more likely to get accomplish. Thanks Clare!

———

ACTION STEP: On a separate piece of paper, start a bucket list. It does not need to be completed today. Spend 5 minutes today writing down all the things you know you want to put on the list. Where will you keep it? How often will you look at it? This is all about having fun!

Time to Reallocate

—∞—

"The purpose of your life is not to get everything done. To have time for what is valuable, you have to stop giving time to what isn't." —UNKNOWN

The three words that jump out at me in this quote are *everything, valuable,* and *giving.* Why do we try to get everything done? We all know it is impossible, right? The pace of the society in which we live is frantic, frenzied, and frenetic. Oh, and I forgot unrealistic.

The second word I noticed was *valuable.* That word made my heart feel heavy. It reminded me that in my effort to get everything done, I was overlooking what was valuable to me—like my family and my friends. I had the order all wrong; I believed that once I got everything done, then I could relax with my family and friends.

And the last word that grabbed my attention was *giving.* I was giving my time to what wasn't necessarily valuable, no one was taking it or stealing it. So, if I am the one giving it away, then the control lies with me, right?

Let's be honest—we aren't going to get everything done today. So, who do you value most in your life? Today is the day we reallocate our time in value-descending order. If your running on empty, this approach is sure to fill the tank!

ACTION STEP: Who or what is getting most of your time? Spend your 5 minutes today journaling about your allocation of time. You are making two lists: who you value most and what amount of valuable time they are getting from you.

Tip for the Day . . .

—∿—

Do you want to do a better job at work, home, friendships, parenting, etc.? I know I do. Here are the four words we need to say to ourselves:

"I can do better!"

That is it. It has been psychologically proven *(Frontiers in Psychology posted on 6/30/16)* that saying these four words will improve our performance. Our potential for personal growth and development is essentially unlimited, so adding these four words to our day taps into our ever-present and infinite resource!

I can do better! I know I can do better.

———

ACTION STEP: Since we already have the sentence, now we need to apply it to something specific. To what do you want to apply this sentence today? Work, home, friendships, parenting, etc.? Pick one person or thing and journal for a few minutes on how you will apply, "I can do better."

The Finish Line

—∞—

I hope you *never* reach the finish line.

I was a big proponent of finish lines, until recently when I realized imposing an end was undermining my own success. Let me explain.

When I set goals for myself, essentially, I am establishing the finish line. As a target for me to reach, the finish line seemed like an important motivational marker, but it has its downside too. The finish line marks the stopping point. Once we stop, it is really difficult to get started again.

This unfortunate phenomenon is observed time and again. The person who signs up for a marathon, successfully completes the marathon, then stops running. The dieter who reaches their target weight, stops dieting, then gains the weight back. The salesman who hits his sales goal then coasts for the remainder of the year. By hitting the goal, we actually undermine the habit we have spent so much time developing.

I am still encouraging us to set goals and I still believe we should have a target, but the target is not the finish line. The habit we create while aiming for the target is what we want to maintain. We believe the finish line is the goal but, in reality, it is the habit we create along the way that makes us a winner.

———

ACTION STEP: Journal about the various finish lines you have crossed in your life. Did you continue with the habit after the task was completed? If your answer is no, journal about how you view it differently now.

I Didn't Catch Your Name

—⚏—

Dale Carnegie, the author of *How to Win Friends and Influence People,* believed using someone's name was incredibly important. He said, "a person's name is the sweetest sound in any language for that person." Our name is the core part of our identity, and so hearing it validates our existence, which makes us much more inclined to feel positively about the person who addresses us.

Greeting someone by name is not only a powerful tool in business, but it is also a personal and meaningful way to engage another person. As we get older, we often fall back on the excuse, "I am awful with names, I never remember anyone's name." That excuse is unacceptable. As soon as we adopt it as a truth, we have given up on the task. I recently decided to put a very strong effort into remembering names and it has worked. Just setting the intention and focusing on the introduction proved fruitful. I was amazed at how impressed people were that I remembered their name.

Greeting people by name, whether at work or at your local coffee shop, not only acknowledges them as the essence of who they are, but also allows us to be connected with them in a deeper way. I used this at dinner the other night with our waiter, Kyle. Immediately, everything changed when I called him by name. We created a personal connection that was not there before. This is a very powerful tool for anyone who wants to be an influential leader!

ACTION STEP: How good are you at retaining and using names, whether it be in a work setting or at the dry cleaners? Remembering names is an incredibly important skill set. "A person's name is the sweetest sound . . . for that person" and therefore worthy of our commitment. Spend a few minutes answering the question: "Where could I be better at addressing people by name?"

Why Are You Here?

—ɯ—

Have you ever thought about why you are on this earth? I, personally, believe everyone is here for a reason and this reason is tied to all the natural gifts we have been given, all the things we are good at doing and enjoy. When we discover the reason, which is tied directly to these gifts, then we will be truly happy.

There is a famous quote from Janet Erskine Stuart, the founder of Stuart Country Day School in Princeton, NJ and its abbreviated version is this:

"Each of our children is destined for a mission in life, to do something for God which will remain undone unless she does it."

I remember hearing that quote every year at Stuart's graduation and it always grabbed my attention and made me think, "What is my special mission? Why am I here?"

The part of the quote that stuck with me most was that the special work will remain undone unless I do it. Have you ever thought about it that way? "Undone" is not a word I take lightly. My wish for you today is that you will explore these words from Janet Erskine Stuart. What is the special work that will remain undone unless you do it? And when you find it, I believe you will be truly happy, to the core.

ACTION STEP: Spend 5 minutes reflecting and journaling on the sentence, *I am **destined** for a mission in life, to do something for God which will remain **undone** unless I do it.* I believe the words *destined* and *undone* were chosen carefully and precisely because we all have unique gifts which we are meant to share with the world.

Life Changes

—∽—

My husband, Doug, purchased tickets for the whole family to see the Kenny Chesney concert on Saturday that included both Old Dominion and Thomas Rhett. After waiting patiently for the rain to subside, we had a great time dancing and singing—all three acts were outstanding!

During one of Thomas Rhett's songs, *Life Changes,* he really got me thinking. The song is about how life is constantly changing, whether we are on board or not. Sometimes we have complete control over life (or so it seems) and at other times we have none. It is when we have none that we tend to struggle, but what if we accept the whole journey? Good and bad.

Rhett recommends, "You can't stop it, just hop on the train, You never know what's gonna happen, You make your plans and you hear God laughing." Rhett forces us to question the struggle. What if we were far more open to the journey as it went up and down? Because the truth is, it's going up and down anyway, why not embrace the ride? There are huge blessings even in the down times—and some would argue more.

————

ACTION STEP: Spend a few minutes journaling about the ups and downs of your life right now. Are you able to let go of the struggle—even just a little bit? What words would you need to write down right now that would allow you to see some of the blessings intertwined with the struggle?

Left Holding the Bag

A funny thing happened while I was on vacation. I found it took all of my willpower to **not** write a post for Motivational Monday. How funny is that? It was more difficult for me to not post, than to post. I learned a lot during my week-long vacation about stress, relaxation, family, time away, and disengaging from the real world.

We arrived at the beach late Saturday night with two of our four children; the other two were arriving late Sunday night, so I could not truly relax until I knew my entire family was safely under one roof. When I woke up Monday morning, I felt like I had been hit by a truck. It took all of my energy to simply make a cup of tea and park myself on the veranda to enjoy the morning. As I sat there, fully aware of how I felt, I realized the intensity with which stress impacts the body. We think we handle stress well, we say we handle it well, but it takes its toll regardless. As I sat there, just taking in the beautiful morning, I took inventory of how my body was processing the stress I had inflicted upon myself. It was as if I could feel my body physically detoxifying itself.

Stress is a funny thing. I feel like I do not know how stressed I am until the stress stops and I am left holding the bag, so to speak. Actually, what I was left holding at the beach was my completely depleted body. Stress is real and we need to treat it as such. We need to stop and recharge our battery regularly. We need to recognize the stress before it wreaks havoc on us. I do not believe we can live a stress-free life, but I do believe we can actively reduce our stress in various natural, healthy, and fun ways.

ACTION STEP: What are you doing in your life to reduce stress? Do not dismiss this question with answers like, "Stress does not really bother/

affect me" because the science behind stress says otherwise. Meditation is the best thing you can do for yourself. Download a meditation app, go for a walk, plan a vacation, make plans with friends to watch a funny movie but please do not ignore stress; whether you realize it or not, it may be impacting your health. Journal below the five things you will add to or subtract from your life to reduce stress!

The Self-Made Man

—∞—

You have undoubtedly heard someone described as, "a self-made man." It is impressive when we hear that description because it eliminates all the thoughts we first may have had which were, "I'm sure he came from money," or "It must be a family business." The term has been used to describe Walt Disney, Milton Hershey, Abraham, Lincoln, as well as Oprah Winfrey, J.K. Rowling, Tory Burch, and many more. I heard it used again the other day which gave me pause. Regardless of our success or lack thereof, isn't everyone self-made?

Self-made. Hmm. That puts me in the driver's seat. No more excuses of my missing trust fund, my bad breaks, or my mean boss. Every person is self-made. Once I accepted that, the power for my future shifted back to me (actually the power had been with me all along, but I had unknowingly relinquished it to the universe).

Does the realization, "I am self-made at all times," change anything for you? It certainly did for me. My desire is that this single truth lights a fire under all of us. Our current "self-made" status does not happen overnight, but it does happen one step at a time. Do we want the world to describe us as a self-made man or woman? Then let us go make it happen, one step at a time. Do not be afraid, we have nothing to lose! Our fear should be that we do nothing and, by default, create that kind of "self-made."

Today, we need to begin embracing our power over our future. If we do not like what we have made up until now, then let's make something new. The power is within us. Do not give up your sovereignty.

———

ACTION STEP: Journal today about self-made. Think about what you have made (or not), but be very careful here. Do not go down the rabbit hole of self-deprecation. Be kind, but be truthful. Be optimistic as well as insightful. In the end, I want you saying, "I did some great things, but I now know I can do so much more!"

Chivalry Is Not Dead

—◆—

We recently took our family and one of our daughter's friends into New York City. The seven of us spent the entire day exploring every nook and cranny NYC has to offer. We went by car, ferry, subway, PATH, and foot. It was a lot of fun, it was a full day, and all of us discovered firsthand that flip flops are not sensible shoes for ten hours in New York City!

After walking the High Line and grabbing a bite to eat in Eataly, we decided to take the subway to midtown to show our Texas-guest Times Square and Rockefeller Center. The subway was empty when we walked on, but it quickly started to fill up. Right before the train began to move, an elderly couple entered the subway car and grabbed hold of the hanging straps in front of my children to steady themselves during the lurching ride. When I saw the couple enter our car, I got my son's attention from six seats away and mouthed the words, "Give up your seat, please." It took him a second to assess the situation and figure out to whom he was supposed to relinquish his seat, but he quickly understood and offered his seat to the elderly woman. She was profusely grateful, sat down with complete relief on her face, and quietly but noticeably exhaled.

My son may have come up with that action on his own had I given him a few more seconds, but I saw it as a teachable moment. He is sixteen and I do not know how much longer I will have to teach him chivalry. He will soon be with his friends more often than with us. I hope this subway lesson sticks with him and he will always remember to give up his seat, hold a door, or get the car when it is raining. It matters. Chivalry is not dead and the people who act as such stand out as exceptional.

ACTION STEP: Regardless of whether you are a man or a woman, doing the right thing will never go out of style. Nor will teaching our young adults old-school manners. As you go about your day, can you embody chivalry, manners, and ways to improve them, all the while modelling this behavior for the next generation? Or Google 'chivalrous acts.' My favorite is that gentlemen should put their hand on the small of the back when introducing their lady.

Be a (Positive) Storyteller

—〰—

What story are you telling yourself? We are constantly telling stories. Some stories we tell out loud to others and some we simply retell in our own mind over and over again. One thing holds true, regardless of how we express our story, the story will either empower us or, very often, diminish us. I say "very often" because most people rarely spend the day ruminating on their awesomeness.

What story are we telling ourselves and others that is limiting us? This story is defining us, so by telling this story over and over again, we are giving it power. Keep in mind, it is likely this story or event happened once, but we are telling it (and thereby reliving it) hundreds, if not, thousands of times.

What story are you telling that is disempowering you? "I can't change jobs/fields/industries, there is too much risk," "I'm not qualified for that," "I'll never meet someone," "I'll never get out of debt," "I'll never be able to afford that," "I'm too old," "I don't have the experience/education for that job," or maybe "I'll never lose this weight."

If any of these stories ring true for you, it is time to put a big wedge between you and your story. "For as a man thinketh in his heart so is he." (Proverbs 23:7). It is time to change our story. We can be victim or victor. It will all depend on the story we choose to tell. Nelson Mandela spent twenty-seven years in jail. What story do you think he told himself over and over again? Shortly after his release, and keeping with his famous dry sense of humor, he said, "I went on a long holiday for twenty-seven years."

———

ACTION STEP: Spend 5 minutes brainstorming how you can change your current story into a new story, your best story. If Nelson Mandela can do it after 27-years of incarceration, so can you.

One of My All-Time Favorite Memories

—∞—

When I went off to college thirty-six years ago (yikes!), things were a bit different. We did not spend thousands of dollars at Bed, Bath, and Beyond. When our parents dropped us off at college, they barely slowed down long enough to let us get out. But one thing does not change, parents miss their children and yes, children miss their parents.

One of my most memorable moments from college occurred freshman year. I invited my father and all of my uncles to come to Rutgers to attend a football game with me and my friends. We organized a bagel breakfast in my dorm room that Saturday morning when they arrived and then we headed out to see some outrageously bad football. My uncles were hilarious and we all had such a great time together. I will never forget that day.

I never thought to invite them up again, but I really wish I had; it remains an all-time favorite memory of mine. The synergy without my mom and my aunts changed everything. My dad and my uncles were so much fun and I am glad I had the opportunity to experience that incredible day. If you are a college student or the parent of a college student, see if you can make this happen. If it is not football, try basketball or no sport at all, just visit. Make it an annual event. I certainly wish I had.

———

ACTION STEP: Journal for 5 minutes on how this idea or a similar one can be adapted into your life. Maybe it is not a college visit, but something else. The key is that you open yourself up to an otherwise unlikely scenario.

450 Minutes (5×90=450)

—ᴍ—

Would you like to double your income? How about switching jobs? Or maybe start your own business? Have you ever had these thoughts, or maybe even more daring ones? What did you do about these thoughts?

If you are like me, it probably ended there. Maybe you had one or two additional thoughts, but then that train (of thought) came to a screeching halt. I have a great tip as we head into the home stretch of this year.

For the next 90 days, or until the year ends, spend 5 minutes a day writing about one particular thought or idea. Just commit 5 minutes a day to reflecting on how you will make this action happen. I started yesterday and I could not believe how many great ideas I came up with in just 5 minutes. We all have 5 minutes—let's put it to really good use. We can do this!!

ACTION STEP: Did you ever wonder why I asked you to journal for 5 minutes a day? I have been training you for this! From now until year end spend 5 minutes a day writing/thinking and all of it will be for your betterment.

A Lesson in Listening . . .

—◊—

Prior to my flight's departure last Friday, I was asked to change my seat to an exit row. I said, "Of course," given the flight was to Orlando and the airline's next choice was likely a 7-year-old little girl wearing Beauty and the Beast pajamas and donning Minnie Mouse ears.

As the plane was preparing for take-off, David, the steward, told me I had to store my two bags that I had positioned in front of me in an overhead compartment. I explained I could not put them in the overhead because they were open bags and everything would be strewn about. He shot me a quick look of disgust and said, "They have to be stored," and quickly walked away. David was of no help, so a fellow passenger offered to put my bags under the seat in front of her, which I did not have available to me.

Later, David was seated for landing in front of me. I leaned over and whispered so as to not make a scene. I tried to explain how I had just needed some help from him, but he would have none of it. He talked right over me and stated two really powerful statements, "You are making a bigger thing out of this than need be and you should be grateful for that seat. Everyone wants that seat for all the leg room!"

I decided not to say another word. He was not listening. I am 5'3" tall. I didn't need leg room—heck, I never need leg room. What I needed was a place to put my bags. I needed someone who knew the plane to be kind and help me. Listening is a really powerful skill, especially if we are in sales, or are a parent, or interact with *people* in any way . This world moves so quickly, we often spit out answers and rules without even attempting to hear the other person. This was a reminder for me, listening is more important than almost anything else. Have you been listening? People want to be heard. I was never heard on that plane. I learned a big lesson from David—being heard is very important.

––––––––

ACTION STEP: Ask yourself, "Have I been listening?" Did you hear your partner? Your co-worker? Your children? Before you say, "Yes," take a moment to revisit what they may have been trying to say and remember, *people want to be heard*.

I Need to Get Motivated

—ɷ—

"I need to get motivated!" "I can't seem to get myself motivated!" "Once I get motivated, then I'll start." I have news for you, motivation is not going to arrive on your doorstep one day in a pretty little package with a bright red bow, nor is it going to be handed to you by a friend, a family member, or even your boss.

Motivation is deceptive. We believe once we get it, then we can start, but just the opposite is often true. Waiting for motivation is a trap. We need to start, take action, or as Nike says, "Just do it," and then motivation will follow. Action creates momentum and momentum triggers motivation which will then make it easier for us to continue.

What is it you have wanted to do/be/have but are waiting for the arrival of your long-lost friend, motivation? I am strongly encouraging you to start without her. Move past the fear, and the excuses, and the procrastination and take bold action. When we take that brave first step, I assure you, motivation will show up on your doorstep almost instantly. She is a reluctant friend at first, but she comes around quickly, as a result of our actions.

———

ACTION STEP: Journal for 5 minutes on that very thing you have wanted to be/do/have but have not had the motivation to move forward. Finish up by testing the assertion that motivation will show up after you start. Start the wheels in motion, and see if motivation arrives as expected.

Two Sides to Every Story

—∭—

For a second, imagine the last person who made you angry, got on your nerves, or just plain annoyed you. Most people, as they went on about their day, would do one or both of the following things without fail.

1. Continue to ruminate over what took place.
2. Engage other people in the story.

Either way, you have allowed yourself to own this. The other person, regardless of what took place, does not own your destructive mental conversation. You allowed him to bring you down if you are still talking about him either internally or externally.

We have been told for years, "Just let it go." Easier said than done, but knowing we are holding onto this negative emotion might encourage us to let it go. I will give you my universal mantra that allows me (most times) to let it go:

I do not know the whole story.

That one line helps me remember, regardless of what just happened, I do not know the whole story of the other person. Maybe they are having marital or financial problems. Maybe they had an abusive childhood. I do not know the whole story.

Whether it is our boss or our sister-in-law, we are best served if we let it go. Stop talking about it and thinking about it. All of us have at least one person who we have allowed to fester and today we should all just let it go! We don't know the whole story.

———

ACTION STEP: Today is a very simple journaling day. Who is the person you are struggling with? Now spend 5 minutes journaling about all the ways in which you do not know the whole story.

Going Through a Rough Patch

—∞—

Having a bad day? Month? Maybe even a bad year? I can help.

Dr. Karl Menninger said it best, but I will paraphrase his poignant words: "If you find yourself in a bad way, lock up your house, walk across town and find someone in need and help them. By doing that, we get out of our own way."

We all have bad times. Most of us believe we have to wait until we are in a better place before we can help others, but just the opposite is true. When we find ourselves in a bad place, there is nothing better for both of us, than if we offer a helping hand to another person.

Dr. Karl Menninger is also quoted as saying, "Love cures people—both the ones who give it and the ones who receive it." As we mull over his enlightening words, let's think about "locking up our house and walking across town." Maybe, just maybe, it will help us just as much as it will help them. Love cures, of that I am certain. And the more we help others, the happier we become. Here's to your happiness!

———

ACTION STEP: Journal for 5 minutes about what thoughts were triggered when you read, "Love cures people—both the ones who give it and the ones who receive it." By helping others, "we get out of our own way." Who could use your help?

"Have No Fear, Superman Is Here."

—⚊—

Fear is an emotion that was given to us so we would not be maimed or killed by a saber-toothed tiger. OK, that is a very helpful tool and I am sure the cavemen found it invaluable. Fear continues to be very helpful today, although I am not generally in need of avoiding physical harm or death.

We have taken this incredible impulse for safety and warped it into our own way of feeling more emotionally comfortable. We did not do it on purpose, but I feel compelled to shine some light on the truth. Think of all the fears that are stopping you right now and list how many of them are actually saving you from physical harm or death. None, right?

We can let fear serve us when we truly need to be safe, but we should overrule it when it's just keeping us comfortable. Fear was created to save us, **not** keep us small. Definitely do not walk down the scary alley at night, however, say yes to the new job offer. We cannot reach our potential when we continue to acquiesce to fear.

We can all benefit from taking a really honest look at our fears. Dark alleys are always a **no**, everything else, well, you tell me? I am thinking most are a **yes**.

———

ACTION STEP: Journal about what came up for you as you read this entry. Was it a heart to heart with your boss? Maybe a job change? Was it fear of failure or rejection? Pick one and dig in deep. Is the fear real? Write down what is most likely to happen if you take this risk. Are you less fearful now that you wrote about it? Can you take an action step?

An Unproductive Enemy

—✺—

What are you worried about? Stop and really think about your #1 worry. Do you have it? OK, now ask yourself, "Who would I be and what would I be able to see if I could erase this worry?"

Glenn Turner said it best, "Worrying is like a rocking chair, it gives you something to do but gets you nowhere." Worry is your imagination on overdrive creating scenarios that are often not only unlikely but improbable. How would things change if you knew deep inside of you there existed a supreme self who is always at peace—and that worry is a choice and so is peace?

At any moment we can all tap into this inner peace. The truth is we can all choose peace over worry every single day. Some days will be easier than others for sure, but peace is *always* there. Try to tap into that peace today. Exercise your right. Don't let worry hijack your thinking, it's an incredibly unproductive enemy that is stealing our joy.

———

ACTION STEP: Today, journal for 5 minutes about the question, "Who would I be and what would I be able to see if I could erase this worry?"

School Days, School Days

—⚒—

It's official! School is now back in session.

For me, this means many things. It means the lack of structure from the summer is gone and order will reign again. It means sleeping in can no longer be. And it means I now have time to think about me and my personal growth.

Back to school should not just be for children. Everyone needs to grow and learn. If we are not growing, then, by definition, we must be stagnant. I never want to be stagnant. Stagnant is characterized by *showing no activity*. That is simply unacceptable!

So, when are we going "back to school?" What are we going to take on this fall so we can grow ourselves in some way? Is it something we have wanted to do for a long time or is it a new interest? Is it personal or professional? Whatever it is, we need to know how important it is for us to pursue.

This growth can help us emotionally, physically, intellectually, spiritually, not to mention a big boost to the brain. Some ideas include yoga, a foreign language, technology, cooking/baking, history, etc. The brain loves to learn. So let's go back to school in some way! Our entire body, inside and out, will thank us!

———

ACTION STEP: Journal for 5 minutes about some topics you are interested in or what have you always wanted to learn. This could mean real school enrollment, adult school, a retreat, an online class, books on tape, etc. Learning fills your mind and your heart.

Let's Git 'Er Done Day 1

—ᨳ—

What do you want to accomplish that has been hanging over your head for way too long now? Is it work-related, entrepreneurial, or personal? Let's put our finger on one thing we want done in the next month because, starting today, we are going to spend the next thirty days getting this thing done!

This is not a to-do list item, this is a real goal. It might not even be completed in 30 days but this challenge will help us get the momentum we need. Let us challenge ourselves by choosing the goal we really want completed, not the easy one.

The key to this challenge is *action*. We will be creating an action guide. Without action, we will go nowhere. Today, we pick the goal. Choose a goal that can be completed in thirty days (if yours is longer, that is ok, but not too much longer). Invite friends to join the challenge as well. *Let's Get 'er Done!* Once we have picked the goal, we must put it in writing. Once it is written, we have committed.

*Note: Although this is a thirty-day challenge, I am only going to write on it for five days to get us all started.

———

ACTION STEP:
1. Pick a goal that can be accomplished in thirty days.
2. Write down some action steps you need to take. Some people will work forward to the thirty-day mark, and some like to plan backwards from the end date. Most important for today is to **take that first action step**. Make sure that every day for the next thirty days has an action step associated with it.
3. Invite friends to join you. Everything is more fun with friends!

Get 'Er Done Challenge Day 2

—⚇—

I trust you have chosen something to accomplish in the next thirty days. If you are finding it difficult to decide, please recognize that it is likely you are procrastinating. Procrastinating is a form of fear and it will continue to sabotage our goals, if we let it. We need to recognize it when we see it because it will rear its head again and again during the next twenty nine days!

In a journal (or in this book), write down everything you can think of that you need to do for this goal to be achieved. This is a brain dump. Clear everything out of your head and then I want you to think of more. If your goal is weight loss, then eating and exercise are obvious, but maybe you need new sneakers or maybe you need to map out a new route for your walk/run that is more challenging or just more scenic.

We really need to dig deep on what we need to do for this goal to be achieved because here is the most important point for today: It is highly likely that we have attempted to achieve this goal before and we failed. If we do the same thing as last time, we *will* fail again. Albert Einstein's definition of insanity: Doing the same thing over and over again and expecting different results. We must do it differently this time in order to be successful.

After we have all our ideas on paper (yes, we *must* write this out), I want us to pinpoint the potential pitfalls. I do not want there to be any risk of failure. Identify your saboteur; mine is time-management. Once we define the enemy, we will see it before it can wreak havoc on our momentum.

———

ACTION STEP: Today we have three journaling tasks.
1. Brain-dump: write down everything you will need for this challenge.
2. Review your past approaches-do not repeat old sequences.
3. Potential Pitfalls: write them down.

Get 'Er Done Challenge Day 3

—◊—

Today's task is simple, create (in writing) an action list. What are you going to do to get this thing done? We must spell out what we will accomplish each day, starting today. Start with the week in mind. We must be specific. Yesterday's work should help with this step. Again, I will use weight loss as the example. If your action step is to exercise, be specific. Wednesday: 6pm, I will walk a one-mile loop. I will time myself so I know how long it takes to walk this loop.

Carving out the time and sticking to it, is the key. When my goal was to finish writing this book, early morning was the most productive time for me. Scheduling it later in the day would have been a recipe for failure. Be honest with yourself about when you are most productive. You might even have to tell your family what your goal is so they can support you. Tell them, "Don't let me skip a workout," or "Dinner will be later now because I need to get my workout in right after work."

It is also a good practice to design your action steps with the end in mind. For me, it was chapters. Essentially, I had to write a chapter every two days so I could reach my weekly target. Once you have written your action steps for the next seven days, then **Get 'er Done!** As I like to say, "We got this!"

————

ACTION STEP: Today's action step is to spell out what you will accomplish on each day for the next week.

DAY 3:

DAY 4:

DAY 5:

DAY 6:

DAY 7:

DAY 8:

DAY 9:

Get 'Er Done Challenge Day 4

———*m*———

So far we have:

1. Chosen a goal
2. Realized that procrastination is simply fear
3. Written down all that our goal will need from us
4. Concluded that we must do it differently this time in order to avoid failure
5. Identified our individual saboteur(s)
6. Designed an action list with the end in mind

Today, we are going to recognize the difference between our goal and our plan. The goal is firm. The plan, however, can change. It can change daily, if need be. As a matter of fact, it is highly likely that the plan will change. The goal cannot change. It is important to fall in love with the goal and make our emotional attachment to the goal, not the plan. Be open to the plan needing to be tweaked, but never, ever, ever do we change the goal! Covet the goal.

Sometimes when the goal looks out of reach, the tendency is to change the goal. If you find yourself in that spot, commit now to never changing the goal, simply rework the plan. Really give that idea some thought. It is another potential saboteur. It looks like this, "I wanted to lose 10 lbs., but I'm happy with 7 lbs." That is like saying, "I am fifty feet from the summit of Mount Everest, but that's good enough, I can kind of see it from here, so I am going to head back down now."

I'm encouraging you to push yourself a little further and ramp up your goal a bit. If, on the other hand, you are feeling discouraged because the goal was set way too high, I am imploring you to make the appropriate change so your goal is still a stretch but not out of reach. Keep the goal; tweak the plan.

———

ACTION STEP: Since I am explaining goal versus plan on Day 4, I am making an exception today that will allow you to revisit your goal and make an adjustment if necessary. Two important points to remember:

1. The goal must be a reach, but not out of reach. Challenge yourself.
2. A goal that is too easy is no goal at all, it is a to-do list item.

Get 'Er Done Challenge Day 5

—⚬—

Do you remember the Mike Tyson–Buster Douglas fight of 1990? Tyson was the heavyweight champion of the world and unbeaten in 37 fights going into this bout. Douglas' mother had suddenly and unexpectedly died of a stroke 3 weeks before the fight. She had told her son, repeatedly, he could beat Tyson. This was one of the greatest sporting upsets of all time and Douglas attributes his win to his mom; she believed in him and she was his *why*.

Today, we are going to write down all of our *whys*. We will elaborate, in sentence form, why we want to get this thing done, once and for all. We must dig deep on this one. It is likely we have more than one *why*. Figure out which one is most important to you. It is critical that we know what is motivating us and driving us forward.

If we find ourselves "falling off the wagon" during this challenge, we must immediately go back to our *whys*. Why are we doing this challenge? Why did we choose **this** goal? Why? *Why* is what is going to make us successful in accomplishing this goal. *Why* is the motivator. Without a *why*, when the going gets tough, there is nothing to inspire us to carry on.

———

ACTION STEP: Today is a journaling day.

Why am I doing this challenge?

Why did I choose **this** goal?

In Name Only

———✺———

"Call me Diana, not Princess Diana."

—PRINCESS DIANA

August 31, 2017 was the 20th anniversary of Princess Diana's death. She was an amazing woman who endured more in her 36 years than most of us will ever experience in our lifetime. She was an ardent activist, fashion icon, and devoted mother. She was known as *The People's Princess*.

At first glance, one would wonder why I picked this quote. *The Princess* part put her in the spotlight, but the title was empty, meaningless really, until Diana's actions set the bar extraordinarily high. Titles do not define us, we do. If we are putting any amount of weight into our title, we are sadly misguided. We are not our title, we are only as good as our actions. Don't be impressed with your own title. The better question to ask is, "What have I done to raise the bar on what this title means to everyone around me?" *Princess* was just a title until Princess Diana infused it with meaning, purpose, determination, deep caring, and authenticity. What have you infused in your title? What I am trying to say is, don't ever tell anyone your title, show them.

———

ACTION STEP: Today is a thinking/writing day. Forget your title for a moment, and write down what you personally have infused into your current role. Show me your title.

Caddyshack

—⚋—

Who is Michael Greller? In 2015, he was on track to make over a million dollars. Have you ever heard of him? Probably not. He is Jordan Spieth's caddie. And if you do not know Jordan Spieth, he is the twenty-five-year-old American professional golfer who is tearing up the PGA Tournaments.

Prior to 2013, Greller was a sixth-grade math and science teacher at Narrows View Intermediate School in Washington. He caddied for the first time in 2006 and kept it up as a hobby. In 2011, he found himself carrying Spieth's bag in the US Junior Amateur. When Spieth turned pro in 2013, he called on Greller to be his caddie. It was not a simple decision to make. The big payoff for a caddie is when their golfer actually wins. Spieth was a twenty-year-old young man entering a pool of very seasoned golfers. Greller recalls asking himself the question, "What if it takes ten years before Spieth wins a major?" His answer is why he took the risk. His answer was, "If and when he wins a major, I want to be there!"

We all play this game called life way too safely! Very few of us would have made the gutsy decision Greller made. It looked like a no-brainer when Spieth was winning every tournament known to man, but that information was not available to Greller when he made his bet on a long shot! He followed his heart, his love of the sport, and his passion which is more than I can say for most people. What is it you really want to do but are too scared to take on the risk? Remember, Greller did not quit his day job for a number of years, he straddled both. You can do the same. Stop playing it safe—it is not helping you reach your full potential.

———

ACTION STEP: Spend 5 minutes today journaling about the question, "What is it you really want to do, but are too afraid to take on the risk?" Think of ways to move forward but, at the same time, to remain safe. Greller did both. Journal all your thoughts. Put it all on the table.

Busy and Booked

—ɷ—

"I don't have time for that." "I wish I had more time." "I can't fit that into my schedule, I'm already over-booked."

I hear this all the time from my clients. I do not want to pass judgement on any of those statements because I have said all of them, and more, at some point. But here are a few painful truths:

1. Busy and booked does not necessarily equate to being important or successful. It means either we have poor time management, we said, "yes" to too much, or we need to hire more employees.
2. If we would slow down long enough to scrutinize where our time is being squandered, wasted, and poorly managed, we could live a more peaceful life.

Some of you are saying, "Beth, you're wrong! There is nothing I can do to change the demands on my time!" Although my response will always be, "You might be right," I have to add, I strongly encourage you to turn your schedule inside out and decide what needs to stay and what can go.

———

ACTION STEP: Everything seems urgent and important until you truly scrutinize and prioritize. Spend some time analyzing everything you do so you can siphon back some of your precious time.

The Power of "No!"

—ww—

By the time we turn eighteen, we will have heard the word "no" approximately 148,000 times (per Shad Helmstetter, Ph.D.). And that is if we grew up in a reasonably affirmative home. It may have been less, but it also may have been more. In comparison, how many times do you think we heard "yes"? How many times, in those first eighteen years, were we told affirmatively what we can do or what we can accomplish? Was it a few thousand? A few hundred? Or was it more like four or five times?

I know the "no's" were mainly delivered in order to protect us, however it still enforced the negative programming. We received "no" from parents, teachers, coaches, peers, bosses, religious leaders, the news, etc. As a result, and leading behavioral researchers have proven, approximately 77% of what we think is negative (*What to Say When You Talk To Yourself*, Shad Helmstetter, Ph.D.). Almost eight out of every ten of our thoughts today will be negative! That, my friend, has to change! (And we are sadly perpetuating this cycle with our children).

Today, let's be aware of our "no's", the "no's" to ourselves, the "no's" to others, and especially the "no's" to our children. We do not want to continue this cycle of negativity. When we start to say "no," can we be open to the possibility of a "yes"? Yes—you can, yes you are capable, yes—go for it!! I am behind you! We can do this! Empowering ourselves and others with "yes"!

———

ACTION STEP: You see the irony in dismissing this exercise, right? Spend a few minutes thinking about how often you say "no" to your friends, your kids, your spouse, your co-workers, etc. Now try to say, "yes" as many times as possible and see how it makes you feel.

A Lot More than Breathing

—ɯ—

How many of you celebrate birthdays? Birthdays are fun! We get a cake, perhaps a few presents, and celebrate with friends and family. Everyone acknowledges that we are another year older. And, do you know what you need to do to get from birthday to birthday? Just one thing. Breathe.

Now, how many of you celebrate your wedding anniversary? For the longest time, we did not celebrate our anniversary. Maybe it was because the kids were little and we were busy, but we did not celebrate or honor our anniversary in anyway. One day, I had an epiphany. Do you know what we need to do to get from anniversary to anniversary? A whole heck-of-a-lot more than just breathing, I can assure you!

Marriage is not simple, it is a lot of hard work, dedication, commitment, sacrifice, tolerance, compromise, etc. At that moment, I committed to **always** celebrating our marriage. Regardless of how elaborate or modest, our anniversary needed to be honored every year. We have gone on trips and we have gone to dinner, but for the last ten or so years, we have made our anniversary an untouchable priority. What we have accomplished every year as a married couple is something we are very proud of. There are always highs and lows that are part of the journey, but as the anniversary arrives, we celebrate the success of it all. Then, we reset for another year. We are up to twenty-six years at the time of this writing!

ACTION STEP: If you do not currently celebrate your anniversary, please start! While you are celebrating, recap the year; go over the good, the bad, and the ugly. Laugh and cry, but be certain to ask each other, "How can I be a better spouse?"

The Chase Is On

—ɯ—

My husband was watching a video of an acceptance speech by Matthew McConaughey at the Academy Awards in 2014. McConaughey pointed to three things for his success. I loved the speech, although I thought I would make one small tweak.

He said, and I paraphrase, "There are three things I need in my life each day. One is something to look up to. One is something to look forward to. And the last one is something to chase! I look up to God. I look forward to my family and it is them that I want to be proud of me, and the thing I chase is me, ten years from now."

It was the "thing I chase" I thought I'd change. I thought an actual target would be a better choice. But after some intense thought, I decided that I do like the goal of chasing me, ten years from now. It forced me to think about who I want to be in ten years and to dedicate myself to living intentionally without following someone else's path. So let's put on our running shoes and get started. The chase is on!

———

ACTION STEP: Take five minutes and write down who you want to be in ten years. Be specific, creative, and brave. Once you know who you are in ten years, then you will know who to chase!

"You Can't Build Your Reputation on What You Are Going to Do."

HENRY FORD

—⚬—

I love this quote! Let's ask ourselves a few questions today. What *is* my reputation? How am I currently trying to **build** it? What do I need to do going forward to *improve* it? What do I want people *saying* about me that they currently are not saying? We must be intentional in our actions. Remember the old adage: *"Actions speak louder than words."* (Abraham Lincoln)

———

ACTION STEP: Spend a few minutes answering each of the following questions. When you have all your answers, decide how you will *intentionally* improve your reputation.

What *is* my reputation?

How am I currently trying to **build** it?

What do I need to do going forward to *improve* it?

What do I want people *saying* about me that they currently are not saying?

I Hate My Job!

—⬩—

Two-thirds of American workers are disengaged at work, or worse, according to a recent Gallup study. 51% feel no real connection and are, therefore, doing the bare minimum. Another 16% are actively disengaged, resent their jobs, and tend to pull the morale of the whole office down.

Therefore, it must be safe to speculate that around 67% of those reading this hate their jobs. Maybe *hate* is a strong word. Is "unhappy in their job" better? How about feeling unfulfilled, apathetic, disheartened, or disillusioned? Are you in any of these categories?

If this is you or someone you love, I have three thoughts which may help. First, if you hate your job, why are you still there? It is likely killing you, slowly but surely, by eating away at your very soul. You have to get out; no job is worth this. Second, if you hate your job, it is highly likely this is not what you are supposed to be doing anyway, as clearly your passion lies elsewhere, right? And third, find out what your passion and purpose are and you will never feel like this again! Passion and purpose together are the one-two punch toward a meaningful and rewarding career.

———

ACTION STEP: Spend your 5 minutes today simply assessing your situation. Do you hate your job or your boss or your employer? What *exactly* is causing your unhappiness? These important questions will lay the groundwork for you to assess the next possible steps you wish to take with a clear head. No one should hate their job. Seriously, no one.

This Should Open a Few Doors

—✍—

I am not a fan of the questionable advice, "When one door closes, another opens." I object to this adage because it suggests these actions occur simultaneously and, therefore, there is a seamless transition, but I find that this is rarely the case. Often, we are looking at a closed door for a while. Sometimes, we continue to bang frustratingly on the door that is closed, but to no avail. In hindsight, I suppose the saying might bother me less since, by then, I would have found the next open door.

What do we do when our door has closed? Most people will continue to pound on the door, trying to force their way in, but rarely does that pan out. The truth is, a closed door can be a gift. It can be a blessing. A closed door is the universe's way of saying, "This isn't for you anymore, this isn't the way. There is a better way." A closed door requires an entirely different approach and perspective.

A great approach, when we realize we are standing in front of a closed door, is to surrender. This is the hardest part. Surrender and say, "Clearly, this is not the way." Picture your GPS saying, "recalculating." The next thing we need to do is ask, "How can I look at this differently? What am I refusing to accept or entertain as a possibility?" The open door is nearby, we are simply not looking in that direction. We are so focused on the closed door, we are missing the open one. Sometimes this requires that we brainstorm with someone else so we really take advantage of all the possibilities.

If you are currently looking at a closed door, consider it a blessing. Something better is coming your way! Be open to the possibility of something better still.

———

ACTION STEP: Spend 5 minutes journaling on this closed door for you. Put all your thoughts on paper; remember, journaling is safe. Why is this the wrong door? What are some other possible doors that might be right? Allow your mind to think freely, allowing everything to be a possibility.

My Very Own Quote

—◇◇—

I offer this one piece of advice regularly to myself, my family, my friends, and my clients. It is really great advice. My family members have grown accustomed to it and actually have taken to using it. It is not easy advice to hear or take, but it really is powerful. And I live by this advice, so I have zero hesitation to offer it to others.

I was reminded of this advice last night when I watched the movie *We Are Marshall* again for the umpteenth time. The Marshall University coach visited their team's rival, West Virginia University, and asked them for any information that would help them run The Veer, an offense WVU was known for excelling at. The WVU coach ultimately gave them everything: playbook, research, and film. He was so dumbfounded that the Marshall coaching staff would have the audacity to ask for all this information that he declared, "You grow 'em big down in Huntington, I'll tell you."

So what is the advice? My advice is always this: You are already at no. What is it in your life right now that will remain a no unless you decide to ask? This requires a lot of bravery to ask, but truthfully, you are already at no, so why not muster up the courage? Here is the best part of the tip, very often the no that was assumed turns into an actual big fat "Yes"! All because we asked. Pick one thing today and go ask for it! This one sentence has changed my life.

———

ACTION STEP: You are already at no, so who are you going to ask in hopes that the no turns into a yes?

"If It Were Easy, Everyone Would Do It."

What a powerful quote. What are we not doing, not taking on, not jumping into, that we have always wanted to do *but* now find it is too complicated to accomplish? You know what I am talking about, is it the college course or degree, the job, the encore career, the athletic feat, etc.? It was such a burning desire for us, and then it got complicated. We know we would be good at it, but now it is too complicated.

It got complicated because of the kids, work, and life. We pushed our dream away because, to make it happen, we would really need to turn our life upside-down. We said things like, "Who would take care of the kids," "It will take too much time," "I don't have the money," or "I'm too old now."

If it were easy, *everyone* would do it. Every average person will say those lines but you are not average. You know you are not average. You would not be reading this book daily if you were average. You want to grow yourself. You are *not* average.

Today, revisit that dream. Yes, it will be challenging and you will make sacrifices, but do not let your dream fade away. I will make you this promise: If you pursue your dream, your family will survive, your spouse will survive, and your life will still be amazing. What you might not see yet is the "you" that comes out on the other side. This "you" will be stronger, wiser, accomplished and significantly more amazing than today, not to mention an inspiration to all of those around you who had the pleasure of watching your amazing transformation.

You are **not** average. If it were easy, everyone would do it. Do not let this one slip away.

ACTION STEP: Spend 5 minutes journaling about *it. If it were easy, everyone would do it.* What is the *it* in your life you have perhaps intentionally postponed? You can write about why it was put on hold, but please make sure you also write about how you are going to get it started.

You Have to Put in the Work

On Sunday my girlfriend, Kerri, celebrated her 50th birthday Kerri-style! She wanted all of us to go on a 50-mile (or 25-mile) bike ride in and around Hopewell, N.J. I haven't been on a bike ride like this in many years, but it was Kerri's birthday, so Doug and I replied, "Absolutely!"

What struck me while we were gathered to venture out on the bike ride was some of the amazingly expensive bikes people were riding as well as all of the accoutrement that went with them. I looked down at my 25-year old Trek bicycle that I had just replaced the dry-rotted tires on so I could do this ride and thought, "I hope I can make 25 miles."

As I was pulling back into the bike shop exhausted as well as excited after completing the 25 miles, I realized a few things. It doesn't necessarily matter what "bike" you are on in life; when you get to the hills—*you* have to put in the work. And when the ride gets difficult and you don't think you can go on anymore—*you* have to dig down deep inside of you. No fancy bike is going to change that fact. You might not know it, but deep down inside you is the will, the determination, and the persistence you need to be successful. Don't be distracted by all the "fancy bikes" around you, everything you need is already inside you!

ACTION STEP: Reread the last paragraph and journal on what that means to you. Remember, everything you need is already inside you!

Karma

—ᗰ—

Karma is a spiritual principle (Hinduism and Buddhism) of cause and effect where intent and actions influence the future of an individual. I certainly do not believe we have to be Hindu or Buddhist to believe in cause and effect.

If Karma is real, then we should spend each day trying to raise the bar on our intentions and our actions in order to influence our life, and that of others, in a positive way, right? You might be saying, "I already do!" And I agree with you, but I realized this morning that I am not even coming close to my potential on infusing this world with positive actions on my behalf. I can do better, much better.

As with anything in life, "OK," is not what I am shooting for and I know you are not either or you would not be reading this book. I need to raise the bar. I can be nicer, friendlier, more helpful and certainly more forgiving and understanding. "OK" is not the target. Exceptional, remarkable, and phenomenal sound like better goals. Of one thing I am certain, changing my target to *exceptional* will change my karma and all of those with whom I come in contact. Will you join me?

———

ACTION STEP: Give an answer to each of the following questions . . .

Where can I be friendlier?

Where can I be more helpful?

Where can I be more understanding?

Where can I be more forgiving?

Where can I be . . .

Exceptional is the target! Go be exceptional!

The Crossroad

—◊◊—

A sign at the crossroads in a southwestern state reads: "Be careful which road you choose—you'll be on it for 200 miles."

This may be true while traveling the southwest, but it is rarely true in life. There is almost always an alternate route. Sadly, most people will essentially park their car at the crossroad for fear of making either the wrong decision or a decision they cannot reverse.

Here is my advice at the crossroads of life:

1. Do not ever park your car; even the wrong road will be better than standing still.
2. Be courageous and choose. Even the wrong choice is still a choice and it results in action. We never know what adventure could be right around the corner.
3. Nothing is irreversible (well, tattoos maybe). Be gutsy. Pick a road for crying out loud. What do you have to lose? You might be right. What if you are right and you spent all that time just sitting at the crossroad, petrified of being wrong?

Be brave. Act.

ACTION STEP: Are you at a crossroad right now? Are you afraid to make a wrong decision? Our "internal roommate" will always choose the safest route. Do not confuse safe with right. The best advice I can give at any crossroad is to trust your gut; it is always right.

The Perfect 10

—ɯɯ—

Here is a really important quote to memorize and digest, not only for ourselves but also for our children, our spouse, our employees, etc.

> "You will never outperform your own self-image."
> —UNKNOWN

This quote is 100% true, but I would like to add a caveat. The caveat I would like to add to the end of this quote is, "without a coach, a teacher, or a mentor challenging you to do things well beyond your own self-image." If, on a scale of 1–10, our self-image is a 5, we **cannot** perform as if we are a 10. Our self-image will not allow it. We repeat, in our mind, "I will never be successful, I (fill in the blank). Is it "came from the wrong neighborhood" or "don't have the right education" or "am not smart enough"? We want to be a 10, but we can only think like a 5. Argh!!

So how do we get from a 5 to a 6? We need to perform successfully at a 6 over and over again until we believe, "Hey, I **am** a 6!" Once we get to a 6, we need to try things a 7 would do. But here is the amazing part, we were capable of being a **10** all along. No learning curve was necessary. The only thing that held us back from being a 10, was the fact that we didn't believe we could possibly be a 10! Guess what folks? We are all 10's, acting like 5's. Ask yourself this: "If I were a 10, what would I do differently today?" Now go do it!

———

ACTION STEP: Your only task today is to answer that question, "If I were a 10, what would I do differently today?" I believe you will be surprised.

Quote Unquote

—∞—

"You must be the change you wish to see in the world."
—MAHATMA GANDHI

"What great thing would you attempt if you knew you could not fail?" —ROBERT H. SCHULLER

"The journey of a thousand miles begins with one step."
—LAO TZU

Great quotes! We love great quotes. We share them with others, we post them where we will be forever inspired by them. We use them to encourage others. Awesome, right? Well, maybe not and let me tell you why.

Great quotes are only awesome if they inspire us to act. *Inspire* comes from two Latin words: in (in) spirare (to breathe). Inspire is to "breathe life into." Often, we are not breathing life into these great thoughts. We are simply remembering them like we would the lyrics to a song or a friend's birthday. If something truly inspires us, it should move us to act.

Stop memorizing quotes. If a quote moves you to say, "I love that quote," then act on it. Listen to Lao Tzu, "the journey begins with one step". These quotes did not start out as one-liners. Mahatma Gandhi was sharing his wisdom, calling on us to act. Robert Schuller did not want his words posted on our refrigerator, he wanted us to step outside our comfort zone! Find your favorite quote today and take one step, just one step toward that end. In doing so, we not only honor them but ourselves as well.

———

ACTION STEP: Do you have a favorite quote? Grab it now or take one of the quotes from above and dissect what it means to you. Take 5 minutes to journal about your favorite quote and how you will apply it to your life.

Are You a "Yes" Man?

—⚍—

I was home alone one Saturday night for a few hours and I decided to watch a movie. Somehow, I landed on a Jim Carrie movie titled, *Yes Man*. The storyline drew me in; he was a guy who said no to everything. I knew I could relate.

I used to get asked to spearhead fundraisers for local nonprofits, to participate in functions for my church, to help out with various school-related events and I said yes repeatedly. But then it became overwhelming, and I started saying no to everything. The pendulum swung the other way, I stopped even thinking about things and I just said no. What ended up happening was no became a habit and I started to say no to everything, even fun things.

In the movie *Yes Man,* Carl (Jim Carrie) committed to a covenant in which he had to say yes to everything. His life became amazingly enriched and fulfilled, simply by saying yes. The 21st century is about as busy a life as one can have and I am all for the no, but it is definitely time to revisit this uncompromising habit. Are we saying, no to our friends? Are we saying no to fun? Are we saying no just because we have created a habit that had its purpose and it's time but now has overstepped its bounds? I am certain my habit of repeatedly saying no prevented me from having a lot of fun in my life. So, if you want to go see a movie, or play miniature golf, or skydive—I am an emphatic "YES!"

ACTION STEP: Today is an awareness day. Examine what you say more often, yes or no. If you really want the truth, ask a loved one which you say more. The most important thing to recognize is whether the swing of the pendulum has suffocated joy, fun, and happiness or not. Both yes and no can be a problem or a gift. Do not let today end without knowing what you need to say more often!

Honor Your Calling

—⚶—

> "There is no greater gift that you can give or receive than to
> honor your calling. It's why you were born. And how you
> become most truly alive." —OPRAH WINFREY

My colleagues and I have now taught our 7th Finding Your Purpose Workshop. I am so passionate about purpose and calling because I struggled for so long to find mine. Trying to put your finger on your calling is no easy task—yet when you find it, ironically it seems as though it was so blatantly obvious all along you're not sure how you missed it.

I believe the best part of finding your purpose is what Oprah Winfrey calls becoming "truly alive." It is when your soul is on fire. It is doing what you love therefore it's not work. It's beyond fun and exciting. And because it's *your* calling, you are already gifted with everything you need to complete the task. Everything is included (in you).

But the most important part of your purpose is when you realize it is not for you. Your calling is the gift you have been asked to bring to the world. There is no doubt you will thoroughly enjoy doing it, but it is the world that *needs* it. Do you know your calling?

———

ACTION STEP: Spend 5 minutes journaling on your calling. What gift have you been asked to bring to this world? Sometimes it is difficult to see ourselves clearly, so consider asking family and friends: What do you think my calling is?

I Will

—ɯ—

Did you ever have a great idea for a business, only to stop yourself with thoughts like, "I don't have enough money," or "I don't have the expertise," or "It's probably already been done"?

Most people seem to think that entrepreneurs have all their ducks in a row; They have money, influential people and connections, and a great idea. This is rarely the case.

Take the case of Kevin Plank, the founder of Under Armour. He was a walk-on football player at the University of Maryland. In the brutally hot summer of 1995, he hated how heavy his sweat-soaked, cotton T-shirt would get during practice. He exclaimed, "There has to be a better way!"

He went to fabric stores in Maryland and discovered the wicking ability of synthetic fabrics. With $450, he bought fabric and had a prototype created. From there, he went on the road selling his new idea out of his car, and the rest, as they say, is history. Under Armour is currently a billion-dollar company and Kevin Plank earns over four million dollars a year.

Plank did not have millions of dollars, he did not have influential friends, and he was not the valedictorian at Harvard. He was a man who recognized a problem and spent his own hard-earned $450 to try and solve it. How is he different from you or me? What did he have in 1995 that we do not have now? We know the answers to these questions.

What is your business idea? Plank's story should inspire all of us. Would you like to earn $4,000,000 a year? I know I would!

ACTION STEP: Do you know the Under Armour slogan? *I Will*. Hmm. Interesting. Spend 5 minutes journaling on Kevin Plank's story and the slogan *I Will*.

Do It Afraid

—∿—

"The fears we don't face become our limits."

—ROBIN SHARMA

I have decided to perform an experiment, thanks to my sister, Diane. In one of my posts, I asked my readers, "Why would you stay in a job that is eating away at your soul?" That sentence spoke to her. The very next day, she mustered up the courage and gave her notice. She even asked her kids, "Did you think I would actually do it?" They said, "No." As scared as she was to quit, I want all of us to hear some of the words she used to describe how she felt after she faced her fears: "broken out of jail, freedom, gratitude, got my life back, life-changing, and life-saving." She is an inspiration!

So, back to my experiment. I have written down 10 things I am seriously petrified to do for my business. They are all 100% outside of my comfort zone. Over the next two weeks, I am going to do each one of them. What I have observed as well as experienced first-hand is that, over time, when people finally face their fear, rarely do they experience anything but success. But my math brain needs a real number and I am happy to be the guinea pig. Well, maybe "happy" is not the best word. Wish me luck!

———

ACTION STEP: I would like you to join me by writing down 10 things that are outside your comfort zone. Exercise your courage muscle. Let me be clear on "seriously petrified"; a few things on my list are emails to people with whom I would love to do business but I don't have an existing relationship. "Seriously petrified" does not have to mean bungy-jumping.

Lessons from a Puppy

—⚊⚊—

In 2016 we said yes to a puppy, which made our new addition the second dog in the house. Some thought I was crazy, but I now think maybe I was brilliant. Accidentally brilliant, but brilliant nonetheless. LOL, let me explain.

I am not certain why we said yes, but we did. I could not and did not foresee what was to come. Well, the obvious, yes, but not everything. What I did not account for was all the joy. Puppies make everyone happy—seriously everyone. Not only was my whole house deliriously happy, so was everyone who stopped by to visit our new addition. Puppies are little happiness-makers. Our house was really, really happy!

Now, before I get lambasted by all of you about how much work puppies are, and they are a lot of work, I want to be clear. I am not recommending everyone get a puppy (although they are very cute). My revelation was about playing it safe. I could have played it safe, stayed content with one six-year-old dog. Simple. Easy. Zero risk. But I jumped in with both feet (again, here is where crazy crossed brilliant).

It was risk versus reward. Where are you playing it safe in your own life? When was the last big risk you took? Look, I will tell you the same thing I told everyone when they said I was crazy for getting a puppy, "It's not a tattoo." Almost nothing in life is permanent. Today, take a risk! Think about all the joy you might be missing out on. I am really glad I did.

———

ACTION STEP: Journal for five or so minutes on how you could proactively add more joy to your life. A puppy may not hit the top-ten, but let your mind be free to write puppy if you want. You are only writing. No one is going to hold your feet to the fire because you wrote it in this journal. Really let your mind go wherever it wants. We rarely allow that kind of thinking. Today, allow it. Liberate the mind from being practical, realistic, and sensible.

Are You a Fern Living in the Desert?

—∿—

My husband and I were going for a walk on Saturday when he made an off-the-cuff comment, "The ferns in the back of the house look amazing!" He was absolutely right, they really looked spectacular.

Here is the deal with ferns or any other plant, they thrive under certain conditions and they wither and fail under others. What is good for the fern is not so good for the cactus. We might be able to keep a cactus alive in New Jersey, but if we planted it in the desert, that is when we would see the real growth. The ferns are flourishing and succeeding at my home because they are living under the ideal conditions that are natural and authentic to them; they are in the shade, with some sun, moist soil, and plenty of humidity.

The same is true for you and me. Are you a cactus trying to live in the shade? Are you a fern trying to make a go of it in the desert? Our blueprint for what we are supposed to be doing in this life is just as important as the ideal growing conditions for the fern and the cactus. Are you thriving? Are people commenting about how happy you look? If not, you may be a fern who is planted in the wrong environment. It might be time to move to the shade. Flourishing will not be possible otherwise.

———

ACTION STEP: Ask yourself if you are planted in ideal conditions. Are you thriving and flourishing? If the answer to this question is no, then it is time for a change. Spend a few minutes writing about the ideal conditions under which you *would* flourish.

P.S. Please remember: There is nothing wrong with the *fern*. The *fern* is not faulty or broken, it's just not planted in the right spot where *ferns* flourish.

"Everything Is Either Love or a Call for Love"

—⚭—

I read this quote in *A Course In Miracles,* and it changed my life. I am still not great at remembering it 100% of the time, but even if I remember it 10% of the time, it will have an enormous impact on my life as well as those around me. Let me explain.

The "love" part you get, I am sure, as it pertains to those closest to you. But this quote applies equally to complete strangers. Do not lose the meaning of this quote because of the word "love." We can substitute the word "love" with words like kindness, caring, and compassion and still get the same result.

"A call for love," is the other half of everything we experience which is not love, and this happens at home, work, and the grocery store as well. Maybe it is our spouse barking at us before heading to work, or our teenagers rolling their eyes and stomping up the stairs to their room, or the Starbucks barista ruining our morning with her sassy retort. All of these are "calls for love" although they certainly don't look like it at first glance.

"A call for love" gives us all the opportunity to look at everything differently. Maybe our spouse is stressed at work? Teenagers nowadays, for sure, are more stressed than ever before. As for the barista, we might never know her personal backstory; but if her life was blissful, I am sure she would have treated us more kindly. If we change the way we look at these unpleasant situations and say to ourselves, "this is just a call for love," then *we* can change *our* reaction, or at least our understanding of what just happened.

"Kindness is the oil that takes the friction out of life."

—UNKNOWN.

"A call for love" is just someone letting us know he or she needs a little "oil."

———————

ACTION STEP: "Everything is either love or a call for love" is a quote worth writing down. Perhaps even commit it to memory. Then go out in the world and apply it. Who in your life right now is calling for love? Go love them!!

Stop "Networking"!

—ɷ—

I hear people use this word networking all the time and every time I hear it, it makes my skin crawl. The word itself sounds so sterile to me and the concept can be so self-centered.

When I think of networking, I think of speed dating: sprinting from person to person, quickly assessing whether or not they are of value, and then moving on to the next potential candidate. The concept, by definition, is very self-serving, myopic, and has the potential to lack integrity if we use someone for our own benefit. But it does not have to be this way, nor should it.

If I could change the name, that would be a good start. Networking should be relationship building. It is much like the give and receive flow of energy found in the continuous ebb and flow of the tide. We could be developing relationships all the time, not just when we are looking for a job. Get the, "Who can I benefit from now," out of our mind and adopt, "Who is a role model in my field?" "Who would I like to get to know better?" Actively create synergy. When we are done looking forward, we should look back as well and ask, "Is there anyone who could benefit from speaking with me?" Perhaps we could invite them to lunch.

Do not get me wrong, I love relationship-building. It is just the negative word association I have with networking that triggers this personal pet peeve. There will always be networkers and networking, for whatever reason, has a bit of a slimy feel for me. Comparatively, an attention to relationship-building will often leave both parties very glad they met and truly connected.

———

ACTION STEP: How can you build more and better relationships? Who can you reach out to? Relationship building should be on your calendar as a weekly task. Being well connected is a result of proactively connecting. If done properly, it should be a win-win for both of you.

Don't Sweat the (Small) Stuff

—∭—

Stop thinking you are the only one with *stuff*. You look at other people and you believe they have it all together, and then there is you. You are wrong. Everyone has stuff. The pretty girl has stuff, the rich girl has stuff and the smart girl has stuff. We all have stuff and most of it is not pretty!

We are all hurting in some way. Everyone. Most of us cover it up, but make no mistake about it, it is there. And the one you really believe has it all going on, you know the one because it is the one you most want to be like, is often the one that is hurting the most.

Be compassionate and be kind, to yourself and to others. But most importantly, stop thinking you are the only one with *stuff*.

———

ACTION STEP: Today's journaling is going to be done with a light heart. Write down the names of all of the people you have described as having a charmed or easy life. After you have them all written down, I want you to write in all capital letters, 'THEY HAVE STUFF TOO!'

I Am Calling Your Bluff

—m—

"The only thing standing between you and your goal is the story you keep telling yourself as to why you can't achieve it." —JORDAN BELFORT

We stand firmly behind our stories, probably because we have told them to ourselves and others so many times. Today, I want to revisit one of our stories and I want to challenge its premise by disputing and discrediting the grounds on which it stands. Here are some examples of how our stories usually begin:

1. I can't leave my job because . . .
2. I can't change careers because . . .
3. I can't start my own business because . . .
4. I can't pursue my dream because . . .
5. Not now, but maybe when . . .

If you are about to say either, "But you don't understand" or "It's complicated," I hear you, but all I am asking us to do today is to come up with some objections to our story. We are literally just *thinking* and if we want to get outrageous, we can *write down* our thoughts.

What if our story is not totally true? Can we be totally open to the possibility that maybe, just maybe, it is fear that is holding us back? Fear is here to protect us, but we don't need protection today. We are not taking any action steps, we are just thinking. Thinking is 100% safe. I promise. We are completely safe to think. Be brave.

ACTION STEP: Today, I want you to dispute your own story by following the format below.

1. Write out your (potentially false) story: For example, "I cannot . . ."
2. Dispute the story: This story is not totally true because . . .

Are You a Ford–Built Tough?

—⟋⟍—

"You never know how strong you are until being strong is
your only choice."   —BOB MARLEY

Perhaps your response after reading this quote was much like mine:
"Isn't that the truth." So what doesn't kill us makes us stronger? Good
to know after the fact; we can proudly say how strong we were, but during it was rough, really rough.

I don't know anyone who loves rough patches. Getting assigned that
mountain certainly was not our choice, but we, without much choice,
climbed it, overcame it, or moved it. The beautiful part is that studies
show these negative events in our life result in us having better mental
health, prosperity, less anguish, and greater life satisfaction for having
overcome them. I believe difficulties are meant to arouse the human
spirit to grow; they were never meant to discourage us.

Ernest Hemingway proclaimed: "The world breaks everyone and after-
ward many are strong in the broken places." I believe that; I know I am.
How about you? Are you stronger in those broken places? Today, let's
look at our broken places with pride. We were strong beyond our com-
prehension and that's pretty darn impressive!

ACTION STEP: Today is a day to celebrate your strength and courage.
Pat yourself on the back. Take yourself out to lunch. Take a bubble
bath. Whatever you choose, please make sure you take the time to celebrate you. We rarely do.

I Can't

—✦—

I love words, mainly because for every word we use, there is often a better word. For instance, let's take the word *can't*. I use *can't* a lot. "I can't make the meeting," "I can't talk on the phone right now," and "I can't commit." The truth is, I am unintentionally lying because *can't* implies that I lack the ability. I certainly do not lack the ability to talk on the phone. Few, if any, do.

A better word to use is *won't*. *Won't* is a choice and it forces us to take ownership for our decisions, which can be difficult and scary. *Can't* lets us off the hook because we can then make failure not our fault. "I can't quit my job." "I can't lose the weight." "I can't start my own business." "I can't talk to my boss."

Today, we need to think of all the places we use the word *can't* and take a much closer look. Is it really an "I can't" or is it more likely an "I won't"? "I can't" keeps us safely in our comfort zone and lets us off the hook. "I won't" is a really firm decision. Choose wisely.

———

ACTION STEP: Today is an awareness day. How many times do you say "I can't"? How many times do you hear "I can't" from others? Practice saying, "I won't" so you can feel the difference. I won't switch jobs. I won't lose the weight. I won't ask my boss.

"Shoot the Puck!"

—⚏—

Yesterday, I walked into the family room to talk to Doug, who was watching an ice hockey game. Detroit vs. Minnesota. I am not a fan of either team but I love hockey. After I sat down to watch the game, I saw three unbelievable goals. One came from an incomprehensible angle. Another was shot from the point with just a small opening in the upper left hand corner. And the last one was really a fluke, ricocheting off the goalie's glove.

As I sat there in my family room watching the game, I kept thinking, "Yes, take the shot! You never know what will happen. It will never go in if all you do is skate around the ice with the puck. You have to take the shot!" And yes, Wayne Gretzky's quote is still classic; "You miss 100% of the shots you never take."

How does this apply to us? Where in our life are we skating around with the puck? If you have ever watched ice hockey and seen someone do this, it is infuriating and some fan will invariably scream, "Shoot the puck!!!" So today, I am going to yell it out for all of us: "SHOOT THE PUCK!" Dreams, wishes, goals, intentions, etc. are all futile without action. Remember, no one wants the skater to explain **why** he isn't shooting the puck. We all just want him to shoot it.

Here is a great quote to add to today's topic from Zig Ziglar: "You don't have to be great to start, but you have to start to be great."

———

ACTION STEP: Somewhere in your life, you are skating around the ice and you are definitely **not** shooting the puck. Journal about why you are just skating around and spend a few more minutes journaling about shooting the puck.

The Cruel Daily Ritual

—m—

Have you ever had a negative thought about yourself? Insert multiple laughing emojis here! Seriously, who has not? Some of us are more self-deprecating than others, but we all do it. So, how do we stop this cruel daily ritual?

I have a simple trick and it is *not* to flood your mind with equal but opposite positive thoughts. I cannot speak for you, but that rarely works for me. My internal roommate is wickedly smart and sees right through that hogwash, which ultimately increases the intensity of my negative thoughts. So, here is my trick: interrogate the negative thought.

What does that mean? Assume your negative thought is, "I'm never going to get out of this financial hole." Start asking yourself questions like, "Is that really true? When have I overcome something similar before? How can I get out of this situation? What would the plan look like?"

A negative thought plays on and on, like a broken record; it is up to us to pick up the needle so that we do not listen to the same thing over and over again. Start reframing immediately: "I am very proud of how conscious I have been recently with all decisions related to money." Now that is a much more believable statement, as well as kind-hearted.

———

ACTION STEP: Today, if you find yourself listening to negative banter within your own mind, start to interrogate. Question the truth of these cruel statements. Stand up for yourself. If you are like me, there will not be a lack of practice time today or any other day. But things change when you do not accept those unkind thoughts as the truth.

The Candy Man Can

—∞—

Growing up, I lived across the street from a girl named Candy. She was a few years older than I was and she was a child with Down syndrome. Her father, Wayne, and my father were best friends.

Candy adored my dad and my dad adored Candy. When she would see him across the street she would start yelling, "Harry! Harry!" My dad would immediately yell back, "Hello Candy! How's my girlfriend?" She would run across the street and give him a big hug and they would begin a lengthy, laughter-filled conversation during which my dad gave her his undivided attention. Always.

Looking back, I always loved watching Candy and my dad. They had a genuine love for each other. I do not know if my dad knew I was taking it all in. I doubt he even knew I was watching.

Looking through a different lens gives you a very different perspective. My dad was a really intense, serious, and tough man, but not when he was with Candy. He softened instantly when he saw her. This reminds me that kindness and compassion when witnessed can have a profound impact. What we do, especially as parents, is far more important than what we say.

Do more. Say less.

———

ACTION STEP: If you are in any role in which others are looking up to you, journal for a few minutes on what others see when they watch you. Some ideas to consider are work ethic, honesty, composure, stress and deadlines, transparency, and integrity.

Fly! Be Free!

—◊—

"The first step toward success is taken when you refuse to be captive to the environment you find yourself in."

—MARK CAINE

It is certainly not fun to be stuck. We all have been there. We get stuck in unhealthy relationships, dead-end jobs, toxic friendships, and life in general. At some point along the way, we forget we can make a move. We are not captive, even though it really feels like we are sometimes. We are a bird in a cage with the door wide open.

If the door is wide open, why do we stay in the cage? We stay because of fear and, therefore, we accept our situation. But what if today, we accepted instead, Caine's words and "refuse to be captive"? Our wings are not clipped and we should stop protecting ourselves from the many possibilities of joy and success right outside the cage. Fly! Be free!

ACTION STEP: Is there any place in your life you feel stuck? Journal for 5 minutes on your newfound knowledge that the door to the cage is open. What move will you make next to get out?

If You Are Here, You Might as Well Be Happy

—⫘—

Here is an interesting fact based on research completed by two economists, Professor Andrew Oswald from the University of Warwick and Professor David Blanchflower from Dartmouth College, who wanted to measure well-being in terms of happiness:

1. Happiness tends to decline from age 30–50.
2. The peak of <u>un</u>happiness resides at the age of 46.
3. Happiness is on the uptick after 50, leveling off at 70.

I am not sharing this information to bring you down, especially if you are forty-six years old! I share it because we know that the majority of our happiness is within our control. The more aware we are of both our happiness level and the control we have over our happiness, the more we can do to change it.

I know there will be some who will say, "But you don't know my circumstances; mine are different." I will only add this, you are correct. I do not know your circumstances, but you are always in control of your own happiness. Always. It is your choice. My feeling is, if you are here, you might as well be happy.

———

ACTION STEP: It is always a good day to revisit our happiness level. On a scale of 1–10, where would you put yourself? Now that you have your *happiness quotient,* journal about what is keeping you from being a perfect 10 and what changes can you make to raise your score?

Your One Thing

—ɯ—

This weekend I hosted my *Finding Your Purpose* workshop. It was a labor of love that was a year in the making. When I sat down with my partners a few weeks prior to the event, I brought to the table enough exercises to host a week-long event. We quickly eliminated most of them, but there was one exercise I really loved.

Although it hit the cutting room floor for the workshop, I can still share my favorite exercise with you. Can you answer this question: What is your one thing? When friends, family, or colleagues call you, what kind of help are they looking for? You will do yourself a disservice if you try to answer this question in your head. Put a pen to paper. List calls you have received and what they wanted from you. Dig deep. When you hang out with friends, what role do you play? Again, write it down and dig deep, the answer often is not right on the surface.

Email this question to your friends and family and ask them to answer, "What is my one thing?" The answers are often very telling and point to your purpose. Sometimes, we are too close to ourselves to identify our one thing. Your answer may likely not be as tangible as you will want it to be. The painters of this world already know their one thing, but maybe you are a natural leader or coach. Maybe you are the fixer or the compassionate listener. The answer is right there, you just haven't put your finger on it yet, but when you do, you will see how obvious it was all along.

———

ACTION STEP: We will definitely be journaling on this one!

What is your one thing?

When friends, family, or colleagues call you, what kind of help are they looking for?

When you hang out with friends, what role do you play?

Now, select five people you will commit to emailing. The email is as simple as:

I am reading *The Wake Up Call* by Beth Fitzgerald and the task I have been challenged with today is to ask five people what my one thing is. You are someone I respect, so I chose you as one of my five. When you think of me, what is the one thing that I am really good at a doing? The answer does not have to be tangible like math, it could be intangible like listening. What comes to mind first?

Pick Up the Phone

—∽—

Text or call? Which is your go-to? Most of us would likely say text because it's faster, but what if I told you the human voice is an incredible medicine of sorts?

In a recent study at The University of Madison, they had subjects take a stressful exam. After the exam, they allowed each subject to contact their mom—half checked in via text and the other half via the phone. Blood samples which were drawn before and after revealed a surprising difference: The students who had heard their mothers' voices showed far lower levels of stress hormones, & higher levels of calming oxytocin. The students who had only texted their moms showed no change in their blood chemistry. Moreover, talking to their mothers activated the same parts of the brain that hugging them did.

All of this suggests that we should be recognizing how powerful the human voice is of someone we love. Unfortunately, we're moving away from communicating this way. Studies show people are 4x as likely to email or text someone than to call. So pick up the phone & *call* someone you love—your voice is the elixir they need.

————

ACTION STEP: Today's task is simple, pick up the phone and call someone you love. Your voice will likely be exactly what they need. I no longer have the luxury of calling my mother, so please do not take for granted this simple phone call. It's truly priceless.

More Lessons from the Puppy

—⚊—

In September of 2016 we were coerced into purchasing a new puppy by our children. I thought I had weighed the pros and cons of adding a second dog to the household, but I had no idea how many things this puppy was going to teach me. As I learned each one, I would run to Doug with what I believed to be my big revelation and he would invariably say, "I know, right? I was thinking the same thing!"

There is no surprise, puppies need to go out a lot. Like every hour. Getting a puppy in September has its perks because the weather is beautiful, but there are also rainy days, too. As I continued to go outside repeatedly with the puppy, I realized what a positive effect it was having on me. I am definitely happier and I noticed that I slowed down. My pace in life (and maybe yours, too), is way too fast. When we are outside, the puppy looks at me as if to say, "What is your rush? We are having fun. Relax. Stay a while."

So I took her advice. I started soaking up nature. The mornings are cold, but so refreshing. The nights are dark, but so peaceful. The sunny days are fabulous and I, like her, do not want to come back in. And then there is the rain, as long as it is not a deluge, this too has had its therapeutic effect. I am forced to go outside many times a day now and I am encouraging you to do it more often as well. Studies show getting outside daily will improve our health. And just once, when it rains, grab an umbrella and go outside. It's truly awesome.

———

ACTION STEP: Get outside—at least once a day. If you do not have a pet, pretend you do. Pick a time and stick to it as if the pet (fake or real) depended on it!

Preserving Someone Else's Dignity

—◊—

Some people have a gift. They are naturally good with other people. This gift does not necessarily fall under the category of being friendly or outgoing. This gift is the ability to allow others to preserve their own dignity by not proving them wrong.

Most people, myself included, will point out another's error, regardless of how important it is to do so. We do so to prove we know the right answer, which ironically puffs out our feathers but manages to deflate the person with whom we are speaking. Unfortunately, our win can come at too big a cost and is often unnecessary.

My husband, Doug, is the master of this gift. It may be the primary reason we have been married for over 26 years. I have watched him with me and others; he has the right answer, but says nothing. He preserves the other person's dignity. It's amazing to watch. He does it flawlessly, but I am just learning. This gift requires a quiet self-confidence to be able to say nothing. For me, it is essential that I ask myself a question before I open my big mouth: "Is being right that important?" Almost always, the answer is no. Thank you Doug! XO

ACTION STEP: Today's task is simple; fully absorb a deep and powerful quote from *A Course In Miracles*. "Do you prefer to be right or happy?"

Big Risk; Big Reward

—ᗰ—

I cannot think of a better motivational story than to share a tale of an amazing woman who followed her calling, stuck her neck out, took risks, faced her fears, and came out on top! If this story does not motivate you, then nothing will.

Welcome to the story of Kerri who happens to be one of my dearest and best friends. Kerri surprised all of us this past year when she started to paint. Apparently, she used to paint a long time ago, but none of us knew of her latent talent. Out of the blue, I was gifted with the prettiest painting of pink peonies which happen to be my favorite flower. Our friend Terry was also given a fabulous painting of daisies and sunflowers. Without hesitation, both Terry and I implored Kerri to sell her work, assuring her of her giftedness as a painter.

The next step is always the biggest and the scariest; putting ourselves out there for all to see. I am sure Kerri had thoughts like, "What if no one likes my work?" Doubt and fear usually stop most people. Forging through those two daunting obstacles is no easy task, but Kerri mustered up the strength and belief in herself and her talent to do so. At a street fair in Hopewell, NJ, Kerri hosted her first art show *and* she sold some of her fabulous artwork! Affirmation is a wonderful thing but it rarely comes without stepping outside our comfort zone. Kerri, is an inspiration to us all! Big risk, big reward.

Kerri conquered both doubt and fear and so can you. What have you been afraid to do? You can be brave. You can go for it. Kerri is proof it is worth taking the risk.

———

ACTION STEP: If Kerri can do it, so can you! What is your "it"? Is it painting? Is it writing a book? Spend the next few minutes journaling. Here is your prompt:

If I was as brave as Kerri, I would . . .

I'm in a Funk

—✺—

Have you ever been in a funk? I think I am! I'm not in a *curled up on my sofa in a bathrobe eating ice cream out of the container and watching soap operas* kind of funk, but it's definitely a funk.

I realized last night that almost every night here is the same; dinner-tv-bed. Rinse and repeat. Ugh! I'm not sure if its autopilot or hypnosis but it's not good. Autopilot is almost never good. It's time to shake things up! Did you know that on a daily basis we repeat 75–92% of what we did yesterday? That is not good.

So I need to shake things up—what about you? Tonight, I'm adding the gym before dinner. Maybe we will play Scrabble instead of watching the dumb TV. Or maybe we will head outside to our firepit! Winter and darkness are on their way and it's really easy to get sucked into a routine. I'm encouraging you to fight it tooth and nail—your brain will thank you.

———

ACTION STEP: Write about all the ways you can either get out of a funk or, better yet, avoid getting into one to begin with. Routines can be both good and bad.

It's the Little Things That Matter

—∞—

"Champions don't become champions in the ring—they are
merely recognized there."   —JOHN MAXWELL

We will lose the relevance of this quote if we only relate it to champions or sports. The "champion" can be a boss, a friend, a mom, a dad, a leader, a coach or any other person.

A champion of any kind becomes so because of his or her daily routine. So, whether it is a fight plan or a life plan, it will come down to what we have done every day that matters. Did we cheat or cut corners? Did we think skipping one day did not matter? Are we on our game only when we are under the bright lights?

Every day matters. If we want to be a champion and the best we can be, then every day matters. Even if we are at a job we do not like, this is the prep work necessary for when we are in the job we do like. There are no dress rehearsals. We are live every day. We must ask ourselves, "Am I pursuing greatness or am I simply putting in my time?" There is a difference, a huge difference. Seek greatness.

———

ACTION STEP: In what aspect of your life would you like to be a champion? Is it as a mom or dad? Is it as a boss or someone else? Pick the place where you would like to be the best and journal about what improvements you could make to be the best. There is always room for improvement, isn't there?

A Lesson from the Ritz

—꘠—

Doug and I recently visited Washington, DC for the weekend and we spent a lot of time walking around the city. The Ritz-Carlton was across the street from our hotel. Every time we passed by it, I noticed an ad in the window on the second floor which read, "Commit To Something."

The ad begs the question, "To what am I committed?" Instead of looking at this "something" as a job or some humanitarian effort, which has such a long-term view, can we look at it more personally? Let's think short term. What can we accomplish if we commit to something for 1–3 months? Do you have something in mind?

I started my commitment to writing/editing this book in June 2017. Over the months, I kept setting new deadlines for various parts of the book. I failed to meet almost every deadline, but I kept my eye on the target. Had I not committed, this would have never happened. Commit to something you really want and chip away at it. You will not regret this decision. Committing means you are 100% in, no less. You can do this!

———

ACTION STEP: Spend 5 minutes journaling about commitment. Is there something you would like to commit to? The word commitment is scary, but only if we think of it in the long term. Think short term. Here are some ideas:

- Show up to work on time or early
- Start a vacation fund with weekly deposits
- Pick one day a week to go to the gym or do yoga
- Volunteer once a month
- Update your resume and LinkedIn profile

The Sky's the Limit . . . Or Is It?

—∞—

"The sky has never been the limit. We are our own limits. It's then about breaking our personal limits and outgrowing ourselves to live our best life."　　　　—UNKNOWN

I spoke at Princeton University recently and I shared the fleas in the jar experiment—perhaps you have heard it. Fleas are put in a jar and they immediately jump out. If a lid is placed on the jar, they jump up and hit the lid for a while but then condition themselves to jump just below the lid to avoid hitting it. Later, when the lid is removed, surprisingly the fleas never jump out. They have accepted their limitations. Furthermore, when they have offspring, the baby fleas only jump as high as the parents; they too never jump out of the jar.

At some point, all of us have had a "lid" placed on us. Maybe it was by a teacher, a coach, a boss, or even a parent. But today, I want you to know: THERE IS NO LID! Jump for goodness sake, JUMP! Those limits that we believed in are about as untrue as when we used to believe the world was flat! We need to start jumping, not only for ourselves but for our children; they need to see us jump so they know for sure—THERE IS NO LID!

———

ACTION STEP: For this action it will require two steps. Step one is to write about the lid. What thoughts or beliefs are holding you down? Step two is to now write about the truth of you, your ability, and your potential without the lid. There is no limit for you! JUMP!

The Pressure Cooker

—∿—

What is your guilty pleasure? And what is keeping you from indulging in it more?

Life is stressful, we all agree. But on top of the stress, many of us feel guilty indulging in that thing that actually lets the steam out from the top of the pressure cooker. Why? Why are we so hard on ourselves?

Today I am giving all of us permission to release some steam. Carve out time specifically for this special treat. For some of us, it will be quiet time with a book. For others, it will be the gym. And for some, it will be coffee and a donut. No judgement here. It is time to release stress, not add more. Finally, this guilty pleasure is just for us and us alone. Family time is something altogether different, that is not what this is.

So what is your guilty pleasure? Will you take 20 minutes today (and every day) to indulge yourself? It is going to require that you carve out the time (challenge #1), as well as engage in this pleasure without feeling one bit guilty (challenge #2), because you know it is relieving stress. No one can continue to run on empty. Let's have some fun.

P.S. We **all** should be engaging in some form of stress-relief regularly.

———

ACTION STEP: You need to identify what your indulgence is so you can engage in it daily as a stress-reducer. My twenty-minute-pleasure is reading. I will sit down and read for twenty minutes almost every day. When I am finished, I feel like I have done at least one thing for me today and that feels good!

Rose Colored Glasses

—⟋⟍—

I looked at the world through rose-colored glasses today.

Seriously, I am being literal. I was headed out the door this morning and I grabbed an old pair of sunglasses for the ride because I couldn't find mine. As I was driving, I marveled at the fall foliage; it was spectacular. After about fifteen minutes in the car, I could not comprehend the beauty any longer. I pulled the sunglasses off to see if they were making a difference and, sure enough, they were making all the fall colors pop! I laughed out loud and put the glasses right back on my face to enjoy the beauty.

When I picked up my daughter, Katie, I told her about the "magical sunglasses" and we shared them, back and forth, all the way home from school. We were giggling about how different the world looked with these sunglasses. The experience really gave me pause. Can we put on our own "rose-colored glasses" and see the world through a different lens? Yes, I believe we can and I literally did so today.

Even though I knew the world did not really look as beautiful as my polarized lenses had made it seem, it really made my day significantly more pleasant! What can we look at differently? Is it the story we tell ourselves that determines whether or not we have a pair of magical sunglasses? Today, put on the "glasses" and look right at the story in your life, you know the story that is causing you so much angst, and see it differently, if only for one day.

———

ACTION STEP: Spend 5 minutes writing about this story in your life, but today, try to look at it through a rose-colored lense. Use the prompt: "How can I see this differently?"

Love. Just Love

—⟋ꟷ—

October 23, 2017.

I will never forget that painfully sad day at our house. Within hours, we learned of three deaths. One of the deaths was a magnificent 18-year-old boy who was my daughter's friend. He had been missing for over a month.

Until something jarring like this happens, I can tend to lose sight of what is important. Hearing all of this sad news, I stopped to think about what does and does not matter. I thought of grudges I was holding, which now seem so petty. I thought of things I argued about, that now seem insignificant. Then I thought of all those people in my life who I love and wondered if they really know how very much I love them.

The following day was my 25th wedding anniversary and to say it gave me pause is an understatement. It is easy to love the lovable. This world needs more love—a lot more love. What would happen if we each purposefully attempted to raise the level of love? A great question to ask ourselves is, "In my attempt to add love to this world, does *this* really matter?" This approach is especially important with our children.

———————

ACTION STEP: The world needs more love! "Does this really matter?" is a question we might want to keep close by and visible. Every day each one of us is a giver and a receiver of many kinds of love. Make sure at the end of each day the math works out that you are a net-giver.

Beyond One's Wildest Dreams

—⟋⟍—

As a coach, I talk to people about their dreams and aspirations. Most times, I have to dig deep to help them reconnect to their dream. People dismiss their dreams for a multitude of reasons and then I come in, feverishly and desperately, trying to establish a stronger signal, because I know if I can make the signal strong enough, they will re-establish the connection.

Why do I care so much about reconnecting people to their dreams? We were built for our dreams. Everything about us is perfectly designed for us to excel at this dream in order to make it a reality. Only we think we need more (more money, more experience, more whatever). Our giftedness was preset from the "manufacturer" (God), so it is only we who believe there are missing parts. Here is the most important truth to note: the gift empowers us, we do not empower the gift. That thought is a bit deep, you might need to chew on it for a while. I know I did.

Here's to developing a strong connection to our dream! How many "bars" do you have?

———

ACTION STEP: Get ready to put pen to paper and challenge your comfort zone (all of the italicised words might make you uncomfortable). Spend 5 minutes journaling on your dream. You know the one. Here are your prompts:

I was *built* for this dream—

I am *perfectly* designed to *excel* at this dream—

I *do not need more* of anything to get started -

This *gift* empowers me—

The Game Changer

—ഝ—

I used to hate going to the gym. When I started going to the gym with Doug, I had an accountability partner. We made each other go and we encouraged each other to do better workouts. That was not happening for me when I chose to do my workouts at home, alone. An accountability partner changes everything. As a coach, that is essentially what I do for a living; I hold people accountable for achieving the positive changes they want in their life.

What changes do you want in *your* life? Who is holding you accountable? I assure you, an accountability partner is a game-changer, but choose wisely. This person needs to be tough and challenge you. He or she needs to be someone you can trust as well as someone who is available to you.

For my work, I have an accountability partner, too. Her name is Susan and in one accountability meeting, everything changed. I told Susan I wanted to create a *Finding Your Purpose* one-day workshop. She told me I needed to pick a date and book the venue. What? I had not even started to craft the workshop yet. She said, "You won't do it until you pick a date and book the venue." I went home and, with as much trepidation as is humanly possible, I called the Nassau Club in Princeton and booked October 8, 2016. And the rest, as they say, is history.

I do not know what you want in your life, but it might be time to choose an accountability partner. If you are brave enough to do that, then you know you are finally ready to get this thing done.

———

ACTION STEP: There are a few easy steps to hiring an accountability partner.

STEP 1: Answer the question, "What do I really want to get done

STEP 2: Think: "Who would I like to have as my accountability partner?"

Call/email them now.

STEP 3: Pick one day a week for your recap and stick to it. Pick a format to follow so this call is no more than 20 minutes. My call with my accountability partner includes:

- Sharing a win from the previous week and setting actions steps for the upcoming week
- My three month goal is broken down into three categories (minimum. target, and outrageous) so I am able to succeed as long as I can hit the minimum, but outrageous is still a possibility
- My longer term goal (more than 6 months) is broken down into the same three categories
- My actions steps for the coming week are outlined toward those three month and longer goals.

P.S. Susan and I have been accountability partners for about 3 years now, and we talk every Monday morning at 8 am.

Can We Talk?

—∞—

Today is Doug and my wedding anniversary! Every year we recap by discussing what went right, what went wrong, and how we can improve. This year I asked him an additional question: "What three words would you use to describe why our marriage works?"

The first word he said was "communication." I had been thinking of the same word. Not only in marriage, but in life, how often do we fail to communicate? Sometimes we are afraid to share our truth. Sometimes we assume the other person knows what we are thinking or what the right thing to do is. And, as a result, we let things fester. Festering is never good.

Festering is when our emotions continue to eat away at us. Festering is the body begging us to communicate. Have you ever been so mad/sad/frustrated and finally decide to speak your mind, only to find out it could have been resolved a long time ago had you just spoken up sooner? Yes, me too.

Today is the day we no longer let that thing fester. Today is the day we find the right words to speak our truth. How long has this thing festered? Too long? The only one it is eating away at is us. Let us liberate ourselves from this thing once and for all. We can do it. But remember, we get more flies with honey than we do with vinegar.

Speaking our truth does not mean we have to bite someone's head off. A great conversation starter could be, "Do you have a moment?" That first line is never easy, but if we can get that far, I am certain, the freedom that follows will be well worth it.

———

ACTION STEP: Today, spend a few minutes thinking about what has been festering within you. Who are you mad/sad/frustrated/angry with? Freedom from this festering is within reach. Can you muster up the courage to say, "Do you have a moment?"

Are You a Catalyst?

—⚹—

Last night, on his way to Trenton for a board meeting, my husband's car was hit from behind by a young boy who clearly was not paying attention. Our bumper (and Doug's neck) indicated this inexperienced driver was traveling at a decent speed when the impact occurred.

When I arrived at the scene of the accident to see if Doug was ok, he had already been treated and released by the EMT (Emergency Medical Technicians) that had arrived. To be safe, we decided I would follow Doug home, but he announced he would have to stop for gas first.

When I pulled into the gas station, Doug was already out of his car, assessing the damage under the bright lights of the gas station. He opened the trunk but, after doing so, realized he could not close it. This was certainly not what we needed at this point. The gas station attendant was trying, unsuccessfully, to help with our dilemma, when a truck hauling gasoline pulled in. When the truck driver saw us he instantly jumped into "fix it" mode. He found a bungee cord in his truck. Quickly he assessed the situation, climbed **under** our car to attach the cord, then jumped back up and returned to his truck. Doug and I were so grateful for his help. Doug ran over to hand him some cash as a thank you; of course he refused, but Doug insisted.

This stranger is a catalyst. He incites change. He is a "doer," as I like to call people like him. He is not afraid to jump in, get involved, mix it up. He is a guy I would want on my team. He is not too busy, and he never says, "It's not my problem."

Are you a catalyst or a bystander? The world certainly does not need any more bystanders. Being a catalyst is a muscle that we all have and we all can exercise. Today, get involved. This may simply mean engaging with the world of strangers out there. We have to stop looking at the ground; we need to pick up our head, make eye contact, and actively engage. Bystanders fill up the world, catalysts make it better.

———————

ACTION STEP: There are only two journaling prompts for today.

Am I a catalyst or a bystander?

How can I become a better catalyst?

Take the Shot, for Crying Out Loud!

—◁ɷ▷—

Kobe Bryant's basketball shooting percentage is 45%. Stef Curry's is 46%. And the all-time-great, Michael Jordan's was 50%. Baseball future hall-of-famer, Miguel Cabrera, has a batting average of .333. Babe Ruth had a lifetime average of .342. Why am I telling you this?

When we think of some of the greatest athletes of all times, we might not think about how often they failed. Michael Jordan was only successful 50% of the time, while Babe Ruth failed to get a hit two-thirds of the time. Trying and failing was part of their success. Wayne Gretzky said it best, "You miss 100 percent of the shots you never take." By the way, in Gretzky's **best** year, his shooting percentage was 26.9%!

I am not suggesting that we shoot for a 50% success rate at work because we would likely get fired (unless we were a weatherman). What I am asking is, "Where, in our life, are we playing it safe? Where are we *passing the ball* when we should be shooting?" No one is asking us to take the 3-point shot, just a lay-up. Take the lay-up! What if it actually goes in?

"No one has ever achieved greatness by playing it safe."

—HARRY GRAY

ACTION STEP: The greatest of all athletes took risks and failed in front of thousands of people. Their greatness is in direct relation to the risks they were willing to take. Can you agree to take a risk? Today, journal about one risk you are willing to take. There is no crowd watching. Just pick one. Now, commit to a date to actually do it. You did not think I was going to forget about the due date, did you?

Do You Want to Know a Neat Little Trick?

Is there anyone in your life you are struggling with? Sometimes it is the ones we are closest with who make us the angriest. Maybe it is not angry, maybe it is frustrated. Maybe it is your spouse or your children. If so, try this . . .

Keep a picture of this person handy (it can be on your phone) that was taken when they were little. It is really difficult to get angry at an adorable little child. This is a picture of me from 1st grade. How angry can you get at her? Not that much, right? Good luck asking your boss for a childhood photo!

ACTION STEP: No journaling today! Today, your task is to get pictures of each of your family members when they were little and put them in a place where they will be easily accessible. Do it today, because on the day you really need this picture, you will be in no mood to ask for it.

My Parenting Advice

—⟋∞⟍—

I sent a baby gift to friends of ours who recently had their first child. In her thank-you note to me the mother said, "We should get together; I'm sure you have lots of great parenting advice to offer." I laughed out loud.

My first thought was, 'You really don't want my parenting advice now. You can't handle it." As a new parent and probably up until recently, I was driven. I wanted the best for my kids, and I was going to make that happen with all of my being. But the words I failed to say to myself were, "At what cost?"

I have four children, the youngest of whom is seventeen years old. Over time, I have evolved as both a person and a parent. All my kids are seeing a new and different mom now. I am using words like relax, have fun, don't take things so seriously, enjoy yourself, you're perfect as is, find your passion, take risks, fail, lighten up, do what makes you happy, slow down, it will all workout, nothing is permanent (except a tattoo), and we love you and will always have your back.

So that is my advice. Finish this sentence with your own words, "Life is short, . . .".

ACTION STEP: Very few of us will ever be asked to give a commencement speech, but with that in mind, what advice would you give to our youth today? Write down your thoughts.

Let's Play Ball

—∽—

> "Progress always involves risk; you can't steal second base
> and keep your foot on first." —ROBERT QUILLAN

If you have ever played softball or baseball (or watched it, for that matter), you know how stealing a base goes. It is a big game of calculated risks. How much of a lead-off of first base can you take without getting picked off? How good is the catcher's arm? How fast are you? All of these risks gets assessed in milliseconds as we linger at first base. Regardless of these answers, the risks of getting picked-off or thrown out always exist, but sometimes you have to take the risk!

Make the catcher throw a strike to second base. Make the shortstop make the tag. Test the waters, see how fast you are. Here is the answer from a former base-stealing softball player (me): There is no greater feeling than taking that risk, sliding into second base, and hearing the umpire yell, "Safe!" There you are, standing on second base perfectly gratified, smiling to your coach and your team as you fully understand the risk-reward relationship.

Look, the truth is I have been thrown out at second, as well. I know that feeling too, but once you have arrived safely at second **once** in your lifetime, you understand that some rewards are well worth the risk! What risk is out there right now that you are not taking? Are your feet planted firmly on first base? Stop playing it safe. Start calculating the risks because I bet you are *faster* than you think!

———

ACTION STEP: Answer just one question . . .

What risk is available to me right now?

A Friendly Reminder

—⚉—

This morning I was swapping out the old pages of my daily planner to make room for the new when I stumbled across a daily routine I clearly stopped doing when the madness of school began in September.

Daily, I wrote down snippets of where joy and abundance were present in my life. It was so much fun reading through all my notes. I wrote things like: Shopping for my sister-in-law's birthday present, walking home under the full moon with Doug, having fun in the pool with all my kids, and trying to catch a toad that brought back amazing memories of being a child at the beach.

I am guessing the start of school distracted me from this daily habit. I am going back to it now. Reading these journal entries reminds me how amazing life is on a daily basis. Ironically, almost none of the things I wrote down required money. That alone speaks volumes! Here's to our abundant lives!

———

ACTION STEP: Think back over the last few days and write down one or two things that illustrate the joy and abundance in your life.

Polar Opposites

—w—

Happy Halloween. Oct 31. Another month gone by. What did you want to accomplish this fall? I am sure you had plans for the fall. Did you get them done?

There is one *big* month left before we head into December when things tend to wind down dramatically as we near year's-end. If you did not accomplish everything you wanted to, why? What is the one thought in your mind that keeps you away from your goals? This thought is like a little prison, keeping you in the exact same place, which results in a cruel form of self-punishment. This thought is likely manifesting itself as doubt or fear or both. I know, I've had the exact same thought.

What is the opposite of that thought? What if the opposite thought is not only possible but probable? What if the opposite thought is the road to success and we are the only one holding us back? What if it has never been finances or education or time? What if it has only been this little nagging, negative, doubting, fearful thought all along? What if we have been sitting in this little prison *and* we have had the key the whole time?

Today, think the opposite thought. This new and positive thought could be the key that unlocks the door to a whole new world of possibilities. Now you know you have the key, but you have to use it! Let's go!

———

ACTION STEP: What was your first thought when I asked you what you had wanted to accomplish this fall?

Was there a second thought that held you back?

If so, write the opposite of that negative thought.

Coach K

—◦◦◦—

Yes, I mean *the* Coach K, Mike Krzyzewski, the head coach of Duke University's men's basketball team for the last thirty-eight years. Feel free to try to pronounce his last name, although it sounds nothing like it looks. Let's stick with Coach K.

In 2015, heading into the NCAA championship, the Duke basketball team was bogged down with injuries and the players were searching for some inspiration. The coaching staff had a plan. Coach brought in one basketball and told the team, "Write on the ball all the names of the people who made it possible for you to be here—people who mean something to you."

All the players and coaches wrote down somewhere between three to eight names. They carried that ball with them for the whole tournament. The public knew nothing of the ball. The players carried it everywhere, some even slept with it. It was a powerful reminder of how many people were responsible for their success.

Duke went on to the NCAA championship and had a huge come-from-behind win against Wisconsin. After winning the championship, the players sent an autographed ball from all the players to each of the people on the ball with a letter explaining what they had done. The note from the team captain said, "Thanks, you were with us every step of the way." Coach K described it as a great lesson in showing gratitude. The recipients were, understandably, amazed by the gesture.

————

ACTION STEP: What names would you have written on the ball? Who are the people who have brought you to where you are today? I believe it is important to know the five most influential people in your life. Is a thank-you note in order? Take it one step further, ask yourself "Would anyone put my name on the ball?"

It's All in Your Approach

—〰—

The other day I was outside working in my garden when I heard a rapper spewing the most inappropriate lyrics from our outside speakers. Instantly, I was both angry and mortified; angry because my children know better than to play that music in front of me and mortified because this offensive language was being broadcasted outside for all my neighbors to hear!

I stormed into the kitchen and immediately conveyed my displeasure. I rebuked their music selection and reminded them of the two young boys living next-door. My daughters apologized instantly; they thought the music was only playing in the house and they changed the song to a much more acceptable one.

I came back outside and ranted to Doug. He quickly responded by saying, "It's all in your approach, Beth." Honestly, I wish he wasn't always the voice of reason! He explained that I could have accomplished the same thing with kindness. Have you ever chosen the wrong approach? Have you ever chosen the hardline when it could have been handled with a softer touch instead of a heavy hand? It's all in your approach. Lesson learned—yet again!

———

ACTION STEP: Spend five minutes today journaling about your approach. Do you, too, often choose a hardline approach when perhaps a softer and kinder version would have achieved the same result?

Calling It a Win

—◊—

I was at a lacrosse showcase this past Sunday at The Episcopal Academy near Villanova University. It was a huge showcase with lots of people and minimal parking. There were a number of people directing traffic, telling us where we could and could not park. The same people directing me as I arrived were the same people directing me as I left. It was a very cold day and it appeared as though they were braving the elements all day long.

Between games I decided to leave to get a hot cup of tea and thaw out a bit. As I was heading toward the exit, I pulled over to drop Liam off with his team. I decided to ask this very surly man guarding the coveted coaches parking lot if it was ok if I stopped to drop Liam off. He was quite the curmudgeon, approximately five feet in height, and about 60+ years old. In a stern voice, he barked, "Yeah, just pull up a bit." He was not happy about allowing me to do so and he let me know it with his look of condemnation.

Liam grabbed his equipment and ran off. As I went to put the car in gear, I thought of how cold this man must be. I put the car back into park, jumped out of the car as cars continued to maneuver around me, and headed toward the old man. As he saw me, I watched his jaw clench, readying himself to right my wrong. Quickly, I said, "Would you like a cup of coffee? I am headed to Wawa." The surly man softened, just a bit. I could only see it around his eyes and jaw. "No thank you," he replied, more softly this time. "It would be my pleasure," I responded, trying to get a yes out of him. He repeated, "No thank you."

Although I was not able to buy this man a cup of hot coffee, I tried. I did not let his brusque manner dissuade me. It was cold and it was the very least I could do. No one will likely remember this guy and, if they do, it will likely not be a pleasant memory. I will remember him. I saw him soften for a split second. I am calling it a win.

ACTION STEP: Who is the curmudgeon in your life? Journal for a few minutes about this person and about how you can try and find a crack his or her facade. Please stay away from any judgement like, "Why bother" or "It's not worth it." I will give you one fabulous sentence that helps me when I am judging another—'You don't know the whole story." That always makes me soften a lot. (We talked about this sentence back in June)

Who Is the Happiest Person You Know?

—𝔪—

Hoda Kotb, the anchor from the Today show, says she does five things every day toward her personal happiness and they are:

1. Write down three things you feel grateful for.
2. Write down something great that happened within the past 24 hours.
3. Exercise a little each day.
4. Meditate for a few minutes each day.
5. Perform a random act of kindness.

I wholeheartedly agree with all five things! I will add that the random act of kindness for me has had a profound effect, but so has the search for the random act. If we have our mind set on finding an act to perform, large or small, our mind is already positioned in a place of kindness.

Do not skip over the first question. Who is the happiest person you know? Tell them. Mirror them. Ask them how and why they are so happy. Happiness is a choice, it is not a gene and it is not luck. It is a choice. Go choose happiness!!

———————

ACTION STEP: Your first task is to answer, "Who is the happiest person you know?" Write down your answer here. _____
Now, look over Hoda's list of five tasks. Focus on numbers one and two. Number five is your task for today, and perhaps every day, if you choose to adopt the Hoda-5. Finally, go back to the name you wrote in the space above, and reach out to them in the manner most comfortable to you, letting them know they are the happiest person you know!

You Are Being Played

—⚬—

"You're being played!" I feel rather confident that no one likes to hear those words, but perhaps it is true. I realized while speaking with a client yesterday, how often we get played both personally as well as professionally via our cell phone and email.

Those two means of communication were created for our convenience, not others. Unfortunately, we have become Pavlov's dogs. (Pavlov was a Russian physiologist who studied classical conditioning by pairing food with a bell for dogs.) The notification rings and not only do we grab our phones to see what just arrived, we generally tend to respond immediately. Yup, sadly, we are the dog!

So do you want to be Pavlov or the dog? I turned off the notification ringer on my cell phone. I don't like being the dog. I want to be Pavlov. I want to answer when it is convenient for me not them. I believe it is fair to say, no one likes to be played, but if you are grabbing your phone every time it buzzes, you, my friend, are being played. You're the dog.

P.S. Additionally, consider how often we look at our phones when we are in the company of other people. Indirectly, we are saying, "Whatever is coming in on my phone right now, I think it may be more exciting than you!"

ACTION STEP: Today, spend 5 minutes deciding if your cell phone and email are ruling you or you are ruling them. Consider challenging yourself by turning off some of your notifications. You can always turn them back on.

"I Saw That."

KARMA

—⚈—

"How people treat you is their karma; how you react is yours."   —WAYNE DYER

I feel like I was beaten over the head with this message this week! And I can tell you exactly why I was failing to learn the lesson. When I get mistreated, I feel justified in returning the favor. Ahh, *justified*—that can often result in doing wrong and feeling moral about it, at least for me.

Most of us have heard the quote, "An eye for an eye will leave the whole world blind." And some would argue that if we fight fire with fire we will get more fire. So *justified,* as I learned this week, is a slippery slope.

I lost a tennis match on Wednesday in a third set tie-break in part, due to an egregiously bad call by my opponent. I had tolerated her other bad calls up until then, but on this one, I let her have it. I felt fully *justified* in berating her. Looks like I need to handle myself better especially when I am *justified!* Ugh, I hate karma. Lesson learned—I hope!

———

ACTION STEP: Today, spend 5 minutes journaling about the word *justified* and what it means to you. Tie in Wayne Dyer's quote as well— "How people treat you is their karma; how you react is yours."

Which Route Will You Take?

—⟋⟍—

I spent 5-hours traveling home yesterday morning from James Madison University. The entire route consists basically of two major highways—Interstate 81 and The Pennsylvania Turnpike. Both of these arteries are heavily traveled by the trucking industry which can make for some rather precarious and sometimes frightening moments!

During my drive, I realized how much this road trip reminded me of life. There were moments when I needed to be courageous in the fast lane as well as times when I needed to be safe in the slow lane. Sometimes I had to remain with the pack and at other times I was free to blaze my own path (so to speak). But perhaps most interesting, was the route itself; had I chosen the safest route by avoiding highways, my route would have taken 8 hours not 5.

What route we decide to take in life really matters. Equally important is the way we navigate the route.

————

ACTION STEP: Here are three really important questions to ask yourself as you travel through life:

Where am I going?

What is the best route I can take?

And constantly ask yourself, "Which lane am I in?"

The slow/safe lane is occasionally the correct lane but it is definitely not the lane to choose for your whole journey. This journey we call life is really worth thinking about. No one should head out on a journey this long without a plan.

The Blank Wall

—⚬—

I saw a picture posted on Instagram by my daughter who is fresh out of college, living on her own in DC, and beginning to decorate her first apartment. When I saw the caption I laughed out loud. "Fear of nailing things into the wall." Really? It's just a wall. There's spackle, paint, strategic picture movement, toothpaste, and, of course, a bigger picture. There are so many solutions—the hole is far from permanent.

It might be helpful if all of us made that picture our screensaver! It could remind us of how scared we are to make a move. And how we let fear keep us from making our lives more beautiful in so many ways. There is nothing gratifying about a blank wall. Yet we leave it blank for fear of a tiny hole that quite frankly is so incredibly easy to fix!

Get out your hammer, folks! We're going to put some holes in the wall. Aren't you tired of looking at this blank wall? How long have you looked at it and said: "I know what I want there, but what if . . ." Hang the picture for goodness sake, we can fix the little holes along the way. We'll use toothpaste if we have to. The wall has been blank for way too long! Be brave. We got this!

ACTION STEP: Today, I want you to think about this metaphor—what is the blank wall that you are afraid to raise a hammer to? It's just fear. Journal about it.

Why?

—∞—

Do you know why you work so hard? Have you ever asked yourself, "*Why* am I doing what I do?" The answers to these questions are really important.

Most will say, "To support my family!" That is the obvious answer, but I am asking you to dig deeper than that, a lot deeper. Really put your finger on the *why*. When you find the *why*, you will have complete clarity and clarity changes everything. For some, the *why* will make you understand that you have lost sight of your priorities. For others, the *why* will rejuvenate you to work harder. The *why* is different for everyone, even within the same household.

I have two *whys*. My first *why* is from childhood and it has defined my work ethic. I came from a lower middle-class family and always hated feeling like the poor kid in town. My second *why* drives me so hard that I will never take my eye off the ball, and at the same time, it fills me with joy. That *why* is my children and my desire to model for them what chasing your dream looks like, all the while being transparent about the ups as well as the downs.

What is your *why*? The answer is deep inside of you and it is not only "to support my family." That is simply the answer that lies on the surface. Your *why* changes everything. German philosopher Frederick Nietzsche once said, "He who has a why can endure any how." Your why is the thing that motivates you to get up every morning, it gives you the courage to take risks, and it moves your life in a more meaningful, rewarding and positive direction.

———

ACTION STEP: Spend a minimum of 5 minutes thinking and writing about your *why*. Dig deep. Your *why* has been within you all along, today you are simply bringing it to the surface of your consciousness. And if you feel you don't have a *why*, then it's time to reassess.

What Really Matters in Life?

—⚬—

I will be the first to admit, I lose sight of this question regularly. Sometimes it is important to pull ourselves out of the rat race and digest not only this question but also the answers behind it that hold meaning for us.

Some of the major themes for what matters in life are: health, wealth, relationships, contribution/achievement, meaning and happiness. Since I certainly need a "what matters in life" refresher course, I am guessing maybe you do, too. I have an exercise that is *so* simple yet so profound—if you engage with it at a deep level. Take each topic, starting with health, and ask yourself, "What really matters here and how can I improve?"

This exercise has such wonderfully grounding elements. It hits on all the core places of our lives. It should remind us of our priorities if we have wandered away from them, or it might affirm that we have our priorities in check. Regardless of where we are, this is not about shame or guilt. If we are off base, it is all about the reset. But we cannot reset if we have not checked in. Take the 5 minutes and check in. You won't regret it. Do them in order. End with happiness. And do not hesitate to press the reset button if necessary.

———

ACTION STEP: What really matters in life?

Health:

Wealth:

Relationships:

Contributions/Achievements:

Meaning:

Happiness:

What Is Enough?

—✠—

*"Be strong enough to walk away from what's hurting you
and patient enough to wait for the blessings you deserve."*

—UNKNOWN

I believe "enough" may, in fact, be the worst word in the English language. We are forever saying or thinking about enough in the negative. We often believe we don't have enough. Most people worry about not having enough money or time, but there are many other "not enough" statements being made that are attached to words like love, strong, young, old, smart, good, brave, and the very worst—I am.

Have you ever thought about what would be enough? Have you ever done the math? What is your "enough" number that would allow you to stop all the worry, anxiety, and fret? You can do the math on any of your "not enough" statements.

The truth is, that word "enough" owns us—but only as long as we allow it to do so. We are only looking in the direction of lack—that which we don't have. Have you ever taken inventory of what you do have? Holy smokes! Enough doesn't even scratch the surface. If you turn your back on "not enough" you will be face to face with your blessings. You get to decide in which direction you will look.

———

ACTION STEP: Today, you will be taking inventory of your blessings, large and small, simply to reassure yourself that you have enough.

If I Knew Then What I Know Now . . .

—◊◊◊—

Hindsight is 20/20. Have you ever thought about how you would do things differently if you could go back 20 years? I know I would definitely do some things a bit differently.

I wish I had not stayed at jobs as long as I did, even though I knew they were not a good fit for me. I wish I had taken more risks. And I wish I had found a really good mentor early on. These are not regrets (I am not a big fan of regret), but had I possessed this wisdom back then, I believe I would have avoided some frustration and discontent.

Here is the good news; it is not too late. Whatever wisdom our hindsight shares with us, there is no reason we cannot apply it now! For me, I am keenly aware of my right job and I am doing it. I am a much bigger risk-taker now. It does not make risk-taking any less scary, but I am doing it. And I have a few incredible mentors. Here is the key—we have to stop long enough to ask ourselves, "What would I have done differently?" Once you have these answers, you can make the changes now. It is never too late.

———

ACTION STEP: What is your biggest regret? I know, dwelling on that regret is not a feel-good moment, but it is where a lot of answers lie. Today is an important and powerful journaling day. Here is an example: If my regret was staying at a job that I was not enjoying until it sucked almost all of the self-confidence out of me, I would journal today on why I stayed. Extract the good! Recognize all the lessons learned. You are bigger, badder, and bolder because of this regret, but we cannot leave it as a regret, we **must** extract the good! And in doing so, maybe it will no longer be a regret.

The Masks We Wear

—ᴥ—

We all portray ourselves to the world with various masks, even though each mask is not necessarily how we truly feel. Surely you have been in a situation where you have put on your happy face even though you were definitely not feeling happy? Me, too.

Wearing a mask protects us from vulnerability; we stand in resistance to our true self. We fear that if we are truly authentic, we will be seen as weak in some way. Becoming authentic is having the courage to acknowledge our limitations, and embrace our own vulnerability.

Five common masks we wear are happy, strong, nice, intellectual, and grumpy. Which one of these masks are you wearing? We believe the mask protects us but does it? I believe those around us see right through our mask. It is quite possible we don't need a mask at all, just a hug. Masks are a sign of weakness; with authenticity comes freedom and strength. Be brave. Take off the mask.

———

ACTION STEP: Today, journal for 5 minutes on the mask you are wearing and with whom. Decide which one you are ready to take off so you can be your truly authentic self.

Food for Thought

—ᗰ—

"I've discovered in 100% of the cases, no exceptions, that people who are *unwilling* to take step #1, never take step #2."
                                          —ZIG ZIGLAR

Zig Ziglar was one of America's most influential and beloved motivational speakers. He believed everyone could be, do and have more. He influenced an estimated quarter of a billion individuals through his 33 books, including the bestseller *See You at the Top*, which has sold almost two million copies.

———

ACTION STEP: Spend 5 minutes today journaling on the Zig Ziglar quote above. Pay particular attention to Ziglar's word choice: unwilling. Are you *unwilling?*

Integrity

—⚬—

"**Wisdom** is knowing the right path to take . . . **Integrity** is
actually taking it."   —W.H. MCKEE

Will we ever see an Abraham Lincoln in office again? Where are the men
(and women) like him? I know they are out there. Have politics become
so corrupt that the good ones have too much integrity to run? It disap-
points me that there is not a candidate I can proudly support with no
reservation. Maybe I am old fashioned or I have lost touch with reality.
Or, maybe I still believe in truth and integrity.

The election aside, integrity is hard to find. Integrity is a firm adherence
to moral values. Incorruptibility. Integrity determines our character and
our reputation. Integrity takes years to develop and can be destroyed
with one single act. And, for all parents, here is the most crucial piece of
information: "Good character, like good soup, is made at home."

Whether we are a parent, a leader, or both, someone is watching what
we say and do. The right way is not always the easy way, but it is always
the way worth taking. It may not pay off quickly, but it always pays off.
Choose wisely.

ACTION STEP: Here are a few ways to check in on your integrity. Do I/
Am I:

- Honor commitments and keep promises
- Truthful at all times, you can trust what I tell you
- Accept responsibility for my own mistakes/failures, then apologizes
- Care about the work, the mission, or the product, more than about self

The Gatekeeper

—ɯ—

Last week, for the first time since I started posting motivational entries on Facebook, I had to ban a user. At first, it was a very uncomfortable decision. I welcome people to disagree with me if my post hits them the wrong way. This person's comment, although not blatantly egregious, came from a very malicious and negative place. I could have just hid the post and moved on, but then I thought about my decision on a larger scale.

We do not always have the choice to shut down negativity in our life, but when we do, I believe we should. The "Ban User" button holds a really important purpose. When I chose "Ban User," I made a statement to myself which was, "I am not allowing your negativity to enter my life." My ban did not come with any hatred or malicious intent in return, it was simply making a stand for what I will allow in.

I wish my life had a Ban User button. I would use it very infrequently, but I would most certainly use it. My ban button would not be permanent either, it would be on a case-by-case basis. Imagine if you had a "Ban User" button in your life. Would you use it? Who is infiltrating your life with their negative thoughts, feelings or actions? You are the gatekeeper of your own life. You decide who and what comes in and who and what does not. It is possible that some of your "users" need to be temporarily or permanently "banned."

ACTION STEP: It is time to identify who is bringing negative thoughts, feelings, or actions into your life. Journal about who this might be. Then determine what action steps, on your part, need to be taken so that you set your own boundaries. Regardless of what decisions you make, this exercise is healthy for the mind, body and soul.

The Rabbit Hole

—⟋⟍—

Have you ever let your thoughts and emotions get the better of you? With Thanksgiving about a week away, I think it's a good time to share a story when that was the case for me! A few years ago, I was hosting Thanksgiving. It was Doug's family who was attending so we had a headcount of about forty. Let me run through a few of the emotions I was feeling leading up to the big day:

ANXIOUS: because there is so much to do

NERVOUS: I am hosting 40 people

ANNOYED: because my kids keep making more messes

OVERWHELMED: what to make, how much, etc . . .

ANGRY: which is really fear that I will screw up

And many more unhealthy emotions!

I decided to take a step back and Google Thanksgiving. The Pilgrims landed in New England in the fall of 1602. The winter was so harsh, they lost half of their people who originally made the journey. The Indians were instrumental in helping the Pilgrims plant and harvest a bountiful crop the following summer. With profound gratitude, the Pilgrims decided to have a harvest celebration to thank God, the Indians, and each other for their success.

So back to all of the unhealthy and unhappy emotions I was wallowing in. Revisiting the history and purpose of this holiday changed my thoughts. I am so blessed to have my home filled with forty family members that I love who have offered to help in so many ways! Maybe I was shooting for perfect, but why? Thanksgiving isn't being judged. It's about spending time with family we don't see regularly. This day is a *gift!* I am grateful. I am thankful! If you are hosting, I hope this helps!

P.S. My mom had the turkey in the oven on Thanksgiving day when she went into labor with me. I am pretty sure that Thanksgiving was not perfect. Although my mom might argue that, to her, it was!

———

ACTION STEP: Today is a journaling day, and you do not get to skip this 5 minutes of writing simply because you're not hosting Thanksgiving! No, no. Spend your 5 minutes on a time when you let your thoughts and emotions get the better of you. I, for sure, went down the rabbit hole on this one, but something made me stop and search for a new perspective. You can, too.

Thanksgiving Thoughts

—ɯ—

Thanksgiving is my favorite holiday! As I get older, I truly believe I like it more than Christmas. The three things that make it so great for me are:

1. It is not commercialized.
2. It is a holiday for **everyone** in America to enjoy.
3. It is all about giving thanks for food, family, and friendship.

Whether we are hosting the holiday gathering or not, Thanksgiving will be upon us in the blink of an eye. Can we pause and ask ourselves, "What does this day mean to me?" What am I truly grateful for?

Today, before we jump on the high-speed express train to Thanksgiving, let us all hit the pause button. Spend five minutes on just two words, *giving* and *thanks*. My guess is we will appreciate those five minutes as they may have helped us pause long enough to remember the meaning of this holiday.

And, if you have an extra minute as well as a little extra money, think about someone who may not be able to afford to celebrate Thanksgiving. Call a local charity and donate a turkey—or a whole Thanksgiving dinner, if you are in such a position. I believe all of our dinners on Thanksgiving will taste a lot better if we know we have put food on another's table that was not going to be there without our help.

———

ACTION STEP: Spend five minutes journaling on the two words, *giving* and *thanks*. Will you step off the merry-go-round long enough to do it? Thanksgiving will be a completely different day if you take the time. Good luck. As always, it is your choice.

Tea with God

—⚬—

I want to share a little ritual I have which has had a profound effect on me, my sense of peace, and my happiness. Sometimes it is not easy, and sometimes I fall off the wagon in a big way, but somehow I always manage to find my way back.

I call it *My Morning Cup of Tea with God.* I wake up around 5 a.m., let the dogs out, make a cup of tea and then let the dogs in. Finally, I settle down on the sofa, usually with one of the dogs cuddled up next to me, and pray. When I start my day with this ritual, it invariably sets the stage for an amazingly peaceful and happy day.

What I used to do after waking up was immediately look at my phone and my laptop, then start working. I didn't have time for this ritual. Did I really say that? I had my priorities completely screwed up and when I started to notice my morning ritual was impacting my health and overall

well-being, I began this more peaceful daily practice. Do you want to reduce stress? Try having a morning cup of tea with God.

Sophie and Ella are my prayer buddies! And if prayer is not your thing, try meditating.

———

ACTION STEP: Entertain whether this ritual will work for you, or find another. Carve out some time for peace and serenity in your morning.

Hate Is a Very Toxic Emotion

—✠—

And the poison is damaging us. Hate is not just in the mind; we can feel it in the body and the soul. Hate affects our organs as well as interrupts the natural processes within the body. In addition, prolonged bouts of anger can have tremendous adverse effects, taking a toll on the body in the form of high blood pressure, stress, anxiety, etc. Research also shows that even one five-minute episode of anger is so stressful it can impair our immune system for more than six hours. (The Huffington Post)

Who do we hate and why do we hate them (or some other strong negative emotion like resentment, disgust, or grievance)? Hate is an emotion like any other and emotions generally serve us. How could hate possibly be *serving* us? Let us suppose our hate is toward our boss. Whatever he or she did to cause us to hate him or her is exactly what we are going to use to become stronger. Pinpoint exactly what it is that you hate. In some way, we can learn from this experience.

Hate is a dangerously broad brush to paint with, therefore if we want to learn from it we need to pinpoint our hate. We need to know exactly what we hate and go fix it or fix ourselves. Hate is poison, but once we find out what we hate and why, we can become the impetus for change and the poison becomes the antidote. It is totally our choice.

———

ACTION STEP: Are you feeling hate, resentment, disgust, grievance or some other strong negative emotion toward someone? Take time to reflect on why. When certain characteristics in someone's personality trigger a negative reaction from us, that is often the very thing we do not like about ourselves and it is coming up because it is ready to be healed.

Perspective

—∭—

I had the good fortune of planning a last-minute trip to London with one of my dearest friends. It was mainly a business trip for both of us, but we did have one day to run around London together and have some fun. Because I planned my trip at the last minute, we were unable to be on the same flight, so I ended up staying an extra day.

On Monday, Terry and I laughed our way through London. From being lost on the Tube, almost getting run over on Abbey Road, making friends everywhere (regardless of whether they wanted to be our friend or not), to just plain silliness.

Then, Tuesday came and Terry flew home. I jumped on the Tube again and headed into London alone. Tuesday was a totally different day without Terry. The juxtaposition was glaring. Tuesday was nowhere near as fun by myself.

As we approach not only Thanksgiving but also Christmas, or any other seasonal holiday, and the busyness begins to distract us, can we stop and think of someone who is alone? Alone has many definitions. Who could use a buddy? Who could use a phone call or a night out? We spend a lot of time thinking about ourselves. It is time to turn the tables. Pick one person. My guess is you knew the one while you were reading this. Alone is not fun. Create joy for you and another.

———

ACTION STEP: Who is going to be alone this holiday? You know what to do. You got this. I am proud of you!

At All Costs

—∞—

Youth sports has spiraled out of control, in my opinion. And I say that as a parent who has spiraled out of control along with it. Our obsession with youth sports is not only unhealthy but has caused us to lose complete perspective!

The Fitzgeralds had quite a weekend here on the east coast. While my son was at The Philly Showcase for lacrosse with his father, I was at his school attending parent-teacher conferences. The day was not going so well in Philly and I was a bit annoyed to be attending my third day of conferences. Then I had my wake-up call. Something in my head said, "You get to hear how wonderfully your child is doing and you only get to hear this for a few more years. Enjoy! Take it all in."

The light bulb finally went off! I called Doug in Philly and said, "You know, lacrosse is great but guess what's even better? Liam's teachers just told me how well he is doing in school, what a great addition he is to class, and how happy he is all the time." I was putting too much weight on our son being recruited and, in doing so, I forgot to recognize what is really important. I wonder what this looks like from the child's perspective? It has to look like we, as parents, have our priorities way out of order. I did, for sure. Not anymore.

Have you lost perspective, too. Maybe it is youth sports, or maybe it is something else. One great question to ask yourself is, "What am I pushing for *at all costs*?" *At all costs* means we have lost sight of balance. Even pushing education *at all costs* means we have lost sight of the power of relaxation and fun that refills the tank.

———

ACTION STEP: Today, spend your 5 minutes journaling about where, perhaps, you have lost perspective. What are you pushing for *at all costs*?

Be Thankful for the Bad?

—⟋⟍—

> "Be thankful for the bad things in life, for they open your
> eyes to all the good things you weren't paying attention to
> before." —UNKNOWN

I love this quote. Sometimes, I believe it is good to immerse ourselves in the bad things (just for a moment), because it is the only place where we can truly get a bird's eye view of all of the good things. I rarely encourage people to bathe in the bad, but today we are going to take a quick dip!

Just for a moment, think of one bad thing. As you think about this negative event, did it actually turn out good in the end? Due to this unfavorable event, were you able to better appreciate all the positive things around you?

I have had my share of bad events and I always try to harvest the good. It is not because I am unrealistically optimistic; it is because I have learned there is always good that comes from bad events, we just need to search for it. Recently, my daughter switched schools. The prior year had been an extremely difficult year for her. I did not know if switching schools was going to be a good thing or a bad thing. Freshman year at the old school was, in fact, painful, but sophomore year at the new school ended up being fantastic. Katie and I have talked about how grateful we both are that freshman year was so bad, for had it not been, she would have never made the move. If we look deep enough, we can almost always be thankful for the bad.

––––––––

ACTION STEP: Do you have a negative story? One that you have never analyzed before? Today is biology 101 and you get to dissect your bad story. Your prompt is this:

Even though _____ happened, here are some of the good things that came from it:

A Gentle Reminder from the Pope

—m—

Never talk about money, politics, and religion. Right! I agree, except if there is a beautiful letter that is inaccurately attributed to the Pope! Apparently this was written by a doctor in the Philippines. I believe this letter applies to everyone, even an atheist, except for the mention of prayer and God once. My favorite part is about life being perfect. Enjoy!

A Gentle Reminder From Pope Francis

This life will go by fast.

Don't fight with people, don't criticize your body so much, don't complain so much. Don't lose sleep over your bills. Look for the person that makes you happy. If you make a mistake, let it go and keep seeking your happiness.

Never stop being a good parent. Don't worry so much about buying luxuries and comforts for your home, and don't kill yourself trying to leave an inheritance for your family. Those benefits should be earned by each person, so don't dedicate yourself to accumulating money.

Enjoy, travel, enjoy your journeys, see new places, give yourself the pleasures you deserve. Allow dogs to get closer. Don't put away the fine glassware. Utilize the new dinnerware; don't save your favorite perfume, use it to go out with yourself; wear out your favorite sport shoes; repeat your favorite clothes.

So what? That's not bad. Why not now? Why not pray now instead of waiting until before you sleep? Why not call now? Why not forgive now? We wait so long for Christmas; for Friday; for Reunions; for another year; for when I have money; for love to come; when everything is perfect . . . look . . .

Everything perfect doesn't exist. Human beings can't accomplish this because it simply was not intended to be completed here. Here is an opportunity to learn.

So take this challenge that is life and do it now . . . love more, forgive more, embrace more, love more intensely and leave the rest in God's hands. Amen.

ACTION STEP: Take 5 minutes to let that powerful note settle into your soul.

"Later" Is the Kiss of Death

—⚇—

Have you ever said, "I'll get to it later"? Sometimes I get a little crazy over a single word and "later" is one of those words. The word "later," as far as hopes and dreams are concerned, is the kiss of death.

You know how it sounds, "I'll write the book later, once the kids are grown," or "I'll pursue my real passion later, once my finances are in order." "Later" would be OK if we tied it to a firm date. Don't get me wrong, I believe people really want their dreams to come true, but I also believe "later" is like saying "someday." "Someday" and "later" rarely ever arrive.

If you have pushed off your dream with the word "later," and we all have, I want to offer plan B. We say "later" because, for some odd reason, we think "now" means "I'm all in" and "full steam ahead" but it does not mean that at all.

So here is plan B: baby steps. That's it. Taking small daily steps toward our goal means, over time, we are getting closer to it, while "later" means we remain idle. Baby steps are action steps and action is the only way we can make things happen. Hoping, wishing, and dreaming are static. Action is how we make our dreams come true. Take a baby step, and then another, and soon a goal originally thought to be too far to be reached becomes achievable.

I wanted to write an audacious letter to a very prominent coach/speaker. I was paralyzed with fear until finally I said to myself, "Just write one sentence a day." I could immediately feel the fear subside. Writing one sentence was something I could agree to do and those baby steps resulted in a full letter that I proudly mailed.

ACTION STEP: Pick a goal you would like to accomplish and begin your journaling by writing, "I can agree to plan B!" It is just baby steps and I can do that! What is the one small baby step you will take toward your goal? Now go do it!!

A Free Bit of Advice

—ɷ—

I learned a really valuable lesson this weekend. *Really valuable* might not even encompass the importance of this lesson, especially if you are a parent.

I was having a deep conversation with a young man about parent-child exchanges. Both of us were conveying our side of the equation when he trumped me. Conversations usually play out something like this: child declares a problem, parent asserts a solution from their years of wisdom. Perfect, right? Well, not always.

As parents, we believe our children are looking for answers and we are so quick to provide such, but what if we are way off the mark? What if our answers are not so spot-on? I asked this young man what he thought would be a better response? His answer was like a light bulb going off in my head; he said, "What would you like me to do to help you?" That question changes everything!

By asking this question, there is no assumption that we, as parents, have the right answer. In addition, we have firmly put ourselves in the camp of our child, we are on their side, fighting on their behalf. We validate their current state and feelings. It is a real deal changer.

I asked my daughter what she thought of this newfound wisdom. She immediately said, "That's perfect. Most often, that is all I need to hear!" So, give it a go.

———

ACTION STEP: "What would you like me to do to help you?" is not only applicable to children; it is great for spouses and colleagues as well. Spend a few minutes journaling about this question and with whom you would like to begin using this response. How will you remember this so it becomes your go-to response?

One Sentence

—∿—

Sometimes, in life, we need to stop and take a look at things in a different way. Unfortunately, we all get tied to our story and we tell it over and over. Have you ever had anyone offer you a different perspective on something, so much so that you were compelled to say, "I hadn't thought about it that way?"

Today, I am going to share one sentence that had a profound impact on me and the way I look at things: "There is another way of looking at this." When we are armed with this sentence, we do not need to wait for our forthright friend to show up and hit us over the head with his or her wisdom. There is *always* another way of looking at something. We can use this sentence at work with our colleagues, at home with our family, and out in the world at large.

What situation is currently distressing you? Use our new sentence! I used it over the weekend when my daughter's carefully orchestrated plans to travel overseas started to unravel at the last minute (all I could think about was the movie *Taken*). I used this new sentence because I refused to freak out and it was remarkably helpful. I thought of all the ways in which she would be safe and all the ways I could make her more safe. I did not allow myself to imagine all the unrealistic ways in which she could be in danger.

Can you apply this new sentence right now to something in your life? There is definitely another way of looking at anything, but it is up to us to choose to look at it differently. This other way is very possibly where peace is. Peace is good.

———

ACTION STEP: Apply this sentence to something in your life: Journal for a few minutes about this other way.

A Difference of Opinion

—◁∞▷—

Ugh! Confrontation. No one really enjoys it, do they? Most people will avoid it at all costs. Ahh and there's the rub—the cost is huge and the only person paying the price is the one who has the bottled up feelings and the unresolved conflict. Holding it in is incredibly unhealthy.

I don't love confrontation but I am certainly not afraid of it—when it is used for the right reasons and handled in the right way. No one wants to be shamed, humiliated, or disrespected, nor should they be. That type of confrontation will only result in everyone staunchly defending him or herself and will usually breed resentment and make matters worse.

The Latin derivation of confront is "foreheads together." It's about having enough self-respect to stand up for yourself & speak your truth. Convey your problem as you see it from your perspective. Take responsibility for your part in this communication breakdown. And always come prepared with some positive outcomes you wish to achieve. Confrontation shouldn't be a fight, it should be a constructive resolution that raises both parties.

ACTION STEP: Today, spend 5 minutes journaling about a communication breakdown that happened recently in your life. Don't give any thought to an actual confrontation—simply lay out your plan on paper as if you will. Be sure to revisit the three steps in the last paragraph. Do this for you—as a sign of self-respect.

Slow Down

—∿—

I had a really unique experience recently. I stayed in an Andean village, 12,000 feet up in the mountains of Peru where farming is the way of life. Electricity is present in the homes for lighting purposes, but the community really operates around the sun. They don't have even 1% of the modern conveniences we have.

I watched them for two full days. They work hard; their work is labor intensive. Nobody looked stressed out; no one seemed to be in a hurry. They are really happy people and they laugh all the time. Meals are a big deal—they are very slow, leaving plenty of time for conversation and connection.

Everything was slower there. I really didn't miss all of my modern conveniences (OK, well I did miss heat at night when the temps hit 25 degrees). I found myself jealous of their slower pace. I knew when I returned home, it would be hard to replicate and maintain this lifestyle. I'm trying though. Long dinners. Real conversations. No T.V. Who has it better? I believe it may be them.

———

ACTION STEP: Today, spend 5 minutes journaling on ways you could slow down the pace of your life. Does a long dinner filled with conversation sound appealing?

Painful Lessons

—ɯᴧ—

"God doesn't give you the people you want, he gives you the people you need. To help you, to hurt you, to leave you, to love you and to make you the person you were meant to be."

—AUTHOR UNKNOWN

Oh, boy! This quote is really going to change things. Of course, we love all the people God put into our lives that make us happy! We want more of those. It is all the other people that we are desperately trying to get out of our lives or at the very least, minimize our exposure to them.

The other people, the ones we would put under the negative category, are people God believes we need to make us better. There is a lesson that must be learned and only will be learned if we accept these people as our teachers. If we can accept this thought, then everything changes!

Think about the most challenging person in your life right now. This person was put into your life to teach you a lesson. This person, unbeknownst to them, is providing a lesson for you that will bring you to a higher level of consciousness. The lesson isn't going away until it is learned. I don't know about you, but I want to learn the lesson as quickly as possible!

ACTION STEP: Today, journal for 5 minutes about this challenging relationship. Apply the label of *teacher* to your challenging person and *student* to you and see if you can look at this person in a different light.

Laughter Is the Best Medicine

—∽—

I talk a lot about stress. Americans are far more stressed than many other countries. One good way to reduce stress is to laugh. Yes, it is true; laughter may be the best medicine.

On average, humans laugh about seventeen times a day, and as far as we know, we are one of the only species on the planet that laughs. Researchers at the University of Maryland have linked laughter to the healthy function of blood vessels—something that can lower our chance of a heart attack. And laughter also boosts our heart rate and the production of certain antibodies, which strengthens our immune system.

So it looks like we need to make laughter a priority. Find ways to bring more laughter into your life like: watch a funny movie, read a funny book, read the comic strips daily, follow a funny sitcom, or find a funny comedian and watch their routines on YouTube. It will not only be good for your brain and your body, but also for your soul!

———

ACTION STEP: Today is a three-minute journaling day. For the next three minutes, brainstorm about all the different things that make you laugh. If it is a person, call them. If it is a movie, plan the night and rent it. Doesn't everyone need more laughter?

What Is Your One Word?

—ᘟ—

"Doubt kills more dreams than failure ever will."
—SUZY KASSEM

You might be buried in holiday busyness right now, but soon you will be staring down New Year's Day and the resolutions that generally come along with it. As you do, keep this quote in mind.

Additionally, think about the one word you want as your mantra or guiding principle in the new year. I am going to suggest that your word be *act*. For now, just chew on this question: "What dream have you wrestled with for years that is still firmly in the 'doubt' folder?" Will you be so bold in this new year and move it to the 'act' file, or better yet, take it out of the drawer and put it right on the center of your desk so you see it every day. Could you be that courageous?

I believe you can!

———

ACTION STEP: Spend a few minutes journaling about the question from above, *"What dream have you wrestled with for years that is still firmly in the 'doubt' folder?"* Spend a few minutes, perhaps with your eyes closed, visualizing the dream. What is your next step? Be brave. Be courageous.

Six Words

—∿—

The other day I was listening to John Maxwell explain how he prepares for a speech. In John's quintessential, easy-going way he stated, "After my speech is written, every day leading up to the speech, I look at it and say, 'How can I make this better?'"

I immediately started using his advice for a presentation I was planning. As I did, it occurred to me that this advice is not only applicable to speeches but it is also applicable to life. Six words that change everything. How can I make this better? Define your "this" and you will be positioned to make little daily changes that ultimately produce big results.

What is your "this"? Your "this" could be work, marriage, parenting, what kind of friend you are, how good of an athlete you can become, etc. Put those six words in your phone so they pop up and greet you every morning. "How can I make this better?" This might very well change the way you look at your day.

———

ACTION STEP: Your task today is to simply put these words where you will see them: **How can I make this better?** We can always be, do, and act better. Sometimes we simply need to be reminded to do so. I know I do.

Restoring My Faith in Humanity.

—◊◊—

On Sunday, Doug and I were driving on a major highway in NJ, headed to my dear friend Bonnie's home for brunch. It was about 12 pm when we saw a pickup truck pulled over on the median. The owner of the vehicle was crouched down beside something and it looked as though he was petting it. When we got closer Doug remarked, "It's a deer! He must have hit it. It's clearly still alive."

I wish you could have seen this. This man was evidently not going to allow this deer to die alone. From afar, it looked like a man and his dog. This highway is Interstate 195, which transports all the New Jersey shore traffic east and west. Pulling into the median and getting out of his car was putting himself in danger. His actions touched my heart. His compassion was not only palpable, but extremely heart-warming.

This morning I googled "restoring faith in humanity." I am encouraging you to do the same but grab your tissues first. Holy cow! My heart feels so much fuller. There are amazing acts of kindness going on and it is worth the few minutes it will take to check it out. Here is one website I really enjoyed:

https://faithinhumanityr.tumblr.com

———

ACTION STEP: Google "restoring faith in humanity," scroll through some amazing acts, and allow your heart to feel fuller.

Who Are You Talking To?

—w—

The person we talk to the most is ourselves. Our inner dialogue accounts for about two-thousand thoughts per hour. This equates to about thirty-thousand thoughts per day (some estimate more). If we are having this many thoughts, it begs the question, "What are we saying to ourselves?"

I would love to believe that your inner dialogue is a lot nicer than my inner dialogue, but I am guessing it is not. I say so many harsh things to myself. I am unkind for sure, but that does not even hold a candle to all the thoughts that fall under categories like defeatist, self-deprecating, criticizing, belittling and condemning. Nice, huh?

How do we stop this self-sabotaging talk? The most powerful tool at our disposal is to simply become aware of it when we hear it. As soon as I hear myself go down a negative path, I need to choose to engage with the part of my mind that has clearly been left unattended for a while. The mind cannot be left alone (think toddler or puppy), because it is certain to be headed down the rabbit hole. I must step in, like any parent or guardian would, and declare, "Enough!" Once I assume an active role, I can direct my thoughts to a more positive and optimistic place. Remember, every negative thought has an equal and opposite positive counterpart. We need to be diligent about directing our mind toward the positive.

———

ACTION STEP: Today is an awareness day. How often do you have a dialogue with yourself that sounds self-deprecating, criticizing, belittling or condemning? Decide what you will say to yourself next time you hear this kind of talk in your head. "Enough!" is a really good start.

The Wounded Warrior

—⊠—

Most people are familiar with the expression Wounded Warrior, which is generally reserved for the brave soldiers who get injured in the line of duty. I am certainly not looking to infringe upon that definition in any way, but after seeing a lot of clients in crisis this past week and thinking about the holidays in close detail, it has occurred to me that it may not be "The Most Wonderful Time of the Year" for everyone.

This world is not for the faint of heart. There are some really burdensome and weighty things that happen to people. Trying to get in the Christmas spirit while carrying this onus is inconceivable for some. It's too heavy. The burden is too great. These wounded warriors may try to be festive on the outside, but the inside will tell an entirely different story.

This year, as we approach the holidays, let us take time to pause and think about those in our life who may be struggling with these holidays. Maybe it is their first holiday without a loved one. Maybe it comes on the heels of some bad news.

Unfortunately, Christmas does not change everything. Sadness doesn't go away or may even worsen during the holidays. I hope we will spend a few minutes today thinking of people around us who could use some extra love. It is like donating blood; we can give of ours until they can create some of their own. Honoring their heavy heart with love might be the gift they need most.

————

ACTION STEP: Who, in your life, might have a heavy heart as the holidays approach? Journal all the possible names that come to mind and all the specific ways you can think of to make it better, lighter, or to simply let them know you are thinking of them.

* We have a family tradition of choosing a person/family in need that will receive an anonymous gift from us each Christmas. In need can mean many things. We all weigh in on who it should be and what we should send them. We have left gifts on doorsteps and we have shipped from distant locations to preserve our anonymity. We never see their reaction, but we hope they find some much needed joy in this random act.

Happiness Is an Inside Job

—⚋—

And so is unhappiness. Think about what makes you unhappy. Is it your bank account? Is it your weight? Is it your job? All of those appear to be outside causes and when they change, you will be happy, right? No.

The bank account/weight/job is not the real problem. It is the "pre-recorded message" we keep playing over and over again in our head that is the real problem. We know what it sounds like, "Once I finally get a new job, one that pays well and where I am appreciated, I'll be happy." We truly believe when those things are better, we will be happy, but that is not necessarily true. Something else will make us unhappy. And then the search for happiness will begin again.

Happiness is a mental choice. Here and now, among the muck and mire, we can choose to be happy. So our bank account is not where we want it to be? Allowing it to make us unhappy today is wasting a day! I cannot speak for you but I have no intention of wasting any of my days. Each and every day is a gift. I am choosing happiness even though my bank account is not where I want it, my weight is not where I want it, and neither is my job. We will never get this day back again, so let us live into it with complete happiness and joy. This is not a dress rehearsal, folks!

———

ACTION STEP: Chuang Tzu believes, "Happiness is the absence of striving for happiness." Spend a few minutes journaling about your happiness as well as what makes you unhappy?

I Could Never Do That

—∞—

We bought a new dresser for our daughter recently. My husband commented in the store, "This is really heavy furniture," but I dismissed his revelation as interesting but unimportant. The dresser would be ready for pick up on Monday.

When Doug arrived home Monday night, Clare, Doug and I went out to the truck to carry the dresser upstairs. I quickly realized why Doug was so concerned about the weight of this dresser. There was no way the three of us could carry this monstrosity upstairs, but we did not want to disappoint Clare.

What happened next still amazes me. We carried weight we believed we were incapable of carrying. We were forced to think very creatively (hint: wheelbarrow). And because we did not want to disappoint Clare, we looked past our limits and carried this heavy and cumbersome adversary from the truck to her 2nd-floor bedroom. It was truly unbelievable!

What limits have you put on yourself? I now know for a fact that the, "I could never do that" statement is very often not true. We are all stronger than we think physically, emotionally, and intellectually. Go ahead, challenge yourself. I dare you.

———

ACTION STEP: Today, spend 5 minutes journaling as many answers as possible to the statement "I could never do that." Some answers might be run a marathon, give up sugar, lose 20 pounds, etc. When you can't think of any more answers, circle one of them. Write a new statement that begins with "Maybe I can do _____." Now go do it!

Affirm: Validate, Confirm.

—cm—

I use affirmations a lot, not only in my own life but also with my clients. An affirmation is a statement of truth, written in the present tense, and it has to be something we believe. Affirmations are dynamic and practical, but not wishful thinking. To me, affirmations are the vehicle through which I can create a new beginning as I set my sights on something I want to attain. Every time I reiterate the affirmation, my entire body hears what I am committed to achieving, all the way down to my subconscious. Here are three general affirmations I like, but consider creating your own:

- My ability to conquer my challenges is limitless; my potential to succeed is infinite.
- I have been given endless talents which I begin to utilize today.
- I am the architect of my life; I am the builder of its foundation and I choose its contents.

Affirmations are amazing, but there is a catch. It is just as easy to consciously create an empowering affirmation as it is for us to create a negative, disempowering affirmation. Sometimes we do this unknowingly because anything we say repeatedly to ourselves is an affirmation. If we declare, "I hate my life!" over and over again, we have created an affirmation. If we conclude, "I have the worst luck!," the universe will happily assist us in making that come true as well. "I can't do this," is another gem.

Every thought and every word affirms something, as does every action and decision. We must choose wisely. A positive affirmation takes us out of the victim role. It wakes us up and helps us to choose our thoughts. What we affirm today sets us up for a new experience tomorrow. We must be careful with what we—and our children—say repeatedly. Only affirm what you truly want in your life.

ACTION STEP: Action step #1 is to cease using all negative affirmations, now that you are aware. Step #2 is to journal various positive affirmations you wish to manifest in your life. My caveat for any affirmation is to make sure you believe it. For instance, do not take, "I can't do this," and change it to, "I will be the best at this." Try something like, "I know I am smart, I will figure this out." Step #3 is to leave your affirmation on your nightstand. Read it in the morning and before bed (which is the best time to affirm, right before sleep). Consider ending your affirmation with: ***I love my life. I am so blessed. And so it is.*** (Thank you Susan for that powerful emphasis).

Mountains Out of Molehills

—⚯—

I met a lovely woman the other day at a local chamber of commerce event. She was explaining how something had gone wrong with her website. She believed Google was involved, but no one seemed to be able to ascertain from where the problem was originating. To make matters worse, she had an outbreak of hives.

I explained to her that according to Louise Hay hives are a manifestation of her website problem. Hay asserts that hives are "small hidden fears as we make mountains out of molehills." She listened politely. I am not certain of her age but she was definitely older than me. It was clear, this problem was weighing so heavily on her mind. So I stated, "I can imagine that in your life, you have overcome a lot more than this little problem?" She quickly nodded and animatedly agreed. I could see the "light bulb" go on.

Sometimes we forget how outrageously strong we really are! We forget the magnitude of the things we have already triumphed over. We lose perspective and allow the small things to become big. Today, I believe it is a really good idea if we all look back over our accomplishments and declare, "Oh that's right, I forgot how CRAZY strong I truly am!" Watch out world, here I come!

———

ACTION STEP: Spend 5 minutes making a list of all the things you have triumphed over so far in life. This page may not be long enough.

Hidden Potential

—ɷ—

It has been postulated that the human potential for growth is unlimited. But, and this is a big but, this potential lies largely untapped. **Why?**

There are many reasons, but I will touch on two today. The first is an internal problem and the reason why I became a coach. People somehow do not see their own strengths, or at least not at the level they should. This is a problem with every client I meet. They are selling themselves short. There is so much more inside of them and it is my job to help them discover this infinite resource so it does not remain untapped.

The second reason applies to anyone who is a manager, a teacher, or a coach. Many people in leadership roles enjoy the benefits of all the talents of their staff but do not try to encourage more. I do not mean more as in draining our resource, I mean more in tapping into hidden potential. There is more. Trust me; there is more. There is always more and the great ones will find it, tap into it, and when they do, it is always a win for both.

———

ACTION STEP: Is it time for you to hire a coach? Is there more inside of you that is largely untapped? Spend a few minutes journaling on that question.

IF APPLICABLE: Does your staff/team have hidden potential? I am surmising they do! How are you going to tap into this resource? Spend another minute journaling about *how* you can tap into this resource.

Two Types of Tired

—⚍—

"There are two types of 'tired,' I suppose. One is a dire need
for sleep, and the other is a dire need of peace."

—UNKNOWN

I can only speak for myself when I admit, I was always seeking both of
these until I had an eye-opening moment recently. I was having a difficult time catching my breath. I saw a doctor, of course, but I also tried
to figure out what was going on in my own life, and at the time my
answer was, "Too much!"

I love it when my body speaks to me! I agreed I was looking for peace.
I was convinced I had to make that my daily mantra so it remained at
the forefront of my mind. I discovered peace is not something you have,
it is something you do. So if you are looking for peace as well, consider
making it your daily intention and build your day around this simple
5-letter word. Base your decisions on whether or not your actions will
bring you peace.

Oh, and P.S., I no longer have any breathing problems!

———

ACTION STEP: Do you feel called to address one or both types of tired
in your life? Journal for 5 minutes on how you will address "tired" in
your life.

Painting Fear with a Broad Brush

—∽—

Rarely does anyone want to stay in a mood that is other than happy, but . . .

I was given some great guidance from my coach the other day. I told her I was afraid. She responded with an unexpected, "Good!" I did not think that was the most appropriate answer and then it got worse. She said, "O.K., now stay there. Stay in the fear." I legitimately thought she had been hitting the sauce at lunch. I looked at her in disbelief and replied, "Really?" I knew clarity was coming, but it was not coming quickly enough.

She finally explained that she wanted me to sit in fear long enough for me to put my finger on exactly what I was afraid of at that moment. I had not only painted fear with such a broad brush that I had made my fear bigger than it truly was, but I had also not really figured out exactly what I was afraid of.

So I sat there in fear. I continued to ask myself, "What are you afraid of?" until no more answers came my way. I arrived at six very well-founded and credible fears. After I had my list, one by one, I wrote out the answer to each fear. By really sitting in this raw emotion, I actually met fear face to face and thereby consciously and rationally made it dissipate.

———

ACTION STEP: What strong emotion are you feeling in your life right now? Maybe yours is not fear, maybe it is sadness, anger, worry, or hate. Regardless, are you willing to sit in that emotion, much like I did? If so, stay in that negative emotional space and continue to ask yourself, "Why am I feeling _____?" I promise you your answers will surprise you. When you are done, write down all of your epiphanies.

Where Do You Spend Most of Your Time?

—m—

The options I am about to give you are probably not what came to mind as you read the question. Do you find yourself "loitering around" in the past, the present, or the future?

This week, in talking with a few clients and friends, I found a lot of people drifting off into the future. The future may sound great and I guess it would be if it was all about hopes and dreams, but I find that people who are in the future are there simply to worry about it. All too often, future thoughts bring worry, fear, and anxiety, and that is certainly not good.

Worry has been described to me as *chewing gum for the mind;* a lot of activity but really nothing to show for it. In addition, worry tends to poison the present. So here is a quick fix for diminishing your worries:

1. Don't live in the future. All the joy (and power) is in the now.
2. If you can do something now, do it. Otherwise, stop thinking about the future "what ifs."
3. Recognize that fixating on the future does not make anyone healthier, happier or more safe. It does not finish tasks. All it does is interfere with your ability to live in the present.

So, if we find our thoughts meandering aimlessly into the future, take the first train back to now. It is a total waste of time to even visit the future briefly. The present is where all the action is!

———

ACTION STEP: So, which are you? Are you a past/regret kind of person or do you tend to be a futuristic worrier? Spend five minutes journaling on why being in the past or the future is causing more problems than it is solving. Write about ways in which you can be more in the present.

The Real You

—∽∿∽—

Who is the real you? As a coach as well as an avid observer of people, I find many people do not pay attention to who they really are and, as a result, they are living an inauthentic life. This really saddens me.

Shortly after getting out of college, I worked in portfolio management at Prudential. I had majored in economics, so it was not a perfect fit but it was a great company with great people. However, I am very much an extrovert, so crunching numbers with my face buried in a computer all day was not exactly tapping into my wheelhouse. Everything in my mind (and body) was telling me this was not a perfect fit, but I carried on anyway at the expense of my confidence and my happiness. I did well financially, however I paid a big price.

A few long years later, my college roommate called me about a financial sales position in The World Trade Center in New York City. It was a perfect fit for me. The job required me to be on the phone all day, cultivating relationships with brokers over the topic of finance. Wheelhouse!! This was where I was able to spread my wings.

Who is the real you? Are you where you are supposed to be? Are you spreading your wings or have they been clipped? Your body and your mind are telling you every day who the real you is. I did not listen for a very long time. Learn from my mistake. Although I unintentionally mismanaged my life for a few years, it was completely reversible.

P.S. Perhaps this would be a good read for any high school or college student—just to be certain they are following their truly authentic path.

———

ACTION STEP: There are two prompts for today:
Who is the real you?
Are you *where* you are supposed to be?

Lessons from My Mom

—⚊—

From my very earliest childhood memory, I remember my mom giving. She was giving of her time, her talent, her money, and her things. If we had it and someone needed it, consider it as good as gone. I should add that we were not living high off the hog. Paycheck to paycheck was a better description of our financial situation, but that did not stop my mom.

One day, when I was about twelve years old, my mom asked me to collect the things in my closet and drawers that no longer fit so we could donate them to the Salvation Army. As I grabbed my bundle of clothes, shoes, etc., I remember feeling so excited to show my mom how much I had to donate. I descended the stairs with a tremendous sense of pride in all that I was willing to give away, not knowing I was about to learn a very valuable lesson.

I was instructed to dump my haul onto the kitchen table where my mom began to go through each piece of clothing, one by one. I was perplexed and asked, "What are you doing?" "I am making sure it is acceptable to donate," my mom responded. Here is where I went terribly wrong. "Mom, they should be grateful for whatever they get!" My mom, in her sweetest and most teachable voice explained, "Beth, everyone wants to be proud of who they are. No one wants to wear stained or tattered clothing. If you would not wear it, then you should never donate it." That was an "Aha" moment for me. I had no idea. She continued, "Stained and tattered clothing belongs in the trash and only the trash."

I am very grateful I learned that lesson on dignity. Thanks Mom!

———

ACTION STEP: Today, you get the day off from journaling. But while we are in this season of giving, can you give some thought to donating. Where, in your home, is there an abundance? Perhaps it is food or clothing—I imagine a warm winter jacket would be well received.

The Four-Step Approach

—◊—

"Decide what you want, decide what you are willing to exchange for it. Establish your priorities and go to work."

—H. L. HUNT

Well, if I was going to design a T-shirt or get a tattoo, this may very well be it. As straightforward as this quote is, I do understand how challenging each of these four steps can be.

Deciding what you want, alone, is complicated mainly because we (falsely) believe we couldn't possibly have it all. We put limits on what we want because we've been taught work words like sacrifice, hard work, and trade-offs.

Then there is the "what you are willing to exchange for it" part. That gets really sticky because often, no one wants to give up anything. For example, we want a great job that gives us financial independence but we don't want a 60-hour work week or we want to be healthy but we don't want to change our diets or live in the gym. There is a cost for everything, or so it seems.

Establishing a firm view of priorities is often a step that is unfortunately skipped. We don't want to move forward with this idea at all costs. Make sure your priorities are in order.

And finally, we have "go to work." If you have been fortunate enough to get through steps 1–3, step 4 should be easy. It is when you have not addressed those first few steps that makes acting difficult.

Four steps. That is it. It is easier than it sounds, but that's the framework to follow. You can do this!!

———

ACTION STEP: Today, journal for 5 minutes on these four steps.
1. What do you want?
2. What are you willing to exchange?
3. What are your priorities?
4. Go to work!

The Shopping List

—〰—

Do you ever write a list before you go to the grocery store? Why do you write it down? I write it down so I save time and money. I am also more efficient, I am more disciplined, and it all results in my feeling accomplished and successful.

Have you ever gone to the supermarket without a shopping list? That is when I feel scattered, disorganized, and ineffective. I waste both time and money without the disciplined direction of my list.

The same is true with life. When we take the time to design our lives with goals and targets, we do not waste precious time roaming around feeling scattered. We become disciplined and laser-focused, which results in win after win and, therefore, a profound sense of accomplishment and success. Why are we more diligent about our grocery list than we are about our own life? I cannot answer that question for you, but I know my life is far more important than my grocery list. I am starting a new list. Are you with me?

———

ACTION STEP: Start your goal list just like you would a grocery list. Add things as you go along. The goal here is to have a list. Goal setting can get pretty intense. Right now, just start your list.

Lean on Me, When You're Not Strong . . .

—◊◊—

At this time of year, it is an onerous task to be in retail; it is Herculean, really. These employees are being asked to work ridiculous hours while the customers are often rude and uncompromising and their entire shift is spent standing on their feet for eight or more hours. I know. My mom worked retail her whole life at Strawbridge and Clothier. I watched my mom during the holiday season come home at 10 p.m. or later as if she had been through a war.

With eleven days until Christmas, can we find a way to extend kindness to everyone working extraordinary hours to make this season "merry and bright?" I went to the mall yesterday and ran into the biggest malcontent working in the jewelry department. It was only 11 a.m. and I thought, "Wow, she is already stressed!" I did my best to engage her with kindness. I even wished her nothing but the sweetest customers! She actually laughed and said, "Thank you."

The Federal Express man arrived at my door on Friday with five packages and my seventy-five-pound dog on his heels acting like Cujo. I signed for the packages and asked if he would like a bottle of water or a soda for his journey. He exclaimed, "Yes, I'd love that," and he truly seemed excited to receive a cold Arnold Palmer.

And then there are my dear friends at the post office. These ladies work like dogs. They shared their daily routine with me which begins at 4 a.m., unloading pallets from UPS, Fed-Ex, and Amazon. The one postal employee described the size of the shipments as "unimaginable." She further explained to me, "My big meal of the day is lunch. By the time I get home, I am exhausted. I grab a glass of wine and a box of Cheez-Its. When the glass of wine is empty, I am out cold until my alarm goes off again at 3 a.m."

Be kind. Be generous. Be grateful. Engage. Connect. Can we help them get through the next eleven days! I am going to deliver a couple boxes of Cheez-Its to my exhausted friend at the post office.

––––––––

ACTION STEP: Spend a few minutes today journaling about all the ways you can bring more joy into the world, not just in December, but all year. It means you have to engage! Strike up conversations with strangers at the post office or elsewhere. Make it your daily mission to raise the level of joy in the world. Have you ever seen the movie *Pay It Forward?* If not, it might be time for a movie night.

Did You Know . . .

—∞—

Federal law, in the United States, does not require employers to give vacation time to their employees. Although most companies offer paid vacation time to their full-time employees, it is not required that it be taken. As a result, research shows that 55% of Americans did not take all their vacation days in 2015, which is up from 42% in 2013.

Are you kidding me? Vacations have been scientifically proven to reduce stress. Studies show relaxation does not even *begin* until day six. Taking two weeks back-to-back has been proven to reduce stress dramatically. Given the crazy world in which we live in and the amount of stress we undergo on a regular basis, I cannot fathom why someone would not take his or her vacation time. However, I do see a lot of people who wear their stressed out life like a badge of honor, as if anything else would be a sign of weakness.

Here are the facts we need to know. Stress is incredibly bad for our health. Other countries do not view vacation like we do. There are over 19 countries, like Austria, Spain and England, that offer over 30 days of paid vacation to their employees each year. Although it is not required, the U.S. offers, on average, 18 days of paid vacation time.

If you get vacation time, take it. When we talk about taking a mental health day, it is no joke. Vacation days are good for the mind, body, and soul. Leaving these vacation days on the table is detrimental to our health.

———

ACTION STEP: Do you take all your vacation days? Do you take two weeks consecutively? Today, revisit your available vacation time and how you are currently utilizing your days. Clearly your health depends on it.

A Special Sign

—✕—

Each of us who has lost someone dear often hopes that, at some point, we will get a sign or a reminder of our loved one's presence in our life. For some of us, it is a rainbow, a bird, a butterfly, or maybe it is pennies. Whatever the sign, it is special to us and when we see it, it warms our heart. It gives us faith and comfort. And the best part is that we never know when it is coming, it always arrives unexpectedly.

My sign for my mom is not retail tags, but she has been on my mind a lot lately. I was in Marshall's recently, looking at coats. I never read the tag, I look at the price, but I do not read all the details. On this day, I did read it all, right down to a note that asserted, "Call your mom." O.K., I admit, I cried in Marshall's.

To all of you this holiday season, my wish for you is that you get your sign. They are so special when they come, very infrequent, but so special!

———

ACTION STEP: Keep your heart and mind open as you actively look and listen for your special moment.

The Light at the End of the Tunnel

—◊◊—

On Friday I drove to Washington, D.C. to pick up my daughter from college. I have made this four-hour trek numerous times. This time though, as I entered the Fort McHenry tunnel which brings me through the Baltimore Harbor, I was struck by the darkness. Because I have driven through it before, I knew how long I would be in the darkness and that there would be the proverbial light at the end of the tunnel, but it did not make it any less dark. It really made me think of my entire journey as a magnificent metaphor.

The tunnel reminded me of times in my life that had been dark. Unfortunately, life does not tell us how long we will be in the darkness although that would be really helpful. As I continued to drive, I thought about what I have learned from the many "tunnels of darkness" I have gone through.

In fact, there is a light at the end of every tunnel, so hold on to the knowledge that tunnels do not last forever. Some tunnels are longer than others, for sure. And it seems like we are in complete darkness when we enter the tunnel but two things are true inside the tunnel: first, there are little lights throughout the tunnel. Let's make sure we notice the little lights; they are there for us and they are so helpful. Second, there are many other people in the tunnel, too. It may feel like we are alone, but we are definitely not alone.

So that is what I did as I traveled through the tunnel: I took note of all the little lights that I had never truly seen before. They had been there all along, lighting my way through the darkness. I'm sorry it took me years to notice.

———

ACTION STEP: Today, journal for 5 minutes about all the *lights* that helped you get through the various tunnels in your life. Perhaps you are in a tunnel right now. If so, take note of all the little *lights* helping you through the darkness.

In the Eye of the Storm

—◆—

We are heading into the home stretch!! We have five days until Christmas and eleven until years end. Maybe the stress level in your home is starting to escalate. Remember, we are in complete control. Here are a few last minute tips to head into this week.

1. Carve out some "me time" even if that means getting up a bit earlier. My favorite time is very early in the morning when it is still dark. I turn on the Christmas tree lights, enjoy a cup of tea, and take in all the peace and quiet. Sometimes I forego the quiet and turn on some Christmas music. Either way, it works wonders.

2. Get connected spiritually. That may mean different things for different people. For some it will mean prayer, for others it will mean meditation, and for others it might mean simply writing in a gratitude journal. These four days are powerful days, it is important to take time to reflect.

3. Create a family night. Make it pajamas required if you are like me— my personal favorite. Sit in front of the fireplace and watch a great movie. Adding hot chocolate with whipped cream and topped off with a drizzle of fudge sauce or sprinkles will make you very popular. The key is that everyone is together and, therefore, spends the night relaxing!

ACTION STEP: Spend your 5 minutes today checking in with yourself. Where are you on the stress scale? Where is your entire household? Journal what steps need to be taken to dial it back. Will it be "me time"? Connecting spiritually? Creating family time? What needs to change?

A Balanced Life

—w—

Over the weekend, a college student said something very profound to me: "I want all of me to graduate." I am not sure if she meant it to be as profound as it was, but something about the simplicity of its truth spoke to me on so many levels.

When I heard that statement, I was floored at her understanding of the big picture. It applies to all of us. Do not let the "graduate" part mislead you into thinking this only applies to students, college or otherwise. Her statement was pointing to balance. She did not want an impressive GPA to be achieved at an expense she was not willing to pay. It was as if she was explaining, "There is more to life than just my GPA."

Her wisdom defies her age and we can all learn from her words. So whether we are in college or well beyond, how is balance going in our life? Are we achieving one thing but at a great cost to another? Can we truly say, "I'm at peace right now?" Are we burning the candle at both ends? Are we saying yes when it should be no? Do we have our priorities in order? Don't just say yes to this question without really taking inventory. We need to stop and assess or perhaps reassess our priorities as it relates to the big picture. This is important. I want *all of you* (and me) to "graduate."

———

ACTION STEP: Answer the following questions thoughtfully and honestly.

Are you leading a balanced life? Would you describe your life as peaceful? If the answer is no, answer the following questions:

What are your priorities? Are they in order? Simply hearing the word *priorities* grounds me. Spend a few minutes on these last two questions; your answers may be revealing.

Doing What You Love

—❦—

Merry Christmas! Whether you are reading this on Christmas Day or not is irrelevant. In fact, it is better if you are not reading this on December 25th; the true meaning of Christmas was never meant for just one day. Today is supposed to be a reminder of how we should be living all year long.

Have you ever given the true meaning of Christmas any thought? We all know it's not about opening perfectly wrapped presents from underneath a beautifully decorated tree. It's not about opening presents at all. I believe it's about opening our hearts and allowing ourselves to feel more deeply about our fellow man.

During the Christmas season we tend to experience strong emotions like kindness, compassion, generosity, patience, forgiveness, and love. What is it about Christmas that opens up our human spirit to such intensely caring emotions? Wouldn't it be great if we could tap into this magical time more than once a year?

———

ACTION STEP: Christmas seems to have a magical way of resuscitating our human spirit. Think about how you could tap into this magical Christmas spirit more than just once a year.

"One Thing at a Time."

—◊◊◊—

Today, we need to repeat these words to ourselves all day long. We really need to stop multitasking. We need to slow down and by slow down, I mean **one thing at a time**. Can we be present to every person, place, or thing we encounter today? In the present, we can actually find peace. When was the last time you took a deep breath? Breathe. And again. One more time. In the present, we can find joy.

Harried is not fun. One thing at a time. Try it out today. It is a "one size fits all" kind of gift.

———

ACTION STEP: As a general rule, how *present* are you? When someone is talking to you, do you ever look at your phone? Being 100% present is not an easy task, but it is hugely important and rewarding. Spend a few minutes journaling about where and with whom you could be more present.

Change? Who, Me?

—∿—

Almost without fail, when I meet a new client who is looking for a change, the first thing they do is essentially oppose the change. Ironic, right? People hate change. I believe what they want is some additional piece of information that they can apply without having to change themselves. Rarely is that the case.

As this next year begins to unfold, what change are you looking for? It is highly likely that you too may fall under the "no change" category because most do. Somehow we believe this time it will work. It's the proverbial square peg in a round hole scenario. Working harder and being more committed but not changing *you* will often deliver the same unfortunate results.

For this thing to change in the new year—YOU have to be different. The change will happen when YOU change. The Keto diet didn't work but Whole30 will? Nope. YOU are the one that needs to change and then everything you want to change will follow suit. It's like dominoes. You'll see.

———

ACTION STEP: Today, spend 5 minutes journaling on what change you are looking for in the new year. Now, write about the part of you that needs to change so your desire for this next year will come to fruition.

Here's One for the Win Column

—⚏—

Do you use a calendar or daily planner to plan your days? I'm an old-school Franklin Covey girl from my Wall Street days. I don't know where I would be without this organizational tool.

There are a few things I write down each day, but one of the most powerful things are my wins. Each day I chronicle the wins of yesterday. Sometimes they are big and other times they are very small, regardless they act as a very empowering daily reminder that I am successfully progressing. It is a tiny act of self-love.

Do you document your wins in some way? I'm sure you remember the big wins, but it's all the small wins that get overlooked and forgotten. We all need a win column. There are no sports teams I know of that only record big wins, they record all of their wins and so should we. Imagine reaching the end of this year and having the pleasure of perusing over 365 wins? All of them yours! As my brother-in-law, Dave, would say, "Yup, that's what I'm talkin' about!"

———

ACTION STEP: Start today by writing down all of your wins from yesterday, big and small. Do your best to make this a daily practice. It's a self-empowering gift you are giving to yourself.

Any Road

—ɯ—

As I was shopping a few days before Christmas, I heard a song playing in the store. The lyrics were very catchy and I found myself engaged with the song although I did not know the words. It was a song by George Harrison entitled, "Any Road," but I believe Harrison gained his inspiration from the famed author, Lewis Carroll, whose quote reads, "If you don't know where you are going, any road will take you there."

The song caught my attention because I had started to think about planning for the new year. Maybe you have thought about next year as well? My goals revolve around my spirituality, family, career, fitness, and home and I keep them in that order to remind me of my priorities.

Today, I am inviting you to join me in thinking and dreaming about next year. It is really important to know where we are headed in the new year. We cannot hit the target if we do not know what it is. Pick a target. What do we really want to achieve next year? We should all have an answer to that question before the new year begins. Dream big!

———————

ACTION STEP: Spend the next 5–10 minutes simply brainstorming and journaling on the following question:

Where do I want to be at the end of next year?

Put It in Writing

—⚹—

- 92% of all New Year's resolutions will result in failure by January 15th.*
- A very small percentage of people (much less than 20%) will actually write down their goals. (Statistics vary)
- We are 42% more likely to achieve a goal if it is written down.***

Given these eye-opening statistics, I am challenging you to write down one goal. Put one goal in writing. There is so much more to goal setting than this, but if you can write down one goal and promise to review it at least once every week, you will likely be a part of the very small percentage of people who will actually achieve their goal.

I hope these statistics, and I, have encouraged and motivated you to take a moment to write down just one goal that you are committed to achieving next year. Start here; taking action is the first step. I truly want this for you, whatever "this" is. Let's go get this thing!

———

ACTION STEP: Write down one goal. Go ahead, write it down. Commit to reviewing this goal no less than once a week.

*A study done by The University of Scranton

**A study done by Dr. Gail Matthews, a psychology professor at the Dominican University in California

As the New Year Approaches . . .

—ɷ—

We are all being bombarded with ideas for the New Year. *Resolutions* and *goals* are the two words trending now. Other headlines are *The Best of,* and *The Top 100.* All of this has a tendency to stir up a lot of unhealthy emotions and to cause us to view the future with angst.

But what if we looked at it differently? What if today, instead of feeling the stress of figuring out how we will make next year *the best year ever,* we simply took stock in how blessed we truly are. If you are reading this post, you are blessed; it means you are alive, you have your vision, and you can read. Begin counting your blessings from here.

New Year's Eve can be a difficult day for many. For now, forget the resolutions and the goals, they come with so many judgements and stress. Take the time to look over the past year with gratitude. If you are drawn to things like a *top 100* list, write out 100 things you were grateful for last year. It will be the best list you could ever write. Gratitude is where next year should begin. As the late Louise Hay would have magnificently stated, "Life loves you," and your list will prove it.

———

ACTION STEP: This day is all about blessings and gratitude. Fill this page with everything joyful in your life. And do not forget the simple stuff like heat and air conditioning, your roof, your bed, clean air, seasons, nature's beauty, etc. Write in the margins. Keep writing until you literally fill this page with blessings.

Index